D1465428

MEMORIES OF MANY MINDS

Memories of
Many Minds

by

M I C H A E L   E L T O N

The Memoir Club

© Michael Elton 2004

First published in 2004 by
The Memoir Club
Stanhope Old Hall
Stanhope
Weardale
County Durham

British Library Cataloguing in
Publication Data.
A catalogue record for this book
is available from the
British Library.

ISBN: 1 84104 111 4

Typeset by George Wishart & Associates, Whitley Bay.
Printed by CPI Bath.

Dedication

Know then thyself, presume not God to scan,
The proper study of mankind is Man.
Placed on this isthmus of a middle state,
A being darkly wise and rudely great:
With too much knowledge for the Sceptic side,
With too much weakness for the Stoic's pride,
He hangs between, in doubt to act or rest;
In doubt to deem himself a God or Beast;
In doubt his mind or body to prefer;
Born but to die, and reas'ning but to err;
Alike in ignorance, his reason such,
Whether he thinks too little or too much;
Chaos of thought and passion, all confused;
Still by himself abused or disabused;
Created half to rise, and half to fall:
Great lord of all things, yet a prey to all;
Sole judge of truth, in endless error hurl'd;
The glory, jest, and riddle of the world!

Alexander Pope, 'An Essay on Man'

Contents

Illustrations

Acknowledgments

I SHOULD LIKE to express my sincere thanks to the following people. Moira Broom is a life-long friend of my wife and myself. By a fortunate coincidence – for me, if not for her – she spent her working life as a professional editor. Both her general advice and her detailed (and always constructive) criticisms were not just invaluable but indispensable. She was generous in the time she gave to ploughing through successive drafts.

Mike Smithurst, the professional philosophy lecturer, was good enough to read Parts III and IV and to give me the benefit of his experience and expertise. He was understanding enough not to judge my efforts by the uncompromising standards he would have applied to, say, a professional philosophy text book. I also picked up a number of useful points from C. David Allen, whose lectures on philosophy I have also much enjoyed.

Lindy Wood surmounted the uphill task of reading my hurried scrawl and used her word-processing skills to produce several drafts of what turned out to be a longer book than I had anticipated when I first sought her assistance. She made some helpful suggestions and did much to sustain my enthusiasm when it was in danger of flagging.

Colin Steward was good enough to check the technical accuracy of Chapter 7 and suggested some important updating of what I had written.

Graham Nye put me right on the technological aspects of our joint venture in producing the CD Rom which I mention in Chapter 8.

By another stroke of luck, Tim Bradshaw (the husband of my niece, Natalie) runs a large pig farm in Yorkshire and so helped to ensure that my conclusions in Chapter 14 were not too wide of the mark.

Closer to home, my brother, John, made some well-judged criticisms of which I took due note. My wife's contribution was her patience with my physical absence for several hours on many a morning and my mental absence for much of the rest of the time. I am grateful, as always, for her understanding.

Michael Elton

September 2004   *Winchester*

Preface

I WROTE THESE MEMOIRS during a period of some twenty months straddling my seventieth and seventy-first birthdays in the years 2002 and 2003 respectively though I have since updated several passages.

People invariably write their memoirs for self-regarding reasons. Amongst my own were the hope that it would be a cathartic process and the need to try to discover the meaning – or meanings – of my life, if such there be.

These are memoirs with a difference, being divided into four Parts. I should, however, stress at the outset that the four Parts are inextricably linked and so should be read in sequence.

Part I is a traditional autobiographical account of my life and the face I presented to the world at large.

Part II describes the deep and often horrifying insights into my unconscious mind which I gained during, and sometimes long after, a prolonged and extraordinary process of psychoanalysis: extraordinary because my insights were aided by the use of drugs.

Part III recounts the views about the human condition which I have reached, partly in the light of subjective insights arising from my psychoanalysis. I analyse the philosophical arguments for and against my views with such objectivity as I can command.

Part IV ranges wide and includes my reflections on the humanist and religious implications of the views I expressed in Part III. It also records some further thoughts about the philosophical arguments in Part III which came to mind as I wrote.

It is not a criticism of professional philosophers to express the hope that my layman's philosophical ruminations are less abstruse than most professional discourses. I should like to think that they are readily accessible to readers who are not well versed in, or are entirely new to, the 'whys and wherefores' of philosophical thinking but are nevertheless interested in exploring the human condition and the meaning of life and death.

Part I

CHAPTER 1

The Lion School

M RS FILLERY has gone away. The first actual words I can remember. It was a sunny morning in the middle of September in 1939. I was seven years old.

I was standing with mum in the porch round the front door of the Lion School in Bereweeke Road. I could spell Bereweeke because I passed a signpost every day on the way to school and back home again. We called it Beer-week. Posh people called it Berri-wick.

It was a big heavy door painted shiny dark green. The porch was made of bricks up to my chest. On top of the bricks the sides and roof were just like church windows with patterns made of dark red, purple and plain bits of glass. The morning sun made the dark bits glow but shone through the plain ones in beams of light filled with tiny flecks of dust floating about in them.

One of these beams shone on a yellowy-brown looking man's face peering round the door, which had been opened a little bit when mum rang the bell. It was him who'd said that Mrs Fillery had gone away, but he didn't explain why she'd gone away or where to and we never found out. I followed mum back along Bereweeke Road wondering what would happen to me now.

In those days there were trees on both sides of the road which made a sort of arch. I thought they looked like the ceiling of the cathedral but didn't tell mum I was thinking that. She wasn't holding my hand.

Mrs Fillery was the headmistress of the Lion School which I'd been at for three years starting when I was four. My brother John was two and a quarter years older than me and had been at the Lion School too but now he'd just started at Peter Symonds School, the grammar school in Winchester. He was nine. I can't remember much about my time at the Lion School. I can only remember a few things that happened there and they're things I didn't like much. Actually I didn't like them at all.

One day some of the boys and me had to have a race down a bumpy stony drive that sloped down from the porch to some garages at the bottom. I ran as hard as I could because I wanted to win the race. Half

3

way down I tripped over a bump and scrazed my knees and hands quite badly. They bled and hurt a lot. Mrs Fillery said I was stupid and should have taken more care not to trip over.

In one of the classrooms there was a high window from the ceiling to the floor that stuck out into the garden. In the space made by the window sticking out there was a big table with a big tray on it and there was sand and bits of plasticine in the tray. We used to play with the sand and bits of plasticine and make things. One day I made some palm trees out of the bits of plasticine and stuck them in the sand. I thought it would look like an oasis in a desert. Mrs Fillery said I had to stand and watch three other boys doing things with the sand and plasticine so I could see the trouble I'd caused. I remember that's exactly what she said, I mean about me causing trouble. I didn't see why I'd caused any trouble or done anything wrong and didn't know why I had to stand all by myself and watch the three boys put right what I'd done wrong. I didn't think I *had* done anything wrong because I thought the sand looked like a desert and it was a good idea to put palm trees in a desert and make an oasis out of them like one I'd seen a picture of. It made me feel sort of silly and upset standing there by myself.

We did school plays every year. One year some of us boys were dressed as red Indians. We wore bands round our heads with feathers stuck in them and carried flags made of coloured paper fixed to sticks with two drawing pins. They had been made by one of the teachers. I felt proud as we paraded round part of the classroom made into a stage and looked for mum and dad in the audience to see if they were watching me. But it was dark in the audience except for a bit of light from the stage shining on one half of dad's face so I could see one of his eyes twinkling but not the other one. It's funny I can remember that so clearly. Then one of the drawing pins sticking my flag to my stick suddenly fell off and the flag nearly fell off too but not quite. It just flapped about. When the play was over, Mrs Fillery told me off for not making sure the drawing pin had been fixed properly to my stick and said I was stupid. You'd think that was her favourite word. I felt all mixed up inside. Part of me felt it wasn't fair to call me stupid because I hadn't made my flag, the teacher had, but part of me felt I must be stupid because the other boys' flags hadn't nearly fallen off like mine did.

Actually, I often thought things were my fault even when I sort of knew they weren't really which really *was* stupid of me, if you see what I mean, but I just couldn't help it.

One of the masters was called Mr Quin. He was tall and going a bit bald and wore a brown suit and glasses. The rims of his glasses were made of some sort of metal which somehow made his eyes look sort of cold and not very kind. I knew he used to beat boys on the bottom with a rubber plimsole in an attic somewhere upstairs. I didn't know how I knew this because I couldn't remember him ever beating me on my bottom. The funny thing was that I could remember seeing the slanting wooden beams that held up the roof of the attic and I could often see them in my mind's eye when I thought about it which I did quite a lot.

One day when it was sunny Mrs Fillery was sitting in the garden at the bottom of a tree covered with white blossoms. A boy who looked rather pretty with fair curly hair was climbing up a branch quite close to her. I wanted to do that too and started to try to. Mrs Fillery said I wasn't allowed to but the other boy was because he was a good boy. He is the only one of all the boys whose name I can remember. It was Antony, not Tony, Hetherington. I wanted Mrs Fillery to think I was a good boy instead of him.

It's funny that I can only remember one more thing about the Lion School and I didn't like that either. It's funny I can only remember things I didn't like. All the boys were going to have to do some boxing. I didn't like the idea very much. Actually I was dead scared at the thought of being punched in the face or anywhere else for that matter. But what worried me a lot more was that I knew John would be even more scared than me. I felt sorry for him because he wasn't the tough guy sort of boy but gentle and I could tell he thought about things a lot. I was glad I wasn't there when he had to box. It didn't turn out too bad for me because I punched some poor kid more than he punched me.

Actually there was one kind old master called Mr Hastings. I could tell he cared for us a lot and wanted us to learn things. When later on I saw a film called *Goodbye Mr Chips*, Mr Chips reminded me of Mr Hastings. Actually I liked wearing the school uniform because it was a nice blue one with a yellowy goldeny lion on my peaked cap and another one on the breast pocket of my blazer. The lions made me feel sort of proud in a funny kind of way it's hard to explain.

It's funny that John and me never told each other about the nasty things that happened at school. I didn't tell mum or dad either and I didn't think John did. As I said, it's funny that John and me didn't tell each other because we loved each other a lot. We never even mentioned it. Dad said he was pleased about the Lion School because I'd learnt to

My brother John and me aged 6 and 4.

read and write so well for my age but I couldn't blame him for being pleased because it was my fault for not telling him about the things that went on there I didn't like.

By the time I followed mum home from the Lion School because Mrs Fillery had gone away, dad had left home a few days ago. Mum said he'd gone to fight the Germans who were wicked and he'd come back soon. I don't remember him leaving or saying goodbye. I guess he thought it would upset John and me if he'd said goodbye.

Of course, I remember lots of other things that happened before dad went away to fight the wicked Germans.

As I said, John and I loved each other a lot. We each had our own bed in the back bedroom where we lived at 6 Milverton Road, Winchester, Hants. We had moved there from a council house at the top of Stanmore

Lane before I could remember anything. We often used to climb into each other's beds and cuddle each other. He put his head on my chest and I put my arms round him in a protective sort of way. After we saw the film *Snow White and the Seven Dwarfs,* we used to pretend we were two of the dwarfs. I was Doc, the wise old leader of the dwarfs with a nice fluffy beard, and John was Dopey, not because he was dopey – I told you he thought about things a lot – but because I thought he needed sort of protecting. We both liked cuddling each other because it made us feel nice and cosy. Mum wasn't the sort of mum who gave you lots of cuddles.

There was one game I liked playing in mum-and-dad's bed when they had got up and hadn't made it yet. I used to fold the sheets up in strips and make them into a circle with a long entrance like an Eskimo's igloo I'd seen a picture of. I would crawl through the entrance and snuggle up inside the circle. If mum came to get dressed afterwards I sometimes watched her putting on her corsets and pulling the laces hard and fixing them into little hooks. This gave me a funny sort of mixed-up feeling. She had such great big bosoms.

Once she became very poorly indeed and dad told me afterwards she'd nearly died. Her face turned all yellowy-brown. I forgot to tell you when I told you about the man's yellowy-brown face peering round the door at the Lion School that when I used to think about it afterwards I didn't like it much and thought it was like mum's face when she was poorly that time.

In the end the doctors said she had to have her gallstones out at the hospital in Romsey Road. When she'd had her operation and was getting better, dad took John and me to visit her. She was sitting up in bed in a ward in a big sort of wooden hut behind the main building. I could hear heavy rain beating down on the roof and making a loud splashing noise. She still looked a bit yellowy but not so much as before. She had some sweets in the cupboard by her bed and gave us one. When she came home she had to stay in bed for quite a long time. When it was fireworks day she couldn't come down to see the fireworks so John and me lit some sparklers and waved them about in her bedroom to cheer her up if we could. Actually I was quite glad because sparklers didn't make a big bang like the other fireworks which frightened me.

What's funny about that is that one day dad said a new king had been crowned and they were going to fire some guns on Saint Giles' hill at the bottom of the high street. He said he'd take me to see them being fired if

John and me on Bournemouth beach.

I wanted to. I said I did so he took me in the car to see them and stood with me as we watched. I was very disappointed. I thought they would be great big guns and make great big bangs but they were only little ones and didn't make much noise at all. You can see why I said that was funny because I was frightened of fireworks making big bangs.

We used to have nice holidays at Bournemouth though really it was Southbourne which was next door to Bournemouth. They were hot sunny days and John and me played on the beach making sandcastles and things and splashing in the waves which we liked doing. Mum and dad sat in deckchairs most of the time but also had swims in the sea and screamed in a laughy sort of way when they first went in because the water was cold. They always said it was lovely once you're in. We had nice picnics with marmite sandwiches and bananas and lemonade and nice things like that with John and me sitting on the car rug which we had to shake the sand out of afterwards. I liked it looking across the shiny sea at three white cliffs sticking out of the water at our end of the Isle of Wight. They were called the Needles because they were supposed to look like needles though I thought they weren't anything like thin enough or pointy enough to look like needles. They looked extra white with the sun shining on them and the blue sky on top of them and behind them too and looking like it touched the sea a long way away where you couldn't see any further. It was extra nice because at teatime dad bought us nice ice-creams in cornets.

I thought I was happy on those days because I liked the days feeling like they were long days which I didn't think I would have liked if I hadn't thought I was happy, if you can see what I mean. I could tell that mum and dad were happy then too which was another reason why I thought I was happy on those holidays by the sea, if you can see what I mean about that too, though it's all a bit complicated. I often used to think of complicated things which I didn't always like but couldn't stop myself thinking which was a bit of a nuisance. Quite a lot of a nuisance actually. I learnt the word complicated from dad when I asked him how the sounds could reach the wireless all the way from London and he said they floated through the air on air waves. When I asked him how waves of air could float through the walls of the house and into the wireless and out again with the same sounds on them as there were when they left London, he said it was all a bit complicated and I would understand it when I grew up. He said never mind not understanding it at my age because I was a clever boy to think of complicated things like that, but the trouble was that complicated things about waves of air floating through walls weren't the sort of complicated things that upset me or that I could ask him about or anyone else for that matter. So when I thought about them I felt I was all by myself in a funny sort of way that wasn't very nice really but it's hard to explain that to you.

We had our holidays in Southbourne because dad's mum Granny Elton lived in a little bungalow there with his sister called Aunty Phyllis. Their bungalow was in Tuckton Road. Granny Elton played nice music on a great big grand-piano that took up most of the front room. I thought it was funny that she and Aunty Phyllis slept together in the same big bed though they were grown-ups. There was no Grampa Elton to sleep in Granny's bed because he had died when dad was a boy. Dad never spoke to me about that, not once, and I thought it was really sad that his dad

Granny Elton and Aunty Phyllis in the garden of
Granny's bungalow in Tuckton Road, Southbourne.

died when he was only a boy. I thought that if Grampa Elton hadn't died he would have slept in Granny's bed and Aunty Phyllis would have had to sleep on her own like John and me did though we weren't really on our own because we slept in the same bedroom and could cuddle each other when we felt like it. I wondered if Granny Elton and Aunty Phyllis ever cuddled each other because they were sad that Grampa Elton had died and felt lonely without him there but I don't suppose they really did because, as I said, they were grown-ups and it would have been funny if two grown-up ladies cuddled each other in bed like John and me did.

On one of those holidays a really really nasty thing happened. It was raining so we couldn't go on the beach so we went to the pictures instead. I can't remember what the main picture was about but the other one was

John and me in the garden of Granny Elton's bungalow.

called *The Mummy's Hand*. It was about a mummy in Egypt that came alive and walked in a slouchy sort of way through long winding passages under the ground. He was made of a sort of muddy stuff with strips of raggy stuff wound round him but you could still see one of his big eyes showing through. He held his right arm sticking straight out in front of him and strangled people to death with a nasty looking hand at the end of the arm that stuck out in front of him. I have never been so scared in all my life. I was sitting in the dark between mum and Granny Elton who somehow knew I was scared stiff though I wasn't crying or anything. She tried to comfort me by saying here comes old muddy every time the horrible creature came on the screen. That night we were staying at Granny's bungalow and I screamed and screamed and screamed in the night. Sometimes Granny or someone came into the little long bedroom I was sleeping in and tried to comfort me and stop me screaming but couldn't.

Sometimes Granny Elton and Aunty Phyllis quarrelled with each other and got cross but mostly they laughed a lot in a nice kind sort of way. Granny's laugh was high up and made a sort of tinkly sound. Aunty Phyllis's laugh was lower down and sort of boomy, not tinkly like

Grampa Keates.

Granny's was. I thought they loved me and John alright but they both kept on about being polite and having good manners which made me feel I must be rude or something and had to be on my best behaviour. I could tell Aunty Phyllis and mum didn't like each other very much and that dad was sort of split in half about it. Sometimes I felt like that too. I thought the reason was that Aunty Phyllis thought mum wasn't posh enough to marry dad and mum didn't like Aunty Phyllis thinking that. Granny Elton didn't seem to mind about mum not being posh enough.

When Grampa Elton died when dad was only a boy as I told you before, dad and Granny Elton and Aunty Phyllis had been looked after by Grampa Keates who was Granny's dad and was rich but wasn't related to the famous poet he sounded like who wrote about misty days in the autumn and things like that. When Grampa Keates died Granny Elton

My father as a boarder at Weymouth College.

and Aunty Phyllis and dad weren't rich any more. In fact they were quite poor but still sort of posh.

Mum came from a family that had always been very poor and lived in Alton. She had five brothers and one sister. Her dad was Grampa Gray who loved John and me a lot, really a lot. We were the first grandchildren he had. We loved him a lot too. We went to Alton for lunch nearly every Sunday and Grampa left the front door open because he could hardly wait to see John and me. He was such a kind looking cuddly sort of Grampa with a bald head. One of his legs was shorter than the other and he wore a great big thick boot on the leg that was shorter than the other. He walked with a walking stick to stop him falling over. We often sat on his knees, John on one and me on the other, and he read us nice stories. Every one loved Grampa and I could tell mum and dad did, especially mum.

Grampa Gray with John and me.

One day when I had just learnt to write young for my age I wrote him a letter but didn't tell anyone. I said Dear Grampa Gray, I love you very much, love from Michael. I must have been very young because I had to stand on my toes and reach up to get the letter in the slit in the red pillar box at the bottom of Milverton Road. I wrote Grampa Gray, Alton, Hants on the envelope and pinched a stamp from mum's handbag and stuck it on the envelope. Everyone said it was funny that my letter got to him because I hadn't put the proper address on the envelope. Mum said that it was because everyone in Alton knew him and loved him so the postman knew where he lived. You would think it was the most important letter he ever got in his life he made such a fuss about it in his nice and kind sort of way and said he would keep it for ever.

His house was in King's Road and was called Assisi and had a statue of Saint Francis over the front door. Saint Francis was his favourite saint because he loved animals. Grampa loved animals too, as well as John and me.

Granny Gray was nice and kind too but always seemed too busy cooking things to take as much notice of us as Grampa did. Most Sundays she made a very nice seed cake for tea. One day I pinched an extra bit

Grampa and Granny Gray in the back garden of 'Assisi'.

from a round green tin in her kitchen when no-one was looking. That's
how much I liked it.

Mum was the first of Grampa's children to get married when she was
only eighteen. John was born when she was twenty and me when she was
twenty two. Often on Sundays some of her brothers were there for the
day especially Uncle Tony and Uncle Bernard because they still lived in
Alton. They were nice and kind too and used to take John and me bird
nesting in Ackender woods. Which reminds me to tell you that the name
of our house in Milverton Road was Ackender which sometimes made
me think about those nice woods with primroses growing there in the
Spring when the birds laid their eggs. There were hundreds of them,
primroses I mean, and they looked extra pretty when the sun shone
beams of light on them through the trees. It was great fun bird nesting
and sometimes Uncle Tony or Uncle Bernard had to climb up trees to
reach the nests but they didn't take eggs out of the nests if there weren't
many in them because it would have been unkind to the mummy birds
not to leave enough eggs to turn into nice little baby birds for them to
look after. I told you they were kind uncles.

When we got back to Grampa's house he always asked John and me if we'd had a nice time and to tell him all about it. My uncles would stick a pin in both ends of the eggs we'd collected and blow through one end so the yolk and stuff came out the other end so they couldn't go bad and stink a lot. Then we put them in a box with cotton wool in it so they didn't get broken and made a collection of as many different colours and sizes as we could find in Ackender woods. My favourites were the smallest ones because they were the prettiest colour, the brightest pure sort of blue you ever saw. I couldn't think how baby birds could be tiny enough to fit inside them. I can't quite remember what sort of birds laid them but I think they were sparrows.

My other uncles were Uncle Francis, Uncle Alfred and Uncle Ernest. They were nice uncles to have too but Uncle Francis sometimes teased John and me a bit too much. Uncle Alfred had a nice tenor voice when he sang and I thought I'd like to have one too when I grew up. Uncle Ernest didn't talk very much as far as I can remember. All my uncles married nice aunties except Uncle Bernard. I don't mean he married a nasty aunty, just that he didn't marry anyone at all. The aunty that Uncle Francis married, Aunty Bessy, had black hairs on top of her lips and round her chin which tickled my face when she kissed me hello and goodbye. Later on Uncle Francis and Aunty Bessie adopted three children and went to live in Australia and Uncle Bernard went to Australia too so we never saw them again. The other uncles all had babies, so did mum's nice sister who married a dentist in Alton called Uncle Percy and had two babies. Her name was Aunty Winnie but later on she changed it to Aunty Jane because she thought it was a nicer name than Winnie. Come to think of it I suppose Winnie did sound rather funny. She and mum saw a lot of each other because they both liked singing a lot and were good at it, especially Aunty Jane who sang solos in the Alton Opera Society. Mum was mostly in the chorus of the Winchester Opera Society but sometimes did little parts and looked very pretty on the stage with her face all made up and dressed in pretty clothes. The operas were written by Gilbert and Sullivan and I liked the nice tunes and laughed at the funny bits like when they did funny dances and things.

Come to think of it, I am running away with myself because some of the things I've told you about my aunties and uncles like getting married and having babies happened after the time I'm supposed to be talking about when I was at the Lion School.

I forgot to say that Grampa Gray and all his family were Roman Catholics so dad changed to be a Roman Catholic before he married

My mother before the war.

mum so they could go to the same church together, Saint Peter's Church in Jewry Street. John and me went to mass with them every Sunday and if it was the eleven o'clock mass which it usually was mum sang in the choir. If I got fed up thinking about God and saying prayers and things or pretending to and began shuffling about and making a nuisance of myself, dad used to hold up some fingers to tell me how long it was before we could go home. What I mean is that if there was seven minutes to go he held up seven fingers and hoped that I would stop messing about if I knew I only had to stop messing about for another seven minutes. If it didn't work doing this he'd look very cross at me which worked alright, I can tell you, because he didn't look cross like that very often.

Before dad went away to fight the Germans we used to have what mum and dad called musical evenings at home. Some of the grown-ups would sing songs with someone playing the piano in the front room we called the lounge. The local violin teacher, Nelly Fulcher, would play the violin. She had flat feet. Dad couldn't sing a single note in tune but liked music very much especially singing. Singing was my favourite too and I thought some of the songs were really nice even though I couldn't understand the ones that were in German.

Actually dad did do what was called a turn. He recited poems like the Charge of the Light Brigade and bits from Shakespeare and what he called monologues. Aunty Phyllis was good at reciting monologues too. Sometimes dad recited some funny ones. There was one about an actor on the stage who kept forgetting what he had to say and got all his things muddled up in his cloak, things like 'the swords and the daggers and the pistols' which I remember exactly. In the end the man in charge behind the stage shouted 'come off, you ass' in a very loud voice which dad put on. We always knew what was coming but the way dad said it all with a more and more desperate sort of look on his face and his voice getting more and more upset in a funny sort of way as everything went wrong made us all laugh every time he did it. Dad said Grampa Keates had taught him and Aunty Phyllis to like poems and monologues and things like that.

Talking about Grampas and teaching things, Grampa Gray hadn't been to school much at all and nor had mum for that matter. But Grampa Gray didn't like it that he hadn't learnt much at school and learnt everything, well not everything but lots and lots of things, by reading hundreds and hundreds of books. In the end he knew enough to write things in newspapers and ended up as an important secretary at Treloar's Hospital in Alton. He must have been important because his boss was a Sir. Mum told us everyone there loved him as usual especially the children of course. He learnt a funny new language called Esperanto and hoped all the people all over the world would learn to speak it too so everyone could understand everyone else and there wouldn't be any more horrible wars which he couldn't bear the thought of.

CHAPTER 2

The Western School

WHEN MUM AND ME got home from the Lion School that day when dad had just gone away to fight in the war against the Germans, mum went round to talk to old Mrs Lansdell who lived next door at 8 Milverton Road. When she got back, she took me down the road to the Western School which was only five minutes walk away. We saw the headmaster in his office but I can't remember his name but he was shortish and thin and had a foxy looking face and wore a brown suit. He said I could go to his school and I stayed there by myself and mum went home.

He took me into a classroom upstairs where the teacher was Mrs or Miss Lovell, I can't remember which, but I'll call her Miss to save me keep saying Mrs or Miss. She was half way between fat and thin and had fair wavy hair which I liked. The other boys were scruffier than the ones at the Lion School and a lot of them talked with what mum called a common sort of voice. But they were nice to me and didn't bully me or do anything nasty like that. There were some girls there too and some were really pretty, I could tell that alright.

I liked the Western School much better than the Lion School. Miss Lovell used to park her car in the drive of a house over the road and I got to school early and met her there and carried her case for her to the classroom. I wanted to be kind to her because she was kind to me. In the first year in her class she taught me a lot of things and I liked learning all about them, mainly sums and writing and reading books but other things besides.

In my second year there the teacher was Miss Scott. She was definitely a Miss. She was tall and had her hair swept back to make a bun at the back of her neck which made her nose look long which made her look strict. Actually she was really really strict and we couldn't mess about or anything. She made me learn a lot of things which I liked a lot. Though she was strict and sort of stern looking she wasn't unkind to me, and wasn't unkind to the other boys either as far as I could tell.

One day she said a funny thing to me, at least I thought it was funny.

My father – a Captain in the Royal Engineers.

What she said was that I had a brain like blotting paper because it soaked up everything I read. I could sort of see what she meant because if I spilt some ink on my desk by mistake my blotting paper soaked it up alright, it certainly did.

At the end of that year in her class she told foxy face that I couldn't learn anything else at the Western School and ought to go to Peter Symonds even though I was only nine like John was when he went there and other boys went there when they were eleven. Somehow foxy face arranged this but I felt a bit worried about it and a bit sorry I wouldn't see Miss Lovell and Miss Scott anymore.

By then I knew that dad was a Captain in the Royal Engineers which was because before he went away he worked for the Hants County Council building roads and bridges and things. Later he became a Major and had crowns on his shoulders instead of three stars and was in charge of the hundred and thirteenth road construction company, I remember that.

Actually he had to mend aerodromes so our aeroplanes could land on them without crashing as well as mending roads and bridges across rivers that had been smashed by the Germans with bombs and big guns as well I suppose.

One afternoon a lady I didn't know called when mum was out. She said she'd heard that dad had got back from a place in France called Dunkirk and I should tell my mum straightaway. I knew she had gone to have a cup of tea with Mrs Payne in Fordington Avenue at the back of Milverton Road so I ran round to Mrs Payne's as fast as I could to tell mum what the lady who'd called had said. Mum looked very pleased and laughed a lot and so did Mrs Payne but she, mum I mean, didn't cry or anything like a lady did in a film I saw about the war when someone told her the man she loved wasn't dead after all but I suppose mum never thought dad was dead anyway.

When dad next came home on leave quite soon afterwards he said he and his soldiers were supposed to get on a particular boat near Dunkirk but everything was in a muddle and the boat was already full up when they got there. They'd had to march another twenty miles to get on another boat which was lucky because the boat they were supposed to get on had been sunk by bombs from German aeroplanes and most of the soldiers on it had been drowned. When he got back to England he'd had to have his boots cut off his feet because they were too swollen for him or anyone else to pull his boots off the usual way.

After this my time at the Western School was when the blitzes on London happened and on other places too like Southampton. Before he went away dad had arranged for a high wall to be built a few feet away from the dining room window at the back of the house. It was made of two rows of bricks more like grey slabs about two feet apart and filled up to the top with sand. This made the room dark of course and we couldn't see the back garden. The idea was to protect us from the German bombs. The room was half filled up by an air-raid shelter which was a big table made of steel with springs underneath it close to the floor like the springs under mattresses on beds. It made a very good ping-pong table. When we got underneath it we could fit bits like the sides of cages round the outside so it was just like being animals in a cage at the zoo.

Every time we were at home when the siren made its funny sort of

haunting wailing sound we all scrambled under the table and fixed the
sides up so we wouldn't get hurt or killed if a bomb hit the house and it
got smashed up and fell on top of us. Night after night we lay there
listening to hundreds and hundreds of German aeroplanes flying
overhead on their way to London to drop bombs on it and smash it all up.
We could always tell it was German bombers because they made a special
throbbing sort of droning noise. We could hear the anti-aircraft guns
firing shells at the aeroplanes. One that was not so far away we called big
bertha because it made the loudest bang.

It was crowded all crushed up together under that table because,
besides mum and John, there were lodgers we had billeted on us. Miss
Allen who we all called Allie looked quite old compared with mum and
had grey nearly white hair without any curls and a kind pale looking face.
She had one of her legs all smashed up in an air-raid on Southampton.
We could feel the springs we were lying on shaking and squeaking a bit,
in fact quite a lot, because Allie was trembling so much because she didn't
want to have her other leg smashed up too, at least that's what I thought.

Once John and me stood on the front doorstep at night-time looking at
a huge red glow in the sky all over Southampton which was being
smashed up and, as Allie said when she came to stay with us, burnt to the
ground. It's funny that I wasn't upset that hundreds of people were being
burnt to death not many miles away in a town we'd been to quite often
and knew quite well. You'd have thought I would have been upset
wouldn't you but actually it just seemed exciting and I didn't have
complicated thoughts about it to upset me. Perhaps it was all too
complicated for me to have complicated thoughts about, if you can see
what I mean. To start with I couldn't understand why some German men
in an aeroplane wanted to smash up Allie's leg. After all, she was nice and
kind and hadn't done them any harm and wouldn't hurt a flea.

Sometimes we watched the beams of searchlights waving about the
night sky and making moving patches of light on the bottom of the
clouds. Sometimes we could see the glint of an aeroplane caught in one
of the beams. Then other beams moved towards the aeroplane and tried
to keep it in a sort of criss-cross of beams. Then the anti-aircraft guns
went off and puffs of smoke appeared round the aeroplane where the
shells from the guns exploded but they never seemed to hit the aeroplane.

There was a time when the German aeroplanes flew over us to London
in the daytime. We could see lots and lots of them coming out from
behind white clouds and glinting in the sunlight with the blue sky behind

them and could hear the special throb throb throb noise their engines made.

Sometimes we saw Spitfires flying in neat patterns like birds do which made us tingle with pride. Sometimes there was just one Spitfire and one German plane chasing each other round and round in circles and firing their guns at each other which was called a dog-fight. Guy Lansdell, the son of old Mrs Lansdell next door, was a pilot in a Spitfire. One day she told us to come out into the garden and not long afterwards Guy flew his Spitfire very low over the roof of her house waggling its wings from side to side. I was afraid it was going to knock the chimney off it was so low and the huge noise was frightening. Mrs Lansdell said he must have gone barmy showing off like that. We heard another pilot had flown his Spitfire under a bridge across the by-pass so we all called it spitfire bridge after that. I didn't think I would be brave enough to do barmy things like that.

If the siren made its wailing noise when I was at school, we all ran or rather walked quickly down the stairs which we practised doing a lot. We weren't allowed to run in case we got all muddled up. We went into one of the air-raid shelters which had been dug in the school grounds which was why they were called dugouts. It was black dark inside our dugout but the teacher lit a lamp like a candle with glass round it. We sat crammed together and sang war songs like 'It's a long way to Tipperary' though I didn't really know what that one meant. It was good fun though.

You'd have thought I'd be frightened when we were told the Germans might invade England any day now and that all the church bells would ring when they started to. Actually we just thought it was exciting. It was cold and snowy whatever Winter it was and me and my friends made some snowballs and piled them up behind our front hedge to throw at the German tanks. We really thought we would, honestly. We also got boxes of tin-tacks from our parents' garages and kept them ready to throw on the road to puncture the tyres of the German lorries. After all we all used to huddle round the wireless in the gloomy dining room and listen to Winston Churchill making speeches about fighting on the beaches and hills and anywhere else he could think of so we thought we should do out bit to stop the Germans capturing Winchester.

When I said the dining room was gloomy I meant really gloomy. It was gloomy in the day time because of the wall I told you dad had got built in front of the window and at night time we just had one light on to save electricity mum said and because of the black-out. The windows had curtains made of what mum called black-out material and had strips of sticky tape stuck all over them so if a bomb landed in the garden it wouldn't make bits of glass blow in our faces and cut them to smithereens. If there was the tiniest chink of light showing from outside men's voices would shout put that light out. Everywhere was completely dark, no street lights, no lights in shop windows, no cosy lights behind curtains anywhere at all. I didn't know a town could be so black, like a ghost town Allie said. The trouble was I was afraid of ghosts.

There were two things that happened that did really upset me actually. One was that I had to have my tonsils and adenoids out because I kept getting high temperatures of nearly a hundred and five. I had to go to the Winchester hospital to get them taken out. One morning mum walked with me to the hospital because we couldn't use the car in the war because our spitfires and tanks and things needed all the petrol. I didn't like having a mask put over my face by men wearing masks and white coats and when I woke up minus tonsils and adenoids my throat still hurt a lot, even more actually. But I didn't mean all that when I said something really upset me. What did was that when I was waiting downstairs in the hospital for mum to fetch me and take me home in a taxi I heard lots of moaning and groaning behind some curtains. A nurse said I was lucky to be fitted in and must have needed my operation badly because the men who were moaning and groaning behind the curtains were soldiers who had just been brought in from France and were going to have to have much worse operations than I had. It reminded me of a scene in a film I'd seen called *Gone with the Wind* where lots of soldiers were moaning and groaning and had to have their legs or arms cut off. It was quite a long time before I got better and lying in bed I kept hearing the moaning and groaning behind the curtains in my brain and feeling sorry for the wounded soldiers because they were real soldiers with real bad wounds and not pretend ones with pretend wounds like in *Gone with the Wind*. I hoped they didn't have to have to have their legs or arms cut off and was glad that dad only had to have his boots cut off like I told you about.

The second thing that really upset me was that John and me had piano lessons with Miss Cobb, Primrose Cobb like the yellow flowers in Ackender woods if you want to know her first name. I don't mean that having the piano lessons upset me though, to tell you the truth, I didn't like them much because I'd hardly ever done my practice properly. John was better at the piano than me and practised a lot more anyway. No, what upset me was that one day I was having my lesson and playing boring scales at Miss Cobb's house when the phone went in the hall and she went out to answer it. Talk about being upset, when she came back she looked more upset than I'd seen anyone be before and a bit white looking in the face. On the piano, just up on my left in a proper frame was a nice photo of a man in light-blue airforce uniform with a peaked cap on. She turned the photo round to face the wall behind the piano and just stood there as if she wasn't there if you see what I mean. After I had done one or two more scales she said would I mind cutting my lesson short as she didn't feel very well. I didn't mind because as I said I hadn't done my practice. When she showed me out of the front door I could tell she was trying not to show she was crying but I could tell she was, not half. I walked home feeling really sad for her because I thought the man in the photo must have been killed or something and that Miss Cobb must have loved him a lot and would be crying a lot now that I'd gone. I bet you she was.

Allie our lodger was very kind to John and me. She taught us to do embroidery and we made some nice serviettes and stuff like that. She tried to stop me biting my nails by cutting them nicely but I still did. She put a notice on her bedroom door saying toenails trimmed as a special favour. I also sucked my thumb a lot till I was quite old and she couldn't stop me doing that either. One day I spilt some ink on the carpet in the front room we called the lounge when mum was out. She could tell how cross mum would be with me when she got home and helped me clean it off by rubbing lots of milk into the inky bit of the carpet which saved mum being cross with me. So you see what I meant when I said she was very kind.

As I said, we had other lodgers too. There was Mister Taylor who was smart looking with wavy silver hair. He was the manager of the Ritz cinema so we were lucky because he let us in free. He always used to listen to the eight o'clock news while he was having his breakfast. The man reading the news always told us what his name was. The one I remember sounded like Alvarledell. He always said this is the BBC eight o'clock news and this is Alvarledell reading it. Mister Taylor told us that the men who read the news always had to tell us their names so that, if the Germans conquered England and one of them read the news, we would be able to tell it was a German even if he pretended to be Alvarledell because we would know it wasn't Alvarledell's voice and that what he was saying was all lies. Alvarledell often used to say that eighty two or seventy six or some other big number of German aeroplanes had been shot down yesterday and every time he said this Mr Taylor always laughed and said that'll teach them.

Miss Wilson was a school teacher and taught art at the girls High School in Cheriton Road which John and me could see from our bedroom at the back of the house. She had black hair and a brown face and eyes and talked a lot but didn't help us draw pictures or anything like Allie taught us embroidery and stuff. She used to annoy mum by talking a lot especially on the phone. She always asked mum if she could use the phone and said she would give mum the tuppence or whatever it cost. Sometimes mum made a really cross looking face when Miss Wilson said this. I thought perhaps she never got her tuppences.

It's funny that letters from dad arrived nearly every day. I can't actually remember mum telling us what was in them and thought perhaps they were love letters saying sexy things she thought John and me weren't old enough to know about and shouldn't know about for that matter because they were naughty things. But I bet you we knew a lot more sexy things than she thought. The letters were delivered by a very nice and friendly postman with a grey moustache who made jokes and funny faces. In fact he didn't put the letters through the post box but made a funny coo-ee noise through it and we could see his twinkly eyes peeping through it. So one of us had to answer the door and sometimes he teased mum by saying no letters from him today even when there were. Most days there was one letter and sometimes two and sometimes even more if there'd been a long gap since the last one. Mum said the postman was a real character and liked trying to cheer us all up.

One day I was ill in bed with one of my high temperatures of nearly a hundred and five when the phone went down in the hall. My bedroom door was open and I could hear what went on. Mum answered the phone and then made a sort of gaspy screamy noise and started to cry a lot. I mean really a lot and quite loud too. She shouted up that Grampa Gray had died from his operation but didn't say any more than that because she was crying so hard. Somehow I knew she was lying on the bottom of the stairs though I didn't actually see her lying there because I was too poorly to get out of bed. I lay there by myself for hours and hours thinking lots of my complicated mixed-up thoughts but it's funny I can't remember what they were this time. I didn't even know Grampa was having an operation and it was the only time in all my life I'd heard my mum crying. It's funny that I didn't cry too because you'd have thought I would have, wouldn't you, seeing that I loved Grampa so much. Actually in a funny sort of way I couldn't understand I didn't really feel much at all really, except that I wanted mum to come upstairs and comfort me. I just kept having all those complicated mixed-up thoughts I can't remember.

There's only one thing I thought that I can remember thinking which wasn't complicated but easy for me to understand which I suppose is why I can remember it. I thought that I would never see Grampa's kind face ever again or sit on his knee ever again or listen to his nice stories ever again, at least not until I died one day too and we would be together again in heaven where he'd be waiting for me like he did on Sundays with the front door open.

CHAPTER 3

Peter Symonds School

THE THOUGHT of going to a big school where there'd be about 600 other kids was a bit scary, though I tried not to show it. What I was scared of was that I might be bullied a lot because I was much younger than all the other boys.

It was lucky that John came with me on my first day and showed me what's what, which was just as well because otherwise I wouldn't have known that the boys who were Roman Catholics like John and me didn't go into the hall for prayers like all the others but queued up in the corridor outside the hall until after we heard the last hymn was finished, when we all filed in and stood at the back while the headmaster, Dr Freeman, read all the notices about this and that. We called him 'Doc', but not to his face, of course. He was far too strict for things like that. It didn't seem funny that Roman Catholics weren't allowed to say prayers and sing hymns with everyone else. No-one took any notice or said we were stupid or anything. It was just the way things were in those days.

Actually, I wasn't bullied at all – well, hardly at all – thank goodness. I did, though, feel a bit lost inside me. All the things we did seemed like separate pieces of a complicated jig-saw puzzle, not all joined together to make one big picture, which would have been a more comfortable sort of feeling to have inside me, if you see what I mean.

There were dozens and dozens of masters but some mistresses too because some of the masters had gone away like dad to fight in the war. They all wore black gowns which made them seem important, at least to start with.

The main thing was that I was quite good at swimming and diving. Actually, I was the under-thirteen swimming champion which was a good thing because most other kids thought better of you if you were good at some sport or other than if you were good at lessons, in which case they though you were a swot which was not very nice and made me feel confused inside because I didn't see what was supposed to be wrong with learning things. Anyway, I couldn't help being 'quick on the uptake', as mum used to say, because of my blotting paper mind, as Miss Scott had called it.

I did OK at most of my lessons in forms 2A, 3A and 4A, but wasn't so good at maths, partly because we had a useless maths teacher who had retired but been called back to help out during the war. He was hopeless at keeping discipline and everyone mucked about all the time. We called him 'daddy' Bishop because he was so old – 'grampa' Bishop would have been a better name. He made the same joke time and time again and we all groaned aloud every time. When he showed us how to do a sum on the blackboard, he always said 'watch the board while I go through it'. Groan, groan!

By the time I reached the fifth form, the one thing I was sure about was that I preferred languages and literature to maths and science, though we had to do maths for the School Certificate.

I definitely wouldn't have got a credit in maths in the School Certificate if 'Cuzzy' Cozens hadn't taken over as our maths teacher. He had a stern, I mean really stern, face with swept-back grey hair and a thick but neat grey moustache nearly as wide as his top lip. His ample body looked far too big for his legs that tapered down to small feet which weren't actually pigeon-toed but looked it because they pointed straight forwards and not outwards like most people's. It was a miracle that he didn't topple over.

When he wasn't in his classroom he kept puffing a pipe that curled down below his chin and dropped ash on the lapels of his checked suit which somehow managed to stay looking smart though, as far as I can remember, it was the only one he ever had. The staff room was at the far end of a long corridor leading from his classroom. Every lesson, on the dot, we could hear his footsteps coming out of the staff room which even such a long way away immediately struck the fear of God into us. You could hear a pin drop. His footsteps got louder and louder till, right on cue, he swept into the classroom with a swirl of his flowing gown which scattered chalk dust in all directions. He did complicated sums on the blackboard with a flourish of hand and chalk explaining what he was doing as he went along in a way the thickest boys in the class could understand. We all got at least passes in School Certificate. We didn't dare not to. You could tell he actually *wanted* us to learn things and wasn't just going through the motions because he was paid to teach us, which is more than you could say for some of the others. Actually, he sometimes made us laugh a lot. One day we were working in the usual deathly silence when the baby belonging to the caretaker whose flat was next to his classroom let out a piercing scream.

Quick as a flash, Cuzzy shouted 'Quiet, Elton!' We all fell off our chairs laughing.

'Perdy' Cooksey was a brilliant Latin teacher with a perpetual sardonic sort of expression on his pale-sallow face which wasn't surprising considering he spent most of his life teaching Latin to kids bored stiff by Virgil and all that stuff. He didn't try to hide that he regarded most of them as thick-heads. There was no mucking about with Perdy, that's for sure. His withering sarcasm was no fun to be on the receiving end of. Sometimes, he literally knocked knowledge into an idle dimwit's brain by banging him on the head with 'Latin for Today' and shouting, 'amo – bang – amas – bang – amat – bang – amamus – bang – amatis – bang – AMANT – BANG!' Like Cuzzy, he really wanted us to learn and kept on at us till we did. He was OK, was Perdy.

'Bill' Sykes taught four of us Greek for our first year. I did Greek because Cuzzy told me they needed someone else to do Greek and I had to because my brother was good at it. Well, you didn't argue with Cuzzy. Bill was slim and tall with whitish grey hair and a scholarly, gentle sort of face. His main feature was a big Adam's apple. Because he'd been gassed in the First World War he made a funny 'humph' noise after every few words and his Adam's apple jumped up and down every time he humphed. You won't be surprised to know that we became brilliant at imitating his humph. I even invented a Greek verb for 'to humph' – ὑμφω (I humph) ὑμφεις (you humph) ὑμφει (he humphs) etc. – and wrote a poem in Greek taking the mickey out of him which was a great laugh. The only time Bill got annoyed with me wasn't my fault. He also taught us Roman history and it was my turn to translate some Latin text about a Roman general called 'Agrippa'. The moment I first said 'Agrippa', Bruce MacMillan, a good friend who was sitting next to me, gripped the top of my leg under my desk and whispered 'I'm Agrippa'! I spluttered and spluttered in a vain attempt to hide my laughter. Bill told me to share the joke which I couldn't without dropping Bruce in it. I just managed to say, 'I'm sorry, Sir', to which he responded with an unusually rapid series of cross-sounding humphs. Somehow he could put different expressions into his humphs. Actually, I liked Bill a lot and felt sorry for him because someone told me that when his wife died his hair turned grey within a few weeks. I hoped he would somehow find happiness again before he died. He was a decent chap who really wanted us to share his enthusiasm for the Classics for our own sakes.

'Tom' Pierce was a decent chap too. At one stage, he taught us English literature and when he read aloud a specially beautiful bit from a poem, his voice choked with emotion and you could tell he was holding back tears. This, of course, was a source of endless hilarity, though I thought that was a bit mean because sometimes I could see why he felt that way, though I kept that to myself in case the other kids thought I was a cissy. Tom used to dish out lists of the first lines of poems and the names of the poems and authors – like 'I will arise and go now, and go to Innisfree – The Lake Isle of Innisfree – W.B. Yeats'. I could see why he thought it was a good idea but was too idle to make the most of it, which was a shame because I must have missed out on a lot of beautiful poems if their first lines were anything to go by.

I need hardly explain why 'Bum' Woodly had that nickname, though he never got near my bum, you have my word for that. He was a rich bachelor, of course – I mean, of course he was a bachelor, not of course he was rich. He always had a pansy handkerchief flopping down from his breast pocket and was a bit of a buffoon. Actually, he was a complete buffoon. Most of the time he didn't seem to care if we messed about, then suddenly lost his temper and gave two or three poor kids a lot of really vicious clouts round the ear which resulted in a stony silence until everything fell apart again, which didn't take long. His idea of teaching us 'Keats and Shelley' for School Certificate was to make us take turns at reading their poems aloud 'over and over again until you damn well know them'. This required the minimum of effort on his part, but I have to admit that in the end I did damn well know them, though any inspiration I had to find for myself. I can quote Keats' Ode to a Grecian Urn to this day and always liked the ending – 'Beauty is truth, truth beauty. That is all ye know on earth and all ye need to know.' I thought a lot about what that meant and I bet you Tom Pierce would have had to choke back a lot of tears if he'd read it to us.

'Hetty' Hammond taught us German OK. His main weapon, apart from his sarcasm which was sort of smarmy compared with Purdy's, was to 'give you the ruler', which meant giving you hard slaps on your cheeks with a ruler which left red marks and stung like hell. I know that, because one lesson he said he'd go round and look at our homework and give us the ruler for our first mistake. He knew darned well we'd all have made at least one mistake. Surprise, surprise – we all got the ruler, which seemed to amuse him no end. I couldn't see how he thought this would make us better at German. As far as I was concerned, apart from being sadistic, it was just plain stupid.

I can't miss out 'Oofy' Priestland because he made a lot of us like Shakespeare, which took some doing. We did Macbeth with him for School Certificate and he made it seem like an exciting thriller. I actually looked forward to the next instalment at the next lesson. He was very strict, with an almost ugly, monkey-looking face that you had to pay attention to. If you didn't, he was a dab hand at striking direct hits with pieces of chalk. He made some of us take the parts of the various characters in Macbeth, which we did pretty well thanks to the atmosphere he created. I particularly remember one of his first lessons when he asked us how we'd say, for example, that Lady Macbeth couldn't wash the smell of Duncan's blood from her hands or that something would last as long as human beings did. The imaginative boys would say something like 'I want to purify my hands with pure water but in vain' and 'until the end of history'. Oofy quoted what Shakespeare said: 'All the perfumes of Arabia will not sweeten this little hand' and 'to the last syllable of recorded time'. This was a good way of showing us that we weren't geniuses and Shakespeare was. He explained how Shakespeare expressed the deepest and most complex thoughts in simple language and took an example from Hamlet. How would we say we didn't know whether there was a life after death and what it would be like if there was? After some feeble and complicated attempts by some of us, he quoted: 'For in that sleep of death, what dreams may come?' Wow! Ten simple words of one syllable, he stressed. Then he asked us why that was poetry when it didn't rhyme. Faced with blank stares, he said it didn't need to *rhyme* because it had *rhythm* like music or your pulse. He wrote it on the blackboard and underlined every other word – For <u>in</u> that <u>sleep</u> of <u>death</u>, what <u>dreams</u> may <u>come</u>? I've gone on a lot about that lesson because I thought it was brilliant teaching and it meant a lot to me, especially comparing Shakespeare with music.

The only subject in School Certificate I didn't get at least a credit in but only a pass was Geography. I've often wondered whether this was just a coincidence or had something to do with my worst experience at Peter Symonds.

Our geography teacher was Miss Noble, who was short and a bit plump and had thick, sexy lips. One day I lost my geography text book. I didn't want to have to admit to her that I'd lost it and so I did something very stupid and very naughty. When Miss Noble left the classroom at the end of one lesson, she left her copy of the book on her desk. When no-one was looking, I pinched it, secretly crossed her name out with lots of strokes of ink and wrote my name underneath. The next lesson she walked round and looked at everyone's book. When she got to me, she asked if I'd crossed her name out and written mine instead. I said I hadn't. She took the book away and at the end of the lesson the next day she called me up to her desk and said she'd used some ink remover and could see I'd crossed her name out and knew I'd stolen her book and lied to her. She sent me to the head master, Doc Freeman, who gave me six strokes of the cane on my bottom. I remember he was wearing his black gown. He had the book with him and told me to give it back to Miss Noble and apologise to her, which I did. I can't tell you how awful and ashamed I felt. I was all muddled up inside and wanted to shrivel up and die. The whole episode haunted me for days and nights. It was so horrible and humiliating to have to bend over while Doc caned my bottom. I kept imagining him holding up his cane and his eyes staring at me as if he despised me, which I didn't want him to. His left eye seemed to bulge out more than his other one in a sinister sort of way, though I don't know whether it really did or whether I just imagined it did. Part of me felt resentful, which wasn't logical because I knew darned well that I deserved the cane because I'd been caught out as a thief and a liar. I thought I must be a real softy because other boys often got the cane without turning a hair. They couldn't have cared less. I couldn't have cared more. I never told anyone about this till now.

If Miss Noble had sexy lips, you should have seen Miss Pugh. I'm not sure if that's how she spelt her name but it was pronounced 'Pew' like a church bench. When she was around, there were more interesting things to think about than how to spell her name. Oh boy, she wasn't half sexy looking. She was a very pretty blonde, wore tight skirts and lots of make-up and wasn't too big up top – and not too small either. She was cool as a cucumber, which only inflamed my emerging pubescent lust all the more. She was the subject of frequent 'bad thoughts' which was a code for solo self-satisfaction – if you see what I mean – every time I went to confession. The first thing I always confessed was that I'd had bad thoughts because I felt so guilty about them. In those days it was supposed to be a mortal sin to indulge in them, which meant that, unless you confessed them, you would go to hell. I wouldn't blame you if you didn't believe what I'm going to tell you now because I wouldn't believe it myself if I didn't remember it so clearly. One of the priests said at the end of one confession that the answer was to wear boxing gloves when I went to bed! One day soon afterwards I happened to see him sneaking

across from St Peter's Church to the Royal Cinema, which was just over
the road. There was a naughty film on and I couldn't help wondering if
he'd taken some boxing gloves with him.

The priest I really liked was Father Mullarkey. Although he was really
holy, he didn't – like lots of priests – have a round innocent face like a
cherub in a religious painting but was tall and thin with a beaky nose and
clever-looking glasses. You could tell he knew what it was like to be a
normal sort of person and commit normal sorts of sins. John told me that
Father Mullarkey once said to him that people's sexual 'peccadillos'
weren't as bad as their other sins like being unkind to people. It was just
that they felt more guilty about them. John and me learnt to be altar
servers and it was useful that we knew some Latin. We were usually the
altar servers at the ten o'clock mass on Sundays and every so often took
turns to serve at the 7 o'clock mass on week-days, which meant getting
up early and cycling to the church quite often in the dark. For some
reason I asked Father Mullarkey one morning how he was and he replied
'As well as can be expected in this vale of tears'. I remember his exact
words because I was surprised that he was unhappy. I thought that a
Catholic priest somehow cut himself off from the sort of sorrows other
people had to put up with and just looked forward to going to heaven. I
often wondered what had happened to make him so sad.

I particularly liked praying in the chapel devoted to Mary. It made me
feel calm and peaceful inside to think that she was the virgin mother of
baby Jesus. There was a lovely big statue of Mary above the altar. She was
holding and comforting baby Jesus in her arms and wearing a blue
garment and a shiny, golden crown. She seemed sort of pure and I didn't
have bad thoughts about her, that's for sure. One day when I went to pray
there, her crown had been taken off to be cleaned. The top of her head
was just a round, bald plaster cast, which really upset me because I
couldn't imagine she was real any more though that didn't make much
sense when I thought about it because I knew it was only a statue in the
first place. I wasn't that stupid.

When the blitz on London and other towns like Southampton was
over, we still huddled round the wireless in the gloomy dining room
when Churchill made his famous speeches or read about them in the
next day's paper. I can't tell you how proud and patriotic he made us feel.
I thought a lot about his words and much later on, after the lesson with
Oofy I told you about, I imagined him writing on the blackboard –
'Never in the field of human conflict was so much owed by so many to

so <u>few</u>.' I thought that Shakespeare couldn't have expressed such an important and complicated thought more simply and beautifully – he could have added it to the play where one of the King Henrys talked about 'we few, we happy few'.

Things at school went on pretty much as usual, but things at home changed a lot, especially when thousands and thousands of American soldiers arrived. They cheered us up in more ways than one. For reasons best known to himself, Doc Freeman told us in one of his classes I'll mention later that he got up early every morning and walked round the bushes in the playing fields picking up scores of used contraceptives. Most families entertained the Americans in their homes and we somehow got to know one who was a professional singer of classical songs and had sung on the wireless in America before coming to England. We had wonderful musical evenings like we did before the war and I was surprised that, though he had a broad American accent, he sang English songs with a perfect English accent. Mum used to sing popular war songs in concerts for the American and English troops, songs like 'There'll be bluebirds over the white cliffs of Dover, tomorrow just you wait and see' and 'We'll meet again, don't know where, don't know when, but I know we'll meet again some sunny day'. Partly I was proud of her looking so pretty and singing so well but partly I felt sort of ashamed of her flirting with the audience as she sang and being whistled at in a sexy sort of way by all those soldiers. After one concert, a nice American colonel we knew walked home with us and John and me went indoors leaving them to talk. When she came in I heard her say to Allie that he'd asked if he could kiss her goodnight. She'd said he couldn't because she was a married woman with children and the colonel had been very upset.

An extra nice American soldier was called 'Mac'. He wasn't like most of the other American soldiers but was a quiet, thinking sort of chap. He spent many evenings with us and sometimes made a pattern on the steel table (which we didn't have to sleep under any more) with packets of chewing gum and even chocolate for John and me to have. Sometime after he'd had to leave Winchester, we heard that he hadn't opened his parachute on a training exercise and had been killed. Apparently he had fallen deeply in love with mum but realized it couldn't lead anywhere.

An important man in our lives was Ronald Smart. He was a really beautiful singer of German and English songs and had sung at our musical evenings before the war and continued to do so. He became a lodger with us – other lodgers must have left by then – and was a good substitute father. He became a Roman Catholic like us and had a special stool in his room that he knelt on to say his prayers. Towards the end of the war he joined the RAF but I didn't understand why he hadn't been called up before. Sometime after the war, John told me that Ronald was a homosexual and had become a Catholic because he needed to try to relieve himself of his guilt. He never, ever tried anything on with John and me and was, as I said, a good substitute father to us. It seems sad to think of such a good man kneeling on his prayer stool all by himself and praying for forgiveness for something he couldn't really help.

We all got very excited when we knew dad was coming home on leave. We used to meet him at the station and sometimes we weren't sure which train from London he was coming on and had to wait or go back to meet the next one. We always looked down the railway lines through several bridges that got smaller and smaller the further away they were, waiting to get the first glimpse of a tiny tell-tale puff of smoke in the far distance. When he eventually arrived, he was always leaning out of the train window and waving. John and I rushed up to him and he picked us up and kissed us. Then he and mum embraced each other and kissed for a long time. Once, he was wearing a beret instead of a peaked cap, which made me feel sort of disappointed and mixed-up inside. His beret wasn't as smart as his peaked cap – nothing like as smart.

Mum looked after us well even though most food was strictly rationed and we had no luxuries, like ice-cream or bananas, and hardly any butter or sweets or chocolate – one small bar a week. She managed to give us nice parties on our birthdays, with jelly and cake and jam sandwiches. Her best friend's husband was in charge of the local slaughter-house and secretly gave her extra bits of meat. I don't know what else she got up to but her friends nick-named her 'the black-market Queen of Winchester'.

In some ways the war made everything confusing, what with all those absent fathers and husbands and the coming and going of soldiers far away from their homes and homelands. Ships that pass in the night, dad once said when he was on leave. In other ways it made things simple. We knew what was right and what was wrong. Hitler was bad and we were good. We were definitely right to fight the wicked Germans and to leave no stone unturned to beat them. It was as simple as that.

Everyone did something for the 'war effort'. Sometimes we stayed on after school to tie bits of brown and green cloth to huge nets to camouflage our guns and tanks. Sometimes we took turns to peel potatoes in the kitchen of the hospital. Men came to take away all the nice iron railings from our gardens to make the guns and tanks with. The factories made bombs and shells for the aeroplanes and tanks instead of cars and other luxuries we had before the war. Women worked in the factories and on the farms so the men could go and fight. Some younger men worked down the mines to help the ordinary miners dig out the extra coal we needed. Older ones joined the Home Guard. All our mums knitted things like socks and balaclava helmets for refugees. Kids like John and me had dartboards on which the bull's eye was Hitler's face and other games like that to 'boost our morale', mum said.

One day a friend of mine who lived higher up on the other side of Milverton Road knocked on the door, breathless with running and excitement. He said his dad, who worked at the railway station, had told him something he wasn't supposed to for strict security reasons and said he wasn't to tell anyone else. Winston Churchill was about to arrive at the station to inspect some soldiers at the barracks. The two of us and John rushed down to the station as fast as we could. Apart from a few policemen, there was only a small crowd waiting by the entrance to the platform for trains from London. Almost straight away a train came in and Churchill himself walked out of the station within literally three or four feet of us. He actually looked me in the eyes and smiled and actually made his famous 'V' sign with a big cigar between his fingers. I could hardly believe that I was actually seeing the great man in the flesh and so close up. I was surprised that he looked a bit thinner than I thought he was and that the hair sticking out under his hat wasn't grey but a bit gingery. I'll never forget his eyes looking into mine.

Leading up to the D-day landings in France, the whole place got fuller and fuller of more and more British and American soldiers. I couldn't think where they all slept. There were often long convoys of lorries packed with soldiers and tanks with an officer standing up through a hole in the top and waving proudly at us. The tanks ripped up the surface of the roads and made such a loud noise that we could hear them when they were a long way off. We always rushed down the road to see them and wave back.

A day or two after D-day, dad was in a convoy of lorries parked along Winchester by-pass, though of course we didn't know that till afterwards. He must have wished he could just pop home instead of going away across the sea back to France. I never quite knew how he managed it but somehow he carried a portable gramophone round France, Belgium and Holland, one of those old ones you had to wind up and played big black records on. He played records of German songs which he loved though he didn't know a word of German and couldn't sing a note in tune. Perhaps they reminded him of the musical evenings he was missing at home.

One day a few months later when John and me were getting dressed for school, we suddenly heard a great roar of aeroplanes and looked out of our bedroom window at the back of the house. What we saw was absolutely breathtaking. Flying towards us low over the trees surrounding the girls' High School were wave after wave of aeroplanes towing enormous gliders attached to long cables. The gliders were much bigger than the aeroplanes and the whole sky was filled with them for ages. When some passed low over our house, the noise of the aeroplanes in front was quickly followed by the eerie sort of silence of the gliders, though we could just about hear the wind whistling against their huge wings. It wasn't like when we saw Southampton burning to the ground, which I told you meant nothing to me. I was old enough now for the dreadful horror of war to sink into my thoughts and imagination. Although it was an inspiring and actually a strangely beautiful sight, I imagined the gliders were packed full of soldiers sitting side by side clasping their rifles pointing upwards. Were they wondering what fate awaited them? Were they feeling brave? Or pretending to be brave but in reality scared out of their wits, wondering whether they'd ever again see their mums and dads, their wives, their children?

We heard on the wireless in the following days that the battle of Arnhem was a disaster with hundreds of our soldiers being killed trying to capture a big bridge across the river Rhine in Holland. Whenever I thought about those huge gliders sailing low and silently through the clear morning air, my mind pictured the mangled, blood-stained bodies of soldiers lying far away from their homes in the fields of Holland. I imagined their silent ghosts, their spirits, their souls leaving their dead bodies and floating up to heaven where there would be no more wars and they'd be at peace with God for ever and ever. I wanted to cry but didn't. I thought of what was my very favourite poem, about a soldier in the First World War, written by Rupert Brooke:

> If I should die, think only this of me:
> That there's some corner of a foreign field
> That is forever England. There shall be
> In that rich earth a richer dust concealed;
> A dust whom England bore, shaped, made aware,

Gave, once, her flowers to love, her ways to roam,
A body of England's breathing English air,
Washed by the rivers, blest by suns of home.
And think, this heart, all evil shed away,
A pulse in the eternal mind, no less
Gives somewhere back the thoughts by England given;
Her sights and sounds; dreams happy as her day;
And laughter, learnt of friends; and gentleness,
In hearts at peace, under an English heaven.

We finally beat the Germans on the sixth day of May, 1945 – two weeks before my fourteenth birthday on the twentieth of May. It was called 'VE Day', which was short for 'Victory in Europe Day'. All I remember about that famous day is that mum had gone out to celebrate with her friends. I expect she felt I'd rather go out and celebrate with mine than be with boring grown-ups. For some reason I can't remember, John wasn't there either. I was left standing by myself in mum and dad's bedroom looking out of the front window at people rushing about all excited and happy. I had never felt so lonely before, so completely and utterly alone in the world. I so desperately wanted to be with my mum, sharing with her – and she with me – what should have been the happiest day of my life. After all, dad would soon be coming back after all those long years away from home and at last we'd all be together again.

I could see myself in the mirror of the dressing table that stood in front of the window, which meant that I couldn't hide my misery from myself. I saw my lips trembling and my eyes filling with tears. Every fibre in my body, every cell in my brain longed, yearned, ached for my mum to be with me, embracing me, enfolding me with joy and love. For once, I couldn't keep the stiff upper lip I remembered dad once said big boys should. I fell on mum and dad's bed and wept and wept, sobbed and sobbed, till there were no more tears left inside me.

I had just turned fourteen when I passed my School Certificate and started in the sixth form where I would remain for four years. After the first two years I passed the Higher School Certificate in Latin, Greek and Ancient History, with German as a subsidiary subject. The following year, I got distinctions in all four subjects and was awarded a State scholarship which would help to cover the cost of going to a University. I spent my last year applying for places at several Oxford colleges and was eventually accepted by Brasenose College. This leisurely timetable imposed no great strain on my 'blotting paper' mind, though I was soon to regret that I hadn't worked harder and especially that I had idled away my time during my final year. Bill Sykes and Perdy Cooksey had both said I should take the opportunity to do a lot of general reading about the Classics but the only book I remember reading was *The Hound of the Baskervilles*, which held such a strange fascination for me that I read it several times. I felt haunted by the sinister, fearsome hound whose menacing baying floated through the gloomy mists from wherever it was lurking in the bleak and mysterious depths of Dartmoor.

Bill and Perdy took four of us for Latin, Greek and Ancient History, and Hetty Hammond a larger group for German. Unlike Bill, Perdy had till then only taught us in his Latin classes of well over thirty pupils. Now he too could treat us as intelligent beings, which he clearly much preferred. As we were leaving the classroom at the end of our last lesson with him in which we'd been reading some Homer, he suddenly said: 'Well, good luck for the future, Elton. I hope I've taught you at least something of value that will stay with you to the end.' I was really quite touched. It showed he cared about me and understood me – better, perhaps, than he realized. It was the sort of thing someone says that you always remember.

Although I was made a prefect, I wasn't as strict as I should have been. I hated the thought of being unpopular. I certainly couldn't bring myself to cane boys as most of the other prefects did. Some seemed positively to enjoy it. I was also promoted to be a sergeant in the cadet force. Somewhat to my surprise, I had no difficulty in being strict. It was quite a thrill to make my platoon drill smartly and a challenge to make it smarter than the other platoons. Besides, wearing a uniform with three stripes on my arms somehow made it possible for me to feel important for once and to adopt an artificial, uncharacteristic role. I didn't have to be myself.

Perhaps that's something to do with why I enjoyed taking part in the school plays. A particular success was Shaw's *Arms and the Man*, in which I played the leading role. Some boys who were super actors had to dress up in women's clothes to play the female characters, which added to the fun. The critic in the *Hampshire Chronicle* said it was the best schoolboy production he'd ever seen. I was particularly chuffed that one day when he was passing me in the corridor outside his study, Doc Freeman stopped and congratulated me and said how much he enjoyed the expressive and amusing looks I'd given the other characters. It made me at last stop feeling rejected by him because of the incident when I'd stolen Miss Noble's book and he'd given me the cane.

Doc took us for one lesson a week. His lessons were riveting – all about evolution and the stars being millions of light years away and the other wonders of the universe. Sometimes he projected fascinating slides on to one of the walls of the classroom, illustrating what he was talking about. He was a distinguished headmaster, in some ways very much of the old school but in others well ahead of his time. He arranged dances in the school hall with girls from the girls' High School and stood watching encouraging us to dance with the girls, which was pretty progressive for that day and age, though I couldn't help noticing that he wasn't exactly averse to making a careful study of the prettiest and shapeliest girls. One of his main hobbies was bird-watching and studying nature generally. He roundly condemned golf as being the ruination of what would otherwise be a decent country walk with your mind on higher things. If you weren't studying a book (or pretending to) when he entered the classroom, he'd point his finger at you and say you'd just wasted sixty seconds of your life which you could never have back. Another of his favourite sayings was that there was 'no fun like work', which was invariably greeted with blank stares of bemused incredulity. He didn't hide his political views and was clearly horrified when Attlee and his Labour government won the election after the war instead of Churchill and the Conservatives. He frequently referred with undisguised contempt to 'the so-called working classes'.

I wasn't particularly good at football or cricket. I much preferred tennis and especially squash, which was by far my best game. I was the school champion for several years. I was only averagely good at athletics, though I came in the first two or three in the annual cross-country race except for one year when I was falling behind and felt so rotten that I stopped running and sat down with my head in my hands. I just couldn't go on and had to be picked up by one of the masters and driven home. Unfortunately, mum was out shopping and wasn't there to comfort me. I felt so churned up inside and scared that the other boys would think I was a wimp.

Although things at school didn't change much after the war, things at home naturally changed a great deal. We no longer had any lodgers and dad was back from the war, though I can't remember the day he actually came home any more than the day he went away. What I do vividly remember is coming home one day and finding that the grey wall outside the dining room window had vanished. Bright daylight was flooding in after all those gloomy years and it was amazing to see the garden again through the window. Never before or since has grass looked so green. The big steel table under which we had spent so many cramped nights during the blitz had been replaced by a much smaller wooden one which made more space to welcome the fresh light.

Inside me, however, there began to be times when my mind became overcast with barely discernible shadows. I couldn't quite put my finger on it, except that I was dimly aware that mum and dad were somehow not as at ease with each other as they had been in those far-off days before the war when we had all spent happy holidays together by the sea at Southbourne. I remembered hearing a lady who lived in Milverton Road telling mum that, since her husband had come home, it was like living with a stranger in the house, and that a friend of hers felt the same way. I tried to say to myself that mum and dad were no different from millions of husbands and wives all over the world whose lives had been torn apart by the war and who had to rebuild the foundations of their relationships starting virtually from scratch. I could see that the casualties of war were not confined to those who had been wounded or killed.

Despite the material deprivations of wartime, mum had had a lot of freedom and fun entertaining the soldiers, singing in the concerts for the troops, flirting – innocently but provocatively – and generally having a taste of what, compared with her deprived and poverty-stricken childhood and youth, must have seemed like a glamorous 'high life'. I could see it was only natural that she should have needed to make up for lost time. She had changed.

Whether or not dad had changed I wasn't so sure. Who knows what war does to a man? He must have known danger and feared death, certainly at Dunkirk and presumably other times, though he never talked about it. Uncle Tony had told us that one of his friends was a private in dad's Company and had told him that dad was the best and best-liked officer he'd ever come across. Had his experience of commanding men, with its enforced comradeship amid the brutality of war, changed him in some way I couldn't detect? Considering his sheltered background, I thought that at the very least his horizons must have been vastly broadened. Yet, for all that, he still seemed to be his old unassuming and gentle self. I instinctively knew he wouldn't regard the 'high life' as glamorous but artificial and shallow. It was not for nothing that he had somehow carted his gramophone and records of lieder round the battlefields of Europe.

HMS Pinafore, *after the war – my mother on the right; Aunty Jane, second from the left.*

Not that anything much changed on the surface. We continued with our musical evenings and Ronald Smart gave mum singing lessons, sometimes shouting at her in his temperamental but inoffensive way. It was just Ronald being Ronald. Often, at the end of a musical evening, the other people would plead with him to sing 'just once more'. He invariably said 'What about a little Mozart?' and proceeded to sing so beautifully the two great arias sung by the Priest in *Die Zauberflöte* (*The Magic Flute*). I was lucky to be quite good at German by then and even then could tell that people missed a lot if they didn't appreciate the subtle beauty of the words. I remember thinking that, even though 'flöte' ('flute') was pronounced almost the same as 'flirter', if you thought it was spelt like that you wouldn't appreciate the beauty of the word, whereas if you realised the 'ir' was a modified 'o' sound, it became, as if by magic, a very beautiful one.

Mum continued to enjoy singing Gilbert and Sullivan in the chorus of the Winchester Amateur Operatic Society and dad became expert at making up the various characters and members of the chorus behind the scenes. They also took part in the productions of the Amateur Dramatic Society and were both good actors. Once I took the part of Bill, the typically troublesome boy in *Dear Octopus*, which was about a family which one of the characters, when proposing a toast at some sort of family gathering, described as 'that dear octopus, from whose tentacles we never quite escape nor, in our inmost hearts, ever quite wish to'. The producer was a larger-than-life character called 'Oscar' Wilde, whose main claim to fame was that he had understudied some of the great Victorian actors. He was a large, temperamental, flamboyant character to say the least, with a flushed veiny face and long, straggly grey hair. Once he made us all stop and shiver in our shoes by shouting louder and louder: 'There are only three rules about acting. The first is to be heard, **the second is to be heard** and **THE THIRD IS TO BE HEARD**'. None of us ever dared mumble our words again.

I also took the part of the son of a character dad played in *The Years Between* about a man going away to the war and then facing the emotional problems of returning home to his family afterwards. I don't have to tell you how true this rang both to dad and me. Father and son playing father and son, especially in this context, gave us a head start, apart from the fact that we obviously looked like a father and son. The critic in the *Hampshire Chronicle* said we had well portrayed how our relationship before the war changed after the missing 'years between' and that I'd really given the impression of having grown up, although the only thing I was conscious of was exchanging short trousers for long ones.

When dad went back to work immediately after his return home, he was quickly promoted several times and quite soon became the Deputy County Surveyor. Being better off financially, we moved to 4 Bereweeke Close, a smartish cul-de-sac leading into Bereweeke Road almost opposite the big house that had once been the Lion School and was a constant reminder of my unhappy time there. Although our new home wasn't very attractive to look at, it was, unlike 6 Milverton Road, a detached house and much bigger; a solid family home. Very luckily for me, its sizeable back garden backed onto the Winchester Tennis and Squash Club. We made a hole in the hedge at the back of the garden so that we could walk straight through to the rather splendid grounds of the Club which consequently felt like part of our 'estate'. Dad was almost obsessive about the back lawn, always raking it, cutting and rolling it in different directions, weeding it, fertilizing it and putting thin, sieved topsoil on it. It was always perfect and the envy of his friends.

It wasn't long after we'd moved that my vague feeling that all was not well with mum and dad was confirmed. One evening I was sitting at the dining room table doing my homework when I heard dad sobbing in the kitchen. Mum was there with him. I could tell he was trying to cry quietly so no-one could hear. His sobbing was interrupted by occasional brief whispers. I strained in vain to hear what they were saying. Dad was clearly inconsolable, so uncontrollable were his tears, so long did they continue to flow.

I had never heard a man cry before, let alone my own dad. I felt physically sick. As I write over half a century later, I can see it may well have been completely unfair to mum but instinctively I sided with dad in what for no identifiable reason I assumed must have been a quarrel about something or other. I felt an increasing bitterness and a blind anger towards her – for what, I didn't know. It was hard to get to sleep that night. It all kept going round and round in my brain and I had to try harder than usual to stop myself crying about it. Wasn't it dad, ironically enough, who once said big boys didn't cry? What had happened that was so awful that a grown man who'd been a brave officer in the war couldn't help crying? I kept saying to myself what I had slowly and painfully come to realize: that I was much too over-sensitive and imaginative for my own comfort, always inclined to think the worst of things. But it didn't help. Not the slightest bit. The shadows in my mind only deepened and darkened.

In my last year at Peter Symonds, Father Mullarkey arranged for the altar servers to go on a pilgrimage to Rome because it was 'Holy Year'. About a dozen of us trekked across Europe by train for hours on end eventually emerging from a tunnel under the Alps into the bright warmth of northern Italy and going on to Rome. Father Mullarkey and two other priests accompanied us and were great fun to be with. We stayed in a convent in the shadow of St Peter's, which we entered via an archway on the left of the Basilica as you look at it from the front. We slept on hard beds in a sparse, dimly-lit dormitory and the food was rather plain, to say the least. The nuns, however, were kindly and gentle with calm, cherubic faces. One morning, I and another chap had to get up early to serve at mass with Father Mullarkey in one of the side chapels in St Peter's. I could hardly believe that I was actually serving at mass in the hallowed surroundings of that famous centre of my holy mother church. The unforgettable moment, however, was when we all trooped into St Peter's with tens of thousands of other pilgrims from all over the world – from over 120 countries, Father Mullarkey said. We stood crammed together for ages waiting with mounting expectation and excitement for the great moment when the Pope himself would appear. Eventually, a huge curtain at the back of the right hand side of the colossal nave was drawn apart and the vast dome was suddenly lit up so that the great message written round its base in enormous letters was ablaze with light: 'TU EST PETRUS ET SUPER HANC PETRAM AEDIFICABO ECCLESIAM MEAM' ('You are Peter and upon this rock I will build my church'). I nearly fainted with emotion at the first glimpse of St Peter's successor, Pope Pius XII, borne aloft on his throne by the Swiss guards resplendent in their colourful uniforms. As he came nearer I could clearly see his pale, serene, saintly face beneath a large white mitre, white robes flowing from his thin body. He looked down at the untold thousands of upturned faces, giving his blessing with signs of the cross to left and right. After a while, we all sang the Latin mass. We all understood what we were singing and knew everyone else, whatever their native language, understood too. I had never known there could be such an overwhelming, sublime sense of unity between the peoples of the world.

Many of the pilgrims had tears streaming down their faces. I glanced at Father Mullarkey who I imagined was transported, in the words that came to my mind from Schubert's great song 'An die Musik' ('To Music'), to 'eine bessre Welt' ('a better world') – a better world, I thought, than the vale of tears he had mentioned so sadly that dark morning before early mass several years ago in Winchester's own humbler St Peter's. This in turn triggered the passing thought that, for me, this vale of tears now included the tears shed by my father that day in the kitchen at home. Nevertheless, the inspiration and elation of the occasion – its sheer magnificence – prevented the hovering shadows from clouding my mind. I was profoundly moved and profoundly happy to feel so close to God.

During the long journey home, I felt full of faith for the one, true, universal church. I thought a lot, as usual. I thought the idea of a Church of England was absurd. I knew enough history to think that it would have been nothing less than farcical if there had been written round the dome of St Paul's: 'Tu est *Henricus Rex* et super hanc petram aedificabo ecclesiam meam.' ('You are King Henry...')

On Saturday evenings once a month, John and I went to dances in the long-gone Cadena Café in the High Street, though I went on my own from the time I was sixteen because by then John had been called up for his National Service. I used to dress up in dad's dinner jacket, which was a lengthy process. It was great struggle to insert a stud to join the two ends of the stiff and uncomfortable winged collar just under my Adam's apple, which, being averse to self-strangulation, I didn't look forward to.

A string trio played old-fashioned dances like waltzes, quicksteps and slow foxtrots. A more exciting dance was the tango because you could push your middle firmly against your partner's. At some stage we always danced a 'Paul Jones', where the girls stood in a circle facing outwards and the boys surrounded them with a bigger circle facing inwards. The girls walked round one way and the boys the other. When the music stopped, you had to dance with the girl opposite you.

One Saturday I stopped opposite a girl with one of her legs in plaster. She had naturally curly hair and a lovely, natural smile. As the Paul Jones was the last dance before supper, I managed so to engineer things that we sat together at the same table. Her name was Isabel Ryott. She went to St Swithun's School, the posh private school on the hill just outside Winchester on the road to Alresford, and had broken her leg playing lacrosse. To say I was enchanted with her would be an understatement. After supper, I tried to dance with her as often as possible but, as she was the undoubted belle of the ball, had a lot of opposition from the other chaps. It sounds corny to say that I'd fallen in love at first sight but I couldn't get to sleep that night thinking about her. The battle between the males of the species was re-enacted at the subsequent dances, a battle I was determined to win. I had a strong willpower when it came to the crunch.

Luckily, Isabel was keen on tennis and she and I and a group of friends arranged to play at the club behind our back garden during that summer holiday. I used to take them home for tea through the gap in the hedge. They were happy days. Mum and dad thought Isabel was a lovely girl in every way – so natural, they said. I had already made up my mind that I would marry her one day, come hell or high water. By the time I was due to go up to Brasenose, we were very much in love with each other. As fate would have it, she was due to attend a smart secretarial college at Oxford run by a Miss Sprules.

CHAPTER 4

Oxford

IN OCTOBER 1950 John and I both went up to Oxford, he to Corpus Christi and I to Brasenose. John had done his national service whereas mine had been deferred so that I could get my degree first.

We were both to read 'Greats', a degree course lasting four years instead of the usual three. It involved two major exams, the first of which was 'Classical Honour Moderations' – 'Honour Mods', for short – which you sat after five terms and comprised Greek and Latin 'language and literature'. The second was the 'finals' which you sat after a further seven terms and comprised ancient history and philosophy in general but starting with the Greek philosophers. In those days, Greats was still regarded as the epitome of academic distinction, especially – if unsurprisingly – by those who taught or read it.

It took only a few weeks for me to come to terms with what high academic standards actually were. My tutor for Honour Mods was Maurice Platnauer whose squat body was surmounted by an impressively large cranium, which manifestly exuded a superfluity of brains. Rumour had it that somewhere in its ample depths was concealed a heart of gold, which wasn't quite beyond the bounds of possibility. More credibly, rumour also had it that when he himself had taken Honour Mods, he had sat fourteen papers instead of the usual twelve taken by lesser mortals, the extra papers involving writing poetry in Greek and Latin. Apparently, he had got 'alphas' in thirteen of the papers but was heart-broken that he only got an 'alpha/beta' in the fourteenth.

His regime was relentless, not to say ruthless. Every week we had to swat up great chunks of Homer and Virgil and/or the other great Classical writers. Their combined length in any given fortnight was equivalent to that of the set books for the Higher School Certificate that we had spent a whole year studying in the sixth form at Peter Symonds. Every Saturday morning we had a written test covering the week's reading. At my weekly individual tutorial, Maurice sat next to me at his desk and went through the passage of Greek or Latin prose that we also had to produce every week, dipping an old-fashioned nibbed pen into a bottle of red ink and

48

covering my masterpieces with corrections in notably neat, precise and actually rather beautiful handwriting. My worst efforts he generally described as 'not too bad'. Once, when I'd made an elementary error, he said 'it's not *your* fault'. He understood, realizing sooner than I did that I was miles behind those of my fellow students who had been to public schools, particularly two of them who had been to 'the other school at Winchester', as John and I used to call Winchester College. I was determined to catch up with them and get a 'first' in Honour Mods as they undoubtedly would.

The pressures on my over-anxious brain were extreme and there were moments when I began to feel I was on the verge of a nervous breakdown. I had to draw on every ounce of my inner strength of mind to ward off the dark shadows ever threatening to overwhelm me. I began to experience a strange, disabling phenomenon whereby high-pitched, sentimental music played by violins was constantly ringing in my ears and undermining my capacity to concentrate.

It wasn't that, as a grammar school boy, I felt socially inferior or had a chip on my shoulder. On the contrary, I felt entirely at ease with most of the public school types, some of whom became delightful friends. The only classic social 'faux-pas' I made was when several of us were invited to dinner with Maurice and, at the end of the meal, his butler placed a decanter of port in front of me. For some reason I knew there was a proper direction in which to pass it round after I'd filled my own glass but couldn't remember which it was. There was a fifty-fifty chance of getting it wrong. Inevitably, I began to pass it to my right. No doubt in the light of experience, the butler had placed himself strategically behind me and instantly leaned forward and whispered in my ear that I should pass it to my left. I felt sure that everyone had noticed and the harder I tried not to blush, the more, of course, I did. Recalling so trivial an incident from the perspective of passing time, it seems absurd and pathetic that my acute embarrassment weighed heavily on my mind for quite some time. Perhaps it was symptomatic of my mental state generally.

Once, in my first year, I went to watch Brasenose playing in the final of the rugby 'cuppers', which was the name of the inter-collegiate 'knock-out' competition. Brasenose was famous for its sport, especially rugby. You might well find yourself sitting next to a rugby international at dinner in hall. Early on there was an incident on the pitch when a penalty was awarded. Having been to a soccer-playing grammar school, I didn't understand the reason for the penalty and asked the chap standing next to me to explain. He was wearing the then traditional garb of a peaked cap and a duffle coat. In a ridiculously exaggerated Oxford accent he replied: 'Are you American or something?' I wasn't in the least offended. I just thought it was hilarious to think that here was a human being who couldn't begin to comprehend that there were actually such things as Englishmen who didn't understand the rules of rugby and that anyone who didn't must be something as patently undesirable as an American or other alien, from another planet, equally beyond the pale.

Another incident roughly in the same vein occurred when quite a few of us were working silently in the college library and it began to snow heavily. An Australian student got up and walked towards the window and stared at the snow with obvious astonishment. Another chap, again with a strong Oxford accent, said in a sardonic tone of voice: 'I suppose you're as surprised to see that as we would be if a f***ing kangaroo walked into the library.' We all broke the mandatory silence and roared with laughter, including, I'm glad to say, the Aussie.

I was selected to play for the College tennis and squash teams and became successively secretary and captain of both. To an extent this took my mind off my anxieties about my academic work. I enjoyed the team spirit and friendship of all concerned. We had a particularly good squash team and in my third year we won the inter-collegiate league, beating the other ten colleges in the first division. That was the year when I was secretary and had to organize trials for the 'freshmen'. One such was a chap called Colin Cowdrey. I had never heard of him and had no idea he was one of the best rackets (as opposed to squash) players in the world and was already marked out as a future England cricketer. By chance, I played with him in the trials and actually just managed to beat him, which wasn't much of a claim to fame considering squash was my main game at which I practised furiously while for Colin it was a casual pastime. When I later found out who he was – Colin being Colin, not from him – I was relieved that the Captain and I had rightly selected him to play for Brasenose. Many years after I'd left Oxford, I went with a friend to a test match at Lords and we were sitting on the grass in front of the pavilion. I happened to glance up to the balcony and there was Colin sitting with his pads on waiting for the next England wicket to fall. He caught my eye and, remembering my name was Michael, leaned forward and asked me what I was doing, how I was and so on. He was going through a bad patch at the time and I was astounded that, with everything that must

Brasenose College Squash Team. Myself on the right with Colin Cowdrey behind.

have been weighing on his mind, his uppermost thought was a genuine concern for my well-being. I was much moved by his premature death and well understood the many references in his obituaries to his sheer human decency. A true gentleman – a truly gentle man – if ever there was.

I was disappointed not to get a blue at squash, though it was some consolation to be appointed what was strangely called a 'Squirrel', which was equivalent to being a 'runner-up'. I was also proud to be invited to be a member of the Jesters Club, which comprised the better players from Oxford and Cambridge.

Isabel was studying at Miss Sprules' posh secretarial college in Oxford and sharing digs with two charming sisters, Annette and Diana, in a smart part of north Oxford. Annette and Diana were always welcoming and became good friends of mine as well as Isabel's. Isabel understandingly realized that I was anxious that our relationship shouldn't undermine my academic work. We normally met up at lunch time on Saturdays and spent the rest of the day together. Often in the evenings we walked through the meadows to 'The Trout', a pleasant pub by the Thames at Godstow. If opportunity presented itself, we used to indulge in what was then called 'heavy petting'. In fact, we did most things short of going the whole hog. This ridiculous compromise was presumably due to my guilt-inducing Catholic upbringing and Isabel's Victorian, Protestant background. I say 'Victorian' because her father married late in life and was fifty when she was born, literally old enough to be her grandfather. He was a dear old chap and a good father, whom Isabel greatly loved. Although I too eventually became very fond of him, the immediate problem was that, now being over seventy, he couldn't – naturally enough – rise above his own narrow Protestant background. The prospect of his beloved daughter marrying a Roman Catholic was more than he could bear. He made it clear that she would not have his consent to marry me, let alone his blessing. The fact that I hadn't been to a public school – as had Isabel and her brother, Richard – didn't exactly help.

I am bound to say that, understanding to a degree though I was, I had moods of great bitterness and anger. I didn't know what my own parents felt but, if such intolerance of love between two human beings was what Christianity was about, I began to wish 'a plague on both your houses'. I began to have doubts about Christianity itself, the very bedrock of my being, of my sanity even. In any case, a university education is as nothing if it doesn't inculcate an attitude of enquiry and objective analytical reasoning, at which – a mixed blessing though it was – I was becoming deft, almost to a fault. In particular, I found it hard to come to terms with the evil in the world, with man's inhumanity to man. After all, I had lived through a world war in which human beings had killed tens of millions of their fellows and the holocaust was indelibly imprinted in my mind ever since, immediately after the war, all the cinemas had been required as a matter of public policy to show pictures of Belsen. Furthermore, the 'Cold War' was at its height and there was a real fear that we would only have four minutes warning of a nuclear attack. I tried to say to myself that either it wouldn't happen, which would be fine, or that, if it did, we would only live in terror for a few minutes before we were all obliterated, which wasn't very long in the scale of things. But such a philosophical approach remained purely theoretical and did nothing to alleviate my anxiety on this score. Perhaps paradoxically, because many people turn to religion when in deep distress, I stopped going to mass.

One evening in my second year I was, unusually, swotting in the small, dingy room in my digs in one of the poorer parts of Oxford in the Iffley Road area, which was all I could afford. I had had to move out of my rooms in College after only one year in residence. My dear old landlady knocked on my door and said a gentleman had called and wanted to see me. She showed him in. To my astonishment, it was Monsignor Elwes who ran the Roman Catholic Chaplaincy where Catholic undergraduates went to mass. He was a superficially charming man who made jokes about the maroon socks his rank entitled him to wear. I was very embarrassed, to say the least, but invited him to sit on the only chair in my room, while I sat on my narrow bed. He said he'd noticed that I hadn't been to mass recently and wondered why. I replied, stumbling over my words, that I had begun to have doubts mainly because of the evil in the world. He said: 'Let's start at the beginning, Michael. If you were walking in a jungle and saw a clock on the ground, you'd know someone had put it there, wouldn't you, Michael?' I could only reply in the affirmative. 'Well then,' he said, 'someone must have put the world here, mustn't they, Michael?' I was flabbergasted and muttered something along the lines that that didn't necessarily follow. After some further conversation, he took his leave with the parting words that he hoped to see me at mass in future. With the arrogance of youth, I was left with the thought that, if that was the simplistic intellectual level on which he hoped to convert me back to Catholicism, it was pathetic and laughable. Indeed, his efforts were, if anything, counter-productive and I felt even less inclined to go to mass. I've always wondered how he'd known that I'd stopped going to mass, even knew my Christian name and had traced where my digs were.

I was distraught that I didn't get a first in Honour Mods but at least it was a respectable second with a clutch of alpha/betas. The two chaps from the other school at Winchester duly got their expected firsts.

———

In my sixth term – the summer term of my second year – I started the second part of the Greats Course. It was then that my nervous system virtually imploded altogether. Against the background of the various pressures and tensions I was experiencing, the last straw was the personality of my philosophy tutor, one Jimmy McKie.

The first task he set me was to write an essay entitled 'The end justifies the means'. I found it difficult to resolve all the contradictions I could see the more I thought about it. At my first tutorial, I had scarcely finished reading my first shortish paragraph when Jimmy McKie interrupted me and walked up and down his room talking non-stop from five past eleven to the ten past one, presumably having nothing better to do. He pointed out that I'd made a logical error in my first few sentences, which I understood almost before the words had left his mouth. I had to sit there for over two hours watching his sloppily moist, yet thin, unkind lips spouting forth, the general drift being to demonstrate his intellectual superiority and, by implication, my own intellectual inferiority. I kept noticing a urine stain on the inside of the right leg of his trousers.

My first Roman history tutorial with Michael Holroyd was also disheartening but for a different reason. Personally he was pleasant enough, but you have to work exceptionally hard to make history boring to anyone with the slightest imagination. He succeeded only too well. I couldn't detect a single spark of inspiration capable of igniting a glimmer of enthusiasm in my exhausted brain.

Unusually for me, I began to be unable to sleep at night. Once, when my landlady asked me if I'd slept well, I said I hadn't and found it difficult to. She liked to mother me and said I was suffering from what she called 'night starvation'. She kindly arranged for me to have a mug of Ovaltine every evening before I went to bed. Though cynical about the likelihood of it being the slightest help, I nevertheless drank it, anxious not to offend her. Much to my surprise, I slept much better and this helped to sustain me. I just managed to soldier on to the end of the term and the beginning of the long summer vacation. It is symptomatic of my mental condition at the time that I can remember little about my academic work apart from the events I have mentioned. I did, however, find some consolation and peace of mind by looking round all the other colleges in turn, observing and absorbing their quiet beauty. I sought spiritual comfort from the concentrated architectural splendour of their 'dreaming spires' and from the seemingly seamless continuity of their peaceful atmosphere of learning rooted so deeply, so surely and so consolingly in antiquity. I used often to end my peregrinations by walking to the back of the 'old quad' of Brasenose, turning round and contemplating the Porter's Lodge and, behind it, the dome of the Radcliffe Camera towering upwards so effortlessly and splendidly: a view unsurpassed even amidst the glories of Oxford.

I was not alone in my distress that term. When I looked round Corpus Christi, I took the opportunity to call on John. We had led our separate busy lives, only occasionally meeting up. On that occasion, he made a remark clearly implying that he felt suicidal. Although he revelled in the academic atmosphere of Oxford, enjoyed the Classics beyond measure and, as I understood it, had tutors sympathetic to his great love of

The Radcliffe Camera behind Brasenose College Porter's Lodge.
(Reproduced courtesy of The Brazen Nose.*)*

learning, I supposed that he was going through a phase when he too felt the stresses of competitive pressure overmuch and I gathered that he had girl-friend problems. There had been a spate of suicides amongst undergraduates, one of which had been close to home. An undergraduate had recently jumped from high up the Radcliffe Camera just outside the entrance to Brasenose. I saw his body on the grass surrounded by a small crowd of people and some policemen. In some magazine or other, I had read that the Vice-Chancellor, Sir Maurice Bowra, had expressed concern about this increasing problem and said he could help undergraduates who felt suicidal. As soon as I left John, I hurried straight to Wadham College, where Sir Maurice was the 'Warden' (the equivalent of the 'Principal' of Brasenose or the 'Master' of some other colleges). I asked at the lodge where Sir Maurice's lodgings were and, having traced them, knocked nervously at the front door. After what seemed like an eternity, the door opened and there stood the great man. I said something like 'I'm sorry to bother you, Sir, but I understand you're willing to help if an undergraduate feels suicidal. I think my brother, who is at Corpus Christi, is suicidal and I should be grateful if you could help.' Roughly speaking, those were my words. Precisely speaking, his reply was: 'When you visit the Vice-Chancellor you should wear your gown.' I was dumbfounded. I was all in favour of Oxford's hallowed traditions but it seemed a somewhat perverse sense of priorities to reprimand me which, in the circumstances, was all I didn't need. He did, however, ask me to wait a moment and went to fetch a card which he handed to me. On it there was a telephone number of a hospital which he suggested John should ring to seek help. I assumed this would put him in touch with a psychiatrist of some sort. I mumbled my rather half-hearted thanks, rushed back to Corpus Christi and gave John the card, explaining what Sir Maurice had told me he should do. I assumed that he did so. At any rate, when I visited him again, much sooner than I otherwise would have, he seemed well enough, much to my relief.

It was a shame that I didn't have time to pursue my passion for lieder and opera as much as I would have liked. Music was amongst the many interests that Isabel and I shared. She was particularly fond of Bach and sang in the Balliol College choir. We occasionally went to concerts in the Music School performed by the University orchestra and conducted by a young undergraduate called Colin Davis, later to become the renowned Sir Colin. I introduced Isabel to opera when touring companies occasionally performed at the New Theatre. Once I took her to the Town

Hall to hear her first lieder recital sung by the great Elizabeth Schwarzkopf. I was delighted that Isabel gradually developed a great love – a shared love – for opera and lieder.

There was another call on my time. I was going to have to start my national service when I left Oxford and Isabel and I intended to get married before then, whatever the obstacles arising from our different religions. The thought of being separated for two years (apart from occasional periods of leave) so early in our married life was yet another cause of anxiety. At least, I thought, I should be in a position to maintain her in reasonable comfort as soon as possible. With that in mind, I joined the University Officers' Training Corps, which was a means of applying for a Commission in advance so that, if successful, I would start my officers' training straightaway rather than having to do my basic training first. This was achievable because, apart from training sessions one afternoon a week during term time, I would undergo my basic training in two periods of four weeks phased over two long vacations. I decided to join the Royal Artillery, which sounded far more interesting than one or other of the infantry regiments. I'm bound to admit that it also seemed rather safer than the front line, should the need for active service arise somewhere in the world, which in those uncertain times was not improbable.

I enjoyed the weekly sessions at which our instructor was a quietly authoritative regimental sergeant major who had become very deaf as a result of his literally close involvement with many bombardments by the staple 'twenty-five pounders' during his active service and especially the greatest barrage in history which turned the tide of war at El Alamein.

The two periods of basic training, in which we were joined by chaps from Cambridge, took place at Catterick and provided an ideal paradise for NCOs who wanted to make life hell for a squad of long-haired Oxbridge types. On neither occasion did we remain long-haired for very long, our first assignment being to be pointlessly scalped. The NCO I remember was a Scotsman with a barely decipherable Scots accent, Sergeant McThingamabob. You could tell that, beneath his short but fearsome exterior, he was a decent sort of chap who saw the funny side of things, including the stereotypical role he was paid to adopt when on parade. His main threat if you failed to come up to his exacting standards – in other words, if you cocked things up – was to 'have your testicles for a bow tie', which displayed a level of creative imagination unsurpassed even by Picasso.

There was a drill competition between the various squads at the end of each of our four week sessions. The other squads were determined not to be beaten by us 'posh prats'. Towards the end of one such competition, we had 'grounded arms' and marched away to do other kinds of drill, leaving our rifles in three neat rows. When we returned to our places exactly beside our rifles, Sergeant McThingamabob gave the order to 'pick up ARMS'. This meant bending down and counting three to ourselves, during which time we had to grasp our rifles without looking down and then stand up to attention with our rifles held firmly by our sides. Unfortunately, I failed to grasp my rifle and stood up to attention without it. Spotting this, Sergeant McThingamabob gave the order to 'ground ARMS' but, unfortunately, I instinctively picked mine up. It took several similar manoeuvres for me to work out that when he ordered 'ground ARMS' my rifle was already on the ground and that, if I was to get in sync with the rest of the squad before the cows came home, I had to mimic grounding it and certainly not pick it up. The thought of me constantly standing to attention holding my rifle when all the others were on the ground – and vice versa – is only funny after the event. By the grace of God, we nevertheless won the competition, otherwise Sergeant McThingamabob's neckwear might have been painful to behold. As it was, he just looked at me with a twinkle in his eyes.

I enjoyed the desk work, plotting angles and distances on large-scale maps and working out how much to 'aim off' to compensate for the strength and direction of the wind. Thanks to Cuzzy's teaching at Peter Symonds, my geometry was up to the task, which was just as well when we translated theory into practice on the ranges. The consequence of getting it wrong couldn't be disguised because, instead of hitting the target, your shells might well head off in the direction of Darlington or Northallerton. If you got it right, it was intriguing and exciting to hit a target well over a mile away. All in all, I quite enjoyed these occasions in a masochistic sort of way, despite all the ridiculous bull-shit. Working round the clock from early morn to late at night at least took my mind off my mental problems.

———•◦•———

I have digressed. One day during that unhappy sixth term, I was just finishing lunch in hall when my father suddenly appeared at the door. I naturally went up to him and expressed my surprise at seeing him there. I never really discovered why but he said he was worried that I might not be feeling all right. Perhaps it was instinctive. We walked round the quad and, restraining tears, I explained the problems I was going through with my tutors. My memory fails me as to how he brought it about but, later that afternoon, I found myself sitting with him in the surgery of the doctor to whom I had been allocated, presumably by the college authorities, but whom I had never even thought of visiting before. After some discussion, he rightly said that, having failed to get a first in Honour Mods, I was probably all the more determined to get a first in my finals. Hence the tensions that were distressing me so much. His diagnosis, if far from complete, was at least better than his cure. He said that, when he felt anxious and under stress, he went out and bought himself a new tie, a remark apparently intended to bring our consultation to a close. When we left, my father said he hoped I was feeling better now. Untruthfully, I said I was, so as not to cause him further pointless anxiety. He had been his usual kind and thoughtful self. I didn't buy myself a new tie.

During the ensuing long vacation, he talked to me further about my problems. I had found it impossible to do any work, waiting in vain for rest and relaxation to revive my energy and interest in learning. I felt no sense of direction. I needed to know what sort of career I would pursue and wanted to earn a decent living after I'd done my national service, presuming that I would have married Isabel before I started it. One day he asked me whether I'd be interested in a career in local government, perhaps as a solicitor. He emphasized the wide range of a County Council's functions and that the County Clerk's department played a central role covering all aspects of the Council's work. I was immediately attracted by the idea of combining the law with public service.

The long and the short of it was that he approached Mr Wheatley, the Clerk of Hampshire County Council, who apparently had great respect for him. Mr Wheatley invited me to dinner with his wife and himself. After dinner he made an excuse to go into the kitchen with his wife and I could hear them whispering, presumably discussing what they thought of me. When they came back, over coffee he said he'd be pleased to take me on as an articled clerk and would ask the Finance Committee to agree that I should be paid half the salary of the 'general grade' – the lowest grade in local government – but I could take it as read that the Committee would agree. The time would come when I would understand all too well that, as far as he was concerned, people would do what they were told. It was quite a generous offer for those days, when it was still quite common to pay a premium to become an articled clerk and receive no remuneration. My father, who hero-worshipped Mr Wheatley, was over the moon.

The immediate task was to get the powers that be at Brasenose to agree that I should change to reading law. I forget who I wrote to but the upshot was that it was agreed that I could. I suspected that Maurice Platnauer, who was the Vice-Principal, would have understood. I felt as if a huge burden, and with it the dark shadows of black despair, had been lifted from my brain and was excited at the prospect of a fresh start in life.

———

With the fresh start came a fresh problem. I had only just over eighteen months to get my law degree instead of the usual three years. Fortunately, however, I soon discovered that it is not the amount of work you do that damages the mind but the frame of mind in which you do it. I was lucky indeed that Barry Nicholas was my main tutor. I was reminded of the contrast with my experience the previous term when I passed Jimmy McKie a few days after the beginning of the new term. All he could bring himself to say was: 'No-one has a right to change courses.'

To my profound sorrow, Barry died at the age of 82 in March 2002, having been associated with Brasenose for half a century. He was one of the great Roman and comparative lawyers of his era. Maurice Platnauer became the Principal of Brasenose after I left Oxford and Barry succeeded him in that post.

I can't do better than to quote the following extract from his magnificent, whole-page, obituary in *The Times* of 7 March 2002.

> As a teacher Nicholas was in his sympathetic element. He taught by the example of his own attitude to learning, and the sensitivity with which he could open a pupil's eyes to the buffers into which an unsound argument was leading. With Nicholas as one's tutor one could neither slack nor flannel. He was a power for good in individual lives.
>
> Brasenose under Nicholas was – as it remains – a dutiful and profoundly decent community, taking its tone from the Principal himself.

When I went to a dinner a few years ago in celebration of his eightieth birthday, he came up to me and said: 'How nice to see you again, Michael'. It says a lot about him that he still remembered his former

John at graduation.

pupils and their names after some forty five years. He was, incidentally, a
Roman Catholic.

We who experienced his dry wit all have our own stories to tell. One I
remember is that, when he once set me an essay comparing a branch of
Roman law with the equivalent branch of English law, he added the
sardonic rider: 'I want a comparison, not a juxtaposition'.

On another occasion, ten years or so ago, the speaker who proposed his
toast at a dinner in his honour told a presumably apocryphal tale which
brought the house down, much to his (Barry's) evident delight. Barry was
attending a cocktail party at one of the colleges on a warm summer
evening and was seen to disappear into the college gardens with a most
attractive young lady. They had walked concealed amongst the trees in the
far corner of the garden. When they returned after about twenty minutes,

Myself at graduation.

the young lady was looking hot and bothered, her face flushed. Another don went up to her and anxiously asked if she was all right and whether she needed some help. She pleaded in reply: 'Thank you so much. Please, please do help me. What is a contingent remainder?'

My blotting paper mind worked at full stretch without tearing apart. In the one long vacation available for me to study, I had – amongst other things – to read up for one of the Roman law papers for myself. I had the distinct advantage over the other students of having read Honour Mods and so could read Justinian and the other Roman sources fluently. At the beginning of the next term, we sat an internal college exam, such exams having the strange name of 'Collections'. Barry said I could take the subject as read and I was awarded a 'Collections prize'. I was allowed to buy books up to a certain value at Blackwell's and chose the complete works of Homer and Shakespeare, as well as Gombrich's well known *The Story of Art*. They were embossed in gold leaf with the College's crest and stand proudly on my bookshelf.

When I had finished the finals, I had sleepless nights agonizing much about the results. I had found some of the papers so problematic that my main concern was that I might only have got a 'third'. I could hardly believe my ears when I heard that I had got one of the eleven 'firsts' in law – or jurisprudence, to use the correct term – awarded that year. I really was completely and utterly stunned, though of course overjoyed. Barry wrote me a short and charming note of congratulation and suggested I might like to come and discuss with him the possibility of an academic career, though he wasn't sure that it would really be my scene. Although I was committed to starting my articles with Mr Wheatley, I nevertheless thought it would be pleasant and interesting to go up to Oxford and have a chat with Barry. After a long talk, he said: 'As I rather thought Michael, it's time you grew up and went out into the real world.' His shrewd judgement of people hadn't failed him. He realized my personality was such that I would have found an Oxford academic career stultifying. That apart, I have often thought that a career, the very essence of which was to be a full-time professional thinker, would have overtaxed my brain which I couldn't stop thinking too much at the best of times.

So it was that I left Oxford on a high note but not without some soul-searching and mixed feelings. It was hard to make a final break from my attachment to that great, ancient and beautiful seat of learning where, despite so much grief and distress, I had also enjoyed times of deep satisfaction and comradeship.

Controlling my emotions, I bade Barry a grateful farewell, thinking that never again would I make more than a passing return to Oxford. How wrong I was, time was soon to tell.

CHAPTER 5

The Local Government World

M R WHEATLEY (later to become Sir Andrew) was probably the outstanding County Clerk of the old school, being remarkably progressive for those days. He was notably distinguished in appearance, his proud poise and upright stance making him seem taller than he was. His strikingly fair hair, always perfectly groomed, combined with his ruddy complexion, belied his years. He was a clear thinker and addressed Committees with a quiet authority not easily gainsaid. He was highly regarded by members of the County Council and by the local government world in general.

To his staff, however, he was the hardest of taskmasters and a single-minded martinet, held in awe – indeed positively feared – by all and sundry in his department, even his most senior lieutenants. If they were summoned to his presence by a flashing buzzer on their desks, they blanched visibly, combed their hair, dusted any resulting scurf, real or imaginary, from their shoulders and straightened their ties, presumably suffering from the delusion that this ritual would somehow reduce the severity of the impending, inevitable bollocking by the big white chief.

I started my articles the day after we knew I'd get the results of my law finals at Oxford on the basis – Mr Wheatley's, not mine – that I shouldn't waste a single day in pursuit of my career. After I'd been shown the desk at which I was to sit and introduced to the staff with whom I would initially work most closely, I was summoned to the presence in his inner sanctum. He delivered a memorable homily about what was expected of me, in the course of which he made two preposterous propositions. He knew I was engaged but said that my work and career came before everything else. I wasn't to get married until I'd completed my articles and qualified as a solicitor, in other words for three years. Secondly, I was to return to Oxford for one term and take the senior post-graduate degree of Bachelor of Civil Law (BCL) in a year's time. As to the former, I was lost for words. As to the latter, I summoned up the courage to say that the BCL was a full year's course, indeed for Commonwealth students often a two year's course, and I couldn't see how it was possible to do it in one term of eight weeks. His peremptory reply was: 'You can do anything if you put your mind to it.'

The full implications of returning to Oxford for one term to study for a BCL took several days to sink in. To start with, in the first year of my articles I had to sit a preliminary Law Society exam on 'Trust Accounts and Bookkeeping', an essential accounting technique – and, for the likes of innumerate people like myself, a complex and difficult one – designed to ensure that solicitors' firms kept their clients' money separate from their own, thereby minimizing the risk of fraud by the few bad apples that any profession contains. This meant that I would have little time to study for my BCL either side of my term of residence at Brasenose, the system being that an articled clerk worked hard at the office all day and swotted in the evenings and weekends for his or her Law Society exams. Conversely, the time I spent swotting for my BCL meant that I would have correspondingly less time to swot for my Trust Accounts and Bookkeeping, as well as for my Law Society finals. It also slowly dawned on me that the BCL syllabus included criminal law which I had missed out on because I had done Honour Mods instead of the 'law prelims', which included a paper on the subject. Compared with other graduates studying for a BCL, not only would I have less time to do so but I would also have to cope with an extra new subject.

While pondering all this with considerable anxiety, I recalled Jimmy McKie's infamous remark that 'no-one has a right to change courses'. I wondered, and rather hoped, that no-one had a right to tell Brasenose that he was going to return for one term to sit for the BCL. I expressed this possibility to Mr Wheatley who said he'd soon see to that. And see to it, he soon did. He wrote to Brasenose, no doubt in his own inimical forceful but reasoned way. The upshot was that the college authorities agreed. Presumably Barry Nicholas thought I could cope.

On top of all this, the structure of the of the Law Society finals was then nothing less than sadistic. In the first place, you had to pass all your exam papers at one sitting. I know people who took the finals several times before they qualified, having previously passed all the papers – some two or three times – but not at the same sitting. In the second place, if you wanted to obtain Honours, you had to sit five extra papers – the 'Honours' papers – the week after you'd sat the 'pass' papers. To add insult to injury, your Honours papers were not even looked at if you didn't get higher marks in the pass papers than were otherwise required. This had the ridiculous consequence that you didn't know how best to divide your time between trying to get the necessary higher marks in the pass papers and working at the Honours papers themselves.

During the first year of my articles, I failed my Trust Accounts and Bookkeeping twice but passed the third time. On the first occasion, I didn't know that I didn't know, while on the second occasion I knew that I didn't know. I have often thought of this as a good lesson for life. Knowing that you don't know is the beginning of wisdom.

It was pleasant in some ways to be back at Oxford for one term as a graduate, though the pressures were even greater than before. Barry Nicholas and others did their best to help me. When the time came for me to take the BCL exams, I had one stroke of luck. The heading on the Roman Law paper said: 'Answer two questions marked with an asterisk and two other questions'. There were four questions marked with an asterisk which were quotations from Justinian and elsewhere on which we had to 'comment', which I could do well enough, aided by my fluency in Latin. The other questions covered a wide range of other subjects about which I hadn't much of a clue. Although it was pretty obvious what was intended, I nevertheless answered all four questions marked with an asterisk. When it came to my 'viva' – an oral examination I had to endure a few weeks later – I found myself sitting in front of four or five professors or other distinguished academics all, like myself, wearing our academic dress. Not to my astonishment, the first question was why in my Roman Law paper had I answered the four asterisked questions instead of just two of them, contrary to the instructions at the head of the paper. It was one of those few occasions in my life when, having nothing to lose, desperation drove me to desperate lengths quite out of character. I heard words on the following lines apparently coming out of my own mouth: 'It seems rather unfortunate that when you sit a senior postgraduate degree in the University of Oxford – let alone a degree in law – you should have to indulge in the subtleties of statutory interpretation to decide what questions you had to answer. I was perfectly entitled to answer the four asterisked questions because the instructions were to answer two *other* questions and not two other questions *not marked with an asterisk*.' In the ensuing stony silence, metaphorical mortarboards metaphorically fell off all over the place, though I can't believe that such a collection of mighty brains hadn't already spotted the ambiguity and guessed what my answer would be. In the train on my way back to

Winchester, I couldn't help seeing the funny side of it and the other passengers must have wondered why I kept smiling to myself. In the event, I was quite pleased to get a respectable 'Second Class Honours' including a 'beta plus' in Roman Law!

———•——

Mr Wheatley had made a decision which was to prove enormously helpful to my mental survival. He had the inspired thought that it would be wise to employ another articled clerk at the same time as myself on the grounds that we could share our experience and knowledge and generally work together more fruitfully than if we'd been the only one. My colleague articled clerk was Bill Moralee who lived in Carlisle and had just finished his law degree at Cambridge. Bill was a heavy, jovial chap, ever seeing the funny side of things and appearing to take life more or less as it came, a delightful counterfoil to my own serious self. Thrown together in the same boat, we developed a deep friendship, gossiping privately about the characters in the office or Mr Wheatley's latest apoplectic fit. Once he came into our office and angrily turned the lights off, becoming redder in the face than usual and opining that we were wasting the ratepayers' money. It was a dull sort of day and we spent the rest of it periodically having a good laugh but straining our eyes in the gloom lest he return to check that we weren't still biting the hands that fed us. Many people are liked and many respected. Few are both. Bill was such a one. I was so pleased that he had a successful career, ending up as County Secretary of the Hertfordshire County Council, but deeply grieved to hear that he had died from a sudden heart attack in his fifties. I was not surprised to hear that the Hertfordshire County Council had arranged for a memorial service or some other such event to celebrate his life as he himself had always seemed to. Had I known, I would have dropped everything to be there with him in spirit.

So ended the first year of my articles.

———•——

So, too, at long last ended my bachelorhood. Isabel and I had decided to get married despite everything. My Catholic faith being on the wane, I became a member of the Church of England and on 24 July 1955 we got married in the Chapel of St Cross, that fine Norman building adjacent to Winchester's lovely water meadows. My parents were fully supportive

Isabel on our wedding day.

and understanding, the irony being that my father had done the opposite by becoming a Roman Catholic when he married my mother. To the extent that I had doubts about the Christian faith itself, becoming a member of the Church of England and getting married in St Cross was, I confess, hypocritical, a matter of social convenience. But at least it removed the tension between Isabel and her parents, which would otherwise have been distressing to her and them as well as, in consequence, to myself.

Father Mullarkey had been such a positive influence on my life that I thought I should tell him why I intended to become a member of the Church of England, rather than just slinking off. As usual, he came up trumps. His reaction confirmed my respect for his understanding of humanity. He made a joke about my prospective parents-in-law liking me but not my politics. He wished me well, displaying a rare absence of bigotry and presence of Christian tolerance that I have always appreciated and will never forget.

In those days, the County Council worked on alternate Saturday mornings. I had screwed up the courage to knock on Mr Wheatley's door on one of those Saturday mornings and, in response to his command to 'come in', I entered his office full of trepidation. I came straight to the point and told him that Isabel and I intended to get married, expecting a volcano to erupt. To my astonishment, he couldn't have been more charming. He wished us well and gave us a splendid car rug as a wedding present.

My best man was Bruce MacMillan of 'I'm Agrippa' fame and the ushers were my brother, John, and Bill Moralee. Isabel's four bridesmaids were two life-long friends, Moira (whom I mentioned in my Preface) and Margaret, and Annette and Diana, the sisters with whom she had shared digs at Oxford.

It was a hot, summer day and the reception was held in the grounds of the Stanmore Hotel. Our toast was proposed by dear old Dr Smythe, who had brought us both into the world. Through his loose, clucking false teeth, he lisped that he had had the privilege of being the first person to be introduced to both bride and groom. After all our anxieties, it turned out to be a very happy occasion.

My parents-in-law lent us their car for our honeymoon. All we could afford was a fortnight in a hotel run by NALGO (then the union for local government officers) in Llandudno in North Wales – hardly as romantic-sounding as the Seychelles. But the weather continued to be perfect and the Welsh coastline and hinterland, including Snowdonia, were dramatically beautiful places in which to start our married life.

————•·•————

It was then back to the grindstone. We rented a gloomy one room flat on the first floor of a big Victorian house in St Cross Road. Our furniture was sparse, the essentials being a 'put-you-up' sofa which could be converted into a double bed and a small desk at which I had to do my swotting most evenings. We also had an unhealthily dank kitchen in the semi-basement, two flights of stairs down from our room. My abiding memory of our first home, if you can call it that, was going down to breakfast one morning and finding toadstools growing out of the floor.

Isabel was doing a secretarial job, coincidentally in the County Surveyor's department where my father was the Deputy County Surveyor.

During these three years of articles, I found that tennis and squash helped to relieve my tensions as they had at Oxford. I was selected to play squash for Hampshire and was proud to receive my County Colours. We used to beat the smaller neighbouring counties, such as Dorset, Wiltshire and Berkshire, quite easily but were beaten almost as easily by the largest counties like Surrey and Middlesex (as it then was).

My experience at the office couldn't have given me a better start for a career in local government. Mr Wheatley ensured that Bill Moralee and I had a taste of most branches of the County Council's work and nearly everyone was unstinting in giving us the benefit of their experience. They were hard-working people of the highest calibre. If you came up to his exacting standards, Mr Wheatley would push you, career-wise, to the end of the earth, using his considerable influence in the process. Several of his senior staff became County Clerks in their own right.

The ridiculous academic pressure, combined with the pressures of work at the office, began to overtax my nervous system once again. The phenomenon of high-pitched violin music in my head returned to haunt me even more distressingly than before. I often felt I had a steel band wrapped tightly round my head trying to prevent the music emerging from my brain. The shadows returned, darker even than during my unhappiest times at Oxford. About a week before my Law Society finals, I felt I just couldn't go on, which was a vicious circle of the worst kind. Not knowing which way to turn, in desperation I made an appointment to see Mr Wheatley and told him how I felt, looking for a pre-emptive excuse if I failed my exams, which seemed inevitable considering the state I was in. My dilemma was that he might regard me as a wimp, the lowest of the low in his eyes. Life is full of surprises. He was thoughtful and understanding. He said he had once felt like that before taking an exam and the remedy was to drink Sanatogen which was good for your nervous system. I immediately dashed down to Boots in the High Street and bought a large jar of Sanatogen. I mixed the specified amount in a glass of water in the gents' loo at the office and guzzled it down, repeating this process every few hours. It was a white, powdery, bitter-sweet drink, more bitter than sweet. I always said to myself that I was drinking 'Mr Wheatley's medicine'. It has never ceased to amaze me that I rapidly felt better, so much so that, by the time the exams started only a week later, I could think quite clearly and calmly. Nevertheless, I only got a pass, not having done sufficiently well in my pass papers to have my Honours papers even read, which only serves to illustrate the absurd crudity and downright cruelty of the system. The Honours papers were more like the Oxford exams, requiring creative analytical thinking rather than 'right or wrong' answers. Theoretically my Honours papers might have deserved first class honours, though in all the circumstances I was sure they didn't. I was bitterly resentful of the time I had wasted studying for them, time which could have been well spent in other directions and relieved me of much unnecessary extra stress. Fortunately for subsequent would-be solicitors, the system was later changed for the better.

Looking back at my academic career, I had sat twelve exam papers for Honour Mods, eight for my law degree finals, seven for my BCL, one (taken three times) for my Trust Accounts and Bookkeeping, seven (each covering several subjects) for my Law Society finals and five unread papers for my Law Society's Honours – a total of 40 major university or professional exam papers since leaving school (42 counting my two failures in Trust Accounts and Bookkeeping). I have sometimes wondered whether this, combined with the radically shortened timescale in which I studied for all of them except Honour Mods, constituted some sort of record. If so, it is nothing to boast about. Rather, dictated though it was by circumstances, it is something I regret to this day, bearing in mind the toll it took on my mental health and the extent to which I could have enjoyed a fuller and richer life at Oxford making more fruitful use of the wide-ranging facilities it had to offer. Nor was it conducive to a relaxed and full relationship with Isabel, which, other considerations apart, was unfair to her.

———•———

The next phase of my life was to be my long-deferred National Service. I had been accepted by the War Office Selection Board for the Commission which had been the purpose of my military antics at Oxford and Catterick. I would go straight to Officers' Training School and would earn a reasonable income sooner than would otherwise have been the case and so would be able to leave Isabel with a decent home while I was away for two years – or at last one that didn't have toadstools growing on the kitchen floor. It was with some feeling of regret and guilt at not 'doing my bit' that I failed my medical, though I would be economic with the truth if I didn't admit that my overwhelming feeling was one of profound relief. I nevertheless hated having to tell people that my eyesight had deteriorated, as a result of my excessive swotting for seven years since I'd left Peter Symonds, to such an extent that I was unacceptable for National Service. What, for instance, would Mr Wheatley say?

He didn't turn a hair or utter a single derogatory word, directly or by implication. On the contrary, he said it was excellent news that I could pursue my career immediately and that I should do just that. The very next week there was an advertisement in the Local Government Chronicle for the post of Junior Assistant Solicitor to the Cumberland County Council, based in Carlisle. I applied for the post and Mr Wheatley was remarkably sensitive in offering to explain to the Clerk of the Cumberland County Council, Cyrus Swift, why I couldn't do my National Service and generally to support my application. I was invited to Carlisle for an interview and offered the post, doubtless due at least as much to Mr Wheatley's influence and support as to such merits as I may have possessed. It was a strange coincidence that he had been the Clerk of the Cumberland County Council before moving to Hampshire. I suppose my academic achievements, in that respect at least, stood me in good stead.

In saying farewell to me and wishing me well on my last day in his department, Mr Wheatley gave me two invaluable pieces of practical advice that I have never forgotten. The first was that the secret of good management was 'plain horse sense' which, though an oversimplification, I later had occasion to remember more than once. The second was absolutely true: 'There are two kinds of solicitors – those who find good reasons for doing things and those who find good reasons for not doing things. You *will* be one of the former.'

It was with such wise admonishments ringing in my ears that I left the Hampshire County Council on the Christmas Eve of 1957, eagerly booking forward to a new life in Cumberland and my first job as a qualified solicitor.

Early in the New Year, Isabel and I took up residence in Carlisle. It was a coincidence that Carlisle was Bill Moralee's home and he and his parents were kind and welcoming to this young couple from the southern hemisphere. Bill had arranged for us to move into a small flat on the top floor of a three-storied house in Strand Road. After only two months or so, our landlady gave us notice to quit on the grounds that people kept ringing us up, which meant that she had to climb two flights of stairs to summon us down to the telephone in the hall. Presumably she chose as our successors people who were hard of hearing or incapable of speech – preferably both – or otherwise incommunicado with the rest of humanity.

We moved to a pleasant enough flat in Warwick Road which was only five minutes walk from my office at 'the Courts', those two round towers either side of the southern entrance to the main street. Our landladies were two spinster sisters – the 'Johnston sisters' – one of whom was thin and severely physically handicapped and the other comfortably rotund. They were jolly characters who took a motherly but unobtrusive interest in our lives.

We had no money to buy a house and eventually the County Council leased us a small, modern, semi-detached house in Skiddaw Road, from whose back upstairs windows we were supposed on the mythical clear day to be able to see the summit of Skiddaw at the northern end of the Lake District. Our friendly neighbours were David, a short, plump engineer in the County Surveyor's Department, and his chatty wife, who provided constant amusement by unwittingly resorting to malapropisms, one I remember being that 'Dave watches too much television because he is *memorized* by it'.

The County Clerk, Cyrus Swift, was the antithesis of Andrew Wheatley, tall and thin, verging on the gangling, grey-haired and grey-faced, less than perfectly groomed and dressed; a gentle, fatherly man. He had been tragically widowed and, though fortified by his Catholic faith, the sadness still showed in his eyes and he harboured a perpetual hangdog expression.

Myself playing King Gama in Princess Ida.

I was singularly favoured to be in the right place at the right time. After six months, the solicitor immediately senior to me left and I was promoted to his position. Amazingly, after a further six months, the same thing happened and I became Senior Assistant Solicitor, ranking next to the Deputy County Clerk, after only one year. Compared with Hampshire the department was very small but the staff were the salt of the earth, hardworking and steadfast in the help and support they gave to this young solicitor from an alien world.

Carlisle was something of a closed community, turned in on itself, inward-looking. Not only was it a long way from any major urban centres but, being surrounded by the Irish Sea, the Solway Firth, the Pennines and the Lake District, seemed cut off – psychologically as much as physically – from the outside world. Nevertheless we quickly broke our way into the social set, partly through my professional contacts within and without the County Council and partly because we joined the pleasant tennis club on the north bank of the River Eden, as well as the Carlisle Choral and Operatic Society. We sang the usual repertoire of choral works in one of the school halls, once broadcasting with 'the BBC Northern Orchestra conducted by Stamford Robinson', nostalgic words to people of my generation who listened to classical music on the radio. In our operatic capacity, we performed the operas of Gilbert & Sullivan in the rather splendid old theatre. There was a nucleus of excellent soloists and our performances were, I think, pretty good. I played the part of King Gama, a hunch-backed misanthrope, in one of the less well-known operas, *Princess Ida*. People's main reaction was one of surprise that the rather dour character I suppose I then gave the impression of being could be so extrovert. We had a full social life and made many good friends whose Christmas cards die out only when they do.

Cumberland had not then been combined with Westmorland and some northern parts of Lancashire to form the single and more sensible administrative unit of Cumbria. A great advantage of working in a small county – small in population and rateable value rather than physical size – was that I gained experience of most of the County Council's functions. I was blooded in speaking on my feet, advising and addressing Committees of all kinds; prosecuting on behalf of the Council in far-flung Magistrates' Courts (in Millom, for instance, near the border with Lancashire some 70 miles south of Carlisle); and representing the Council at public inquiries about planning decisions and compulsory purchase orders. My prosecutions covered offences ranging from the standard ones under the Trade Descriptions Act, such as those committed by butchers who adjusted their scales so that their customers got less meat than they'd paid for, to cases in the Workington and Whitehaven Courts where fishermen used illegal nets whose meshes were so small that they ensnared fish that were smaller and younger than the law allowed, thereby unduly depleting the stocks of fish in that remote part of the Irish Sea.

I can't remember committing any major bloomers, which in a way is a pity because one's mistakes are usually more interesting than one's successes. Except for one. I was asked to give a lecture about local government to newly promoted police sergeants attending a course designed to extend their knowledge of local affairs. I spent several evenings working out what I would say, determined to shine by making my lecture a model of clarity. At some lunch or other a few weeks after

I'd delivered my magnificent oration, I found myself sitting next to the Chief Constable. When I introduced myself, he said: 'Ah, so you are Elton. I should be grateful if you wouldn't talk down to my sergeants in future.' I was distraught with embarrassment. I felt so foolish, so ashamed that I had presumably given the impression of a brash young solicitor, too clever by half, talking to dumb, clod-hopping policemen. Criticisms are more hurtful when they are justified than when they are not. This criticism, by the Chief Constable of all people, hurt more than I can say. For the rest of my life I was nothing less than compulsive in my determination not to repeat such a crass error, to the point that at the end of my career, as we shall see, I made the opposite mistake, much to my detriment.

When we moved to Carlisle, my father lent me £100 (repayable at a rate of £5 a month) to buy, second hand, one of those old, black, upright 'Ford Populars', whose main and potentially fatal failing was that, when you drove up steep hills, the windscreen wipers slowed down almost to a halt. This made the ascent of Shap Fell on our journeys at Christmas to and from Winchester extremely hazardous when it rained or snowed, as one or the other it invariably did. Driving virtually blind wasn't helped by the fact that, being a tall, narrow and light vehicle, I had to cling to the driving wheel for dear life lest we were toppled over in the blustery conditions that also prevailed on Shap Fell. Yet for all that, being my first one, I was prouder of that old banger than of any of the smarter cars I later possessed. And at least it enabled us to explore the glorious countryside that surrounded Carlisle, including that of the valley of the River Eden through the Pennines and of Scotland to the near north. Best of all, it was wonderful to live so close to the Lake District and to be able to explore it, particularly at weekends in the 'off season' on clear, crisp days when there were few tourists about.

Our three and a half years in Cumberland were happy times crowned by the ultimate joy, way beyond words, of Isabel's first pregnancy. She began labour early one evening and I hurriedly drove her to the hospital. I stayed with her until the nurse in charge of the maternity ward said: 'It would be nice if you left now, Mr Elton'. In those days, husbands – as then they usually were! – did not stay to witness the birth of their children. I drove home, half disappointed and half – coward that I was – relieved. I slept fitfully, got up early and immediately rang the hospital, anxious to hear the good news, only to be told that Isabel was still in labour. I pretended to concentrate on my work at the office, phoning the hospital every hour or so. By the time I left the office to go home earlier than usual, there was still 'no news'. In a state of mounting anxiety, I could think of nothing more original to do than restlessly pace up and down in the lounge. I remember thinking it was as if I were playing a role in a third-rate 'B' movie and actually smiling to myself at the thought, though I vaguely recognized that my mind was playing tricks on me in an effort to disguise my unreasoning fears that something might have gone terribly wrong.

There was a sudden knock on the front door. When I opened it, a senior nurse who lived opposite us was standing there. I felt sure that she was the harbinger of terrible news. So fast did my mind race that in no more than a second or two it worked out that someone had thoughtfully decided that it would soften the blow if the sad tidings were conveyed to me personally in my own home rather than via an impersonal telephone call. She looked me steadily in the eyes, held out her hand and said: 'Congratulations. You are the father of a beautiful daughter. I wanted to have the pleasure of telling you myself.' I didn't take her hand but instead embraced her, mumbling my thanks and dampening one shoulder of her nurse's uniform. She exhorted me to drive carefully and not to forget the flowers which she had spotted on the hall table.

When I arrived at the hospital I joined a queue of husbands waiting impatiently in the corridor leading to the maternity ward, most of us clutching our bunches of flowers. After a while, there was an announcement on the intercom: 'If Mr Elton is waiting would he please come to reception.' The sound of that female voice reverberating through the pristinely white-walled corridor again reverberates in my brain as I write over forty years later. I still see in my mind's eye the instant darkening of that clinical whiteness. My imagination ran instantaneous riot.

I am not inclined to panic but panic then I did. I charged back down the corridor, desperately shouting to all and sundry to tell me the way to reception, which I quickly found. A severe-looking bespectacled lady told me in a dead-pan tone of voice, as flat and funereal as that of a weather forecaster announcing impending drizzle, that Mrs Elton and 'the baby' had been taken 'urgently' to the isolation hospital because she (Mrs Elton) had a 'high temperature' which might be due to 'an infection'.

Clearly satisfied that she was being obliging, she told me how to get to the isolation hospital, where I arrived within twenty or so minutes and where the lady at reception was, in marked contrast, thoughtful and sympathetic. She said there was no need to look so worried: the baby was fine and my wife had only been taken there as a precaution in case her infection spread throughout the maternity ward. That, she explained, when I expressed my fears about the 'urgency', was the only reason why it was urgent: it wasn't – she added reading my mind – because my wife or the baby were dangerously ill. She showed me into Isabel's room and said she would bring me 'a nice cup of tea'.

Isabel was lying in her bed with her eyes closed, exhausted by over twenty-four hours' labour. There was a cot next to her bed. I kissed her gently on the cheek, whereupon she opened her burning eyes and looked calmly into mine: no need for words. I then looked into the cot where lay our tiny daughter, Caroline, fast and peacefully asleep. After such a roller-coaster of emotions, it was hardly surprising that unrestrained tears welled up inside me and crept their silent way down my cheeks, to which I could feel blood, in miraculous defiance of gravity, slowly beginning to return. The kindly receptionist brought me the promised cup of tea in which she said she had put 'plenty of sugar' which would 'do you good', adding that she was pleased to see that 'you're getting your colour back'; she was kindness itself. I sat there in a time warp, more serenely happy than I had ever imagined it was possible to be.

I visited 'my wife and daughter' in the evenings, having at once telephoned my parents and parents-in-law proudly to announce the birth of their first grandchild. My parents said they would come up to Carlisle with another couple with whom they had made friends and take the opportunity to have a short holiday. We arranged to meet at the isolation hospital two evenings later, by which time Isabel was already very much better. The couple who were to accompany my parents were very well-off. He was superficially attractive, superficial being the operative word. I already knew that he and my mother were having a flirtatious affair, but not, I believed, an affair in any deeper sense of the word, though Isabel and I called him 'lover boy'.

I arrived at the hospital before they did. While we were waiting for them to arrive, the receptionist explained that they could only come in two at a time. They were a little late and I was impatient with excitement at the prospect of my parents' joy at their first sight of their first grandchild. To say that I was crestfallen when the first to come in were

Isabel, myself and Caroline.

my mother and lover boy would be the understatement to end all understatements. Whereas, with the objectivity of hindsight, my brain is capable of understanding how this might reasonably have come about, at the time my sentient mind felt a degree of bitterness and anger such as I have rarely experienced before or since. As usual, I laid most of the blame at my mother's door, though my emotions were conflicting and tangled: I felt that my father should for once have suppressed his natural courtesy and insisted on coming in first with my mother: that lover boy should also have so insisted if he had had the slightest sensitivity and comprehension of the situation. I was furious with him and loathed him more than I already did for the part he was playing in what was clearly a deteriorating relationship between my parents. I was deeply distressed on my father's behalf. As I said earlier, not for him was the shallowness of 'the high life', however understandably attractive it might seem to my mother against the back-cloth of her poverty-stricken youth. Superficiality was not the hallmark of a man to whom classical music and Shakespeare meant so much: a man who, or whose batman, had carried a gramophone and records of lieder through the overt turmoil of war. No less turbulent was the inner turmoil of the warring emotions which I had to contain in the name of an elementary politeness. I had so wanted it to be so much more than an occasion for platitudes.

———•◦•———

Our time in Cumberland was drawing to a close. We would miss our friends and the accessibility of Carlisle's magnificent environs. One of our nearest and favourite spots was the hill opposite the little church at Howtown on the south-eastern side of Ullswater. On many a day, for many an hour we would sit on its summit, sometimes picnicking but always observing the inverted, seemingly three-dimensional silhouettes of the mountains opposite mirrored darkly in the water's depths and so, by contrast, sharpening the crystal clarity of the unshadowed parts of that gentle lake whose ephemeral ripples meandered silently to our distant right and to our left until soon hidden from our gaze by a higher hill than ours. There is much grander, far more dramatic scenery in foreign lands but none, surely, more lovely in its simplicity and intimate scale than the English Lake District. We are lucky to have known its true and inexhaustible beauty which has for ever imbued our hearts and minds.

———•◦•———

I was appointed Second Assistant Solicitor to the Surrey County Council in 1961. This wasn't the demotion it may sound because Surrey was then one of the very largest local authorities in the country in terms of population and rateable value, not yet having been deprived of the large chunk of its metropolitan area that was soon to become part of Greater London. I later learnt that my application was successful because at my interview William Willis Ruff, the Clerk of the County Council, asked me what I thought was the main principle of good management. Casting around in my mind for a suitable answer, the word 'delegation' found its way to my lips. Such is fate that this was apparently the answer he wanted to hear. He certainly practised what he preached and, failing a crisis, left us well alone to get on with our work.

If I tell you that William Ruff was on the short side and a little tubby with a round, red face and a balding head, I suspect that the last picture that springs to your mind is one of a man distinguished in appearance, manner and mind. Yet such a man he undoubtedly was, exuding a quiet, almost shy, charm interspersed with delightful moments of joviality. He was a big enough man not to be above the occasional risqué joke, provided the occasion was rare and well-judged. On one such occasion, when he had invited the solicitors for a drink in his office one Christmas, he recalled – with evident delight that he hadn't been responsible for its drafting – a clause in one of the Surrey County Council Acts that had preceded the Town and Country Planning legislation of general application which said: 'There shall be no unauthorized erections on Epsom Common.'

We still had insufficient money to put down as a deposit for a house, especially considering the exorbitant price of houses in Surrey. The County Council had compulsorily acquired a row of houses in Grennell Road in Sutton, which were in due course to become part of the site for a new school. In the meantime, they were temporarily leased to staff, fortunately including me.

There could be no greater contrast than that between Cumberland and the then metropolitan part of Surrey. The contrast was not a favourable one. Sutton was a faceless, impersonal borough, largely surrounded by equally undistinguished and indistinguishable boroughs that conjured up in the mind's eye such alliterative, romantic vistas as Mitcham, Morden and Merton. You could only tell you had entered another borough if you came across another Woolworths. Far more people commuted from Surrey than populated the whole of Cumberland, which did nothing to foster any sense of identity or cohesion in our social lives. We did the same things as we had in Carlisle, joining the Sutton Tennis Club and the Wimbledon Operatic Society. Yet having played tennis or attended a rehearsal, everyone disappeared – literally and metaphorically – into their shells to continue their anonymous, pressurized lives, concerned only to get up early enough the next morning not to miss the 7.15 or whatever to Waterloo or wherever. In this respect I was no different. When I didn't take the car, I had to change trains at Wimbledon in order to get to the County Hall at Kingston-upon-Thames and stood day after day on the platform wearing the mandatory bowler hat and carrying the prescribed black, tightly-rolled umbrella. If it is not beyond the bounds of human imagination to envisage a sea of bowler hats, the tide flowed and ebbed at Wimbledon station at the morning and evening rush hours with monotonous, monochrome regularity.

At least when I reached the County Hall it was one of the more splendid of its kind, situated by the banks of the River Thames. With such a large County Council my professional experience was inevitably more specialized than it had been in Cumberland, being confined to the social and 'public protection' services which covered a miscellany of functions such as enforcing the Trade Descriptions Act and some special provisions in private Surrey County Council legislation.

Being so closely involved with the social services, especially those relating to children, was one of the most rewarding phases of my career in local government. Social workers, like members of any other profession, made occasional mistakes in dealing with sometimes impossibly difficult cases about the welfare of the most unfortunate children in our society, only to be lambasted by pompous judges who opined always with the wisdom of hindsight. No-one ever heard of the vast majority of the thousands of good decisions taken by sympathetic social workers, for whom I developed a profound respect. I conducted many cases in the courts defending the decisions they had made, designed to enhance the welfare of, or at least mitigate the harm to, children with appallingly tragic parental backgrounds – decisions, for instance, to take children into the care of the County Council or to assume parental rights over them, which were invariably based on a fine distinction between the lesser of two evils. They could be as damned if they did as they could be damned if they didn't.

It was in the 'public protection' field that I made two 'mistakes' I have never forgotten, though, to be fair to myself, it remains arguable whether they were mine or those of the Courts.

There was a huge dance hall in Purley named the Orchid Ballroom, though orchids don't spring to mind as being the predominant species of flora in Purley. It was owned and run by the powerful consortium called, for short, Grand Met. It was licensed under one of the Surrey County Council Acts designed to control the spread of indecent establishments from central London to leafy Surrey and generally to prevent over-crowding in public buildings with all its inherent dangers, such as the capacity, or rather incapacity, to escape in the event of a fire. The licence granted by the County Council limited the number of people allowed to occupy the building at any one time to 1,800. The exact words of the relevant part of the licence were 'Music and dancing – 1,800'. The problem was that the people in the surrounding areas repeatedly complained that far more people than the permitted limit crowded in on Saturday evenings, with the result that for miles around they were plagued with parked cars jamming up the suburban streets in which they were otherwise apparently content to live.

I was determined to earn some Brownie points by tackling the problem head on. I summoned eight officers from the relevant department to my office and instructed them to sit one Saturday evening in pairs in four cars, each within sight of one of the four entrances, and to count the number of people who went in. I would then, by a process of simple addition, be able to prove conclusively the total number of people who had entered the building. They were agog with excitement at their prospective Sherlock Holmes roles, one even suggesting that he should wear a false beard, which I deemed unnecessary. On the Monday morning following the Saturday in question, they reported back that far more than 1,800 people had entered the building – about 2,600 if I remember correctly. Triumphantly, I launched a prosecution against Grand Met and appeared before the local Magistrates several weeks later.

Having called my eight witnesses, I sat down without further ado, entirely satisfied that the Court couldn't do other than convict Grand Met for a breach of their licence. Grand Met had briefed a QC who then stood up and, to my eternal astonishment, submitted that there was no case to answer on the facile grounds that 'Mr Elton has produced no evidence that there were more than 1,800 people dancing at any one time'. I responded, thinking fast off the top of my head, that the intention of the legislation and licence was perfectly clear and that, if my learned friend were right, there would be nothing to stop 5,000 people attending a dance at the Orchid Ballroom, with all the potentially disastrous consequences for life and limb that the legislation was so unambiguously designed to avoid. Furthermore, the legislation would be impossible to enforce. How could anyone count the number of people dancing at any one time? My learned friend responded by submitting that in a criminal case, any ambiguity in the drafting of the legislation and licence had to be resolved in favour of the accused. After only a brief adjournment, the Magistrates resumed their seats on the bench and their Chairman peremptorily announced that the case was dismissed. Collapse of stout party – in this case, unfortunately, myself. I slunk back to the County Hall with my tail between my legs, older and wiser. William Ruff shared my view that it was a perverse decision, but felt that there was a danger of incurring the substantial costs of both sides if we appealed to a higher court and lost, the possibility of which couldn't be altogether ruled out. Such, unfortunately, is life.

Such, too, was life in another, even more bizarre case for which I was responsible. The Surrey Public Analyst reported to me that he had analysed Hermesetas and found its chemical composition was exactly the same as the other main types of saccharine. Yet it was being advertised as 'sweeter than ordinary saccharine' – as clear a case of misleading advertising as a prosecutor could wish to find.

The chance of an important successful prosecution immediately appealed to me, if only – as a matter of personal pride – to redeem myself for the Orchid Ballroom fiasco. I enthusiastically launched a prosecution against the producers of Hermesetas, confident of success and redemption. From memory, it was the Dorking Magistrates before whom I appeared because the Public Analyst had analysed a tin of Hermesetas that had been bought within its jurisdiction. I simply called the Public Analyst to the witness box and he gave his scientific evidence clearly and concisely. I rested my case.

Once again, the opposition was represented by a QC, who didn't cross examine the Public Analyst, thereby confirming my view that he couldn't offer any defence but only make a plea in mitigation of the penalty to be imposed. Words nearly failed me when he proceeded to call a number of well-known chefs as witnesses, including a famous one they had flown over from Paris. They all swore blind that they used a lesser amount of Hermesetas than of other 'ordinary saccharine' to achieve the same degree of sweetness in their famous, fancy desserts. They all stuck to their guns in the face of such cross examination as I could muster on the spot. After retiring for scarcely longer than the Purley Magistrates in the ill-fated Orchid Ballroom case, they ruled that the defendants were not guilty. The Public Analyst was naturally disappointed, not to say disgusted, and I could hardly face the prospect of returning to the office with a second lot of egg on my face. William Ruff was again entirely supportive of my decision to prosecute and, rightly enough, took the same view as before about the unacceptable risk of appealing.

With the effluxion of time, I can see the funny side of both these cases but I need hardly add that I didn't exactly laugh my head off at the time. I was not, though, incapable of being amused by an episode that occurred soon after the Hermesetas case came to grief. A senior secretary in the office – secretary to the Deputy Clerk no less – was a very prim and proper, but delightful, spinster. A new Xerox copying machine was installed in her office, which she unwittingly and unblushingly referred to as the 'Durex machine'. I leave to your imagination the endless variations on the theme of ribaldry that ensued until some unknown brave soul must have pointed out the error of her ways and spoilt the fun.

Looking after Caroline, a demanding child if ever there was, was a full time occupation for Isabel during the weekdays and I did what I could to help out on the weekends. Looking back, we were not happy in the nondescript physical environs and virtually non-existent social life of Sutton though, such is the strength of the human spirit, we did our best not to recognize this at the time. On the other hand, my professional life was thoroughly rewarding and we made some good friends of some of my colleagues at County Hall.

One weekend my parents came to stay with us. Their marriage had reached crisis point. They were both very distressed and talked openly about their problems. I remember my mother thoughtfully saying that it wasn't fair to impose 'their misery' on us. At one stage of the evening I left Isabel to talk with my mother and took my father for a drive round the dreary suburbs in the dark. It was pouring with rain, the amount and ferocity of which was exaggerated in the garish glare of endless street lights. It was like those plays on television when it always seems to pour with rain at appropriately gloomy moments. He was in tears and clearly on the verge of mental breakdown. I advised him to seek medical help and gave him such comfort as I could. He was pathetically grateful.

Several months later we spent a weekend with my parents in Winchester. As in the case of their visit with lover boy and his wife to the isolation hospital in Carlisle a few years earlier, something happened in relation to which my brain's thoughts as I write diverge from my mind's feelings at the time. My brain now realizes that times had changed: that in society as a whole television had largely supplanted domestic activities such, in our case, as the musical evenings that we had found so fulfilling before, during and after the war: that the middle class society of those days traditionally functioned by way of shallower pastimes such as cocktail parties. When I walked into the lounge I saw what, for my emotional self, could hardly have been a more poignant and corrosive symbol presaging the tragic shape of things to come: a symbol which resurrected the unfeigned hatred I had long harboured for lover boy and the bitter resentment I increasingly felt towards my mother. My fury knew no bounds.

The piano had been replaced by a flashy, ostentatious cocktail cabinet, filled with the futile accoutrements of so-called social life.

——————

After three and a half years in Surrey, I was appointed Assistant Clerk of the Buckinghamshire County council in 1965. I was at last earning enough to raise a mortgage and buy our first new house.

It was a pleasant, brand-new house next to a ramshackle old pub in the village of Granborough near Winslow and some ten miles to the north of Aylesbury, where the County Council's office was located at the lower end of the town square, which was quite attractive until ruined by a concrete monstrosity of a shopping centre on one side. The County Clerk was Richard Millard, a slender figure of moderate height whose walk, with his wrists turned slightly outwards, had a swanky look about it, an impression which, aided and abetted by his suave manner and upper-class accent, compounded his reputation for snobbery. I was not amongst those who assumed it followed that he wasn't intelligent. I learnt much from him.

Once, when in his presence I referred to a chap in the office called Ken Batson as 'Mr Batson', he said, 'I say, Elton, why do you call Batson Mr Batson?' I was stumped for a polite answer to what seemed to me to be a bizarre question and can't actually remember what tightrope I presumably trod in response. I always felt it was as insulting to call men by their surnames as, in those 'pre-Ms' days, it would have been to call a woman 'Jones' instead of 'Mrs' or 'Miss' Jones'. I felt it was impersonal to the point of treating them as objects rather than human beings and, in the case of people like Ken Batson, who were junior to myself in the office hierarchy, rubbed their noses in their inferior status. Looking at it the other way round, Ken would never have dreamed of calling me Elton any more than I would have called my boss 'Millard' rather than 'Mr Millard' or, more usually, 'Sir'. But we should be careful, when we feel inclined to criticize people, to remember the times in which they had been brought up. Upper-class men of two or three generations ago used habitually to call a man they didn't know 'Mr Smith' but 'Smith' when they became on familiar terms. *Sic tempora, sic mores* – such are the times, such are the customs.

——————

Social life in Granborough was as different as chalk from cheese from that which we had enjoyed in urban Carlisle but hadn't in suburban Surrey. The indigent natives were the inter-bred descendants of

Four delightful and beautiful children, left to right: Tim, Louise, Mark, Caroline.

generations who had lived there since time immemorial, with the result that they were certainly psychologically, and perhaps even genetically, incestuous.

Whereas in suburban Surrey there were so many people around that we constantly waited to see if we'd come across more compatible friends, in Granborough there were so few that we had little choice if we weren't to live like hermits. We were thrown together, which made for a pleasantly mixed social life. Even so, the few lifelong friends we made were intruders like ourselves. Among the practical advantages of village life was a ready supply of baby-sitters, which turned out to be just as well.

Our time in Granborough was blessed by the arrival of Tim, Louise and Mark, who completed a family of four delightful and beautiful children. As I sit at my desk recalling and, as if it were yesterday, reliving the sublime joy I felt on each occasion, I find it hard to hold back the tears that are blurring my vision.

Between the arrival of Tim and Louise, Isabel had a miscarriage. The warning signs were there and it happened one night soon after we had gone to bed. I helped her to get to the bathroom and sit on the loo just in time. Having further helped her to clean herself up and return to bed and given her such comfort as I could, I went back to the bathroom and flushed the blood-soaked loo. I stood there for a long time, quietly weeping at the thought of an embryonic human being, in whose miraculous creation I had shared, coursing his or her disintegrating way through the sewers of mid-Buckinghamshire, carried and consumed by urine and shit to an unknown and unworthy grave. I returned to bed and put my arm round Isabel. United in our grief, we did not sleep well that night.

Four demanding children were a handful for Isabel to cope with on weekdays when I had to spend long hours at work. We made three unsuccessful attempts to employ au-pair girls. On the first occasion, I went to Heathrow to meet a young lady from Argentina, with whose photograph I had been provided by the agency. She looked a lovely person in every way. The children had excitedly put flowers in the room she was to occupy. When the relevant flight from Argentina landed, I waited at the exit from Customs with photograph in hand so that I could recognize her. To my dismay, she never appeared and we never heard a word from her explaining her failure to board the plane at the eleventh hour. I drove back to Granborough feeling angry and frustrated. Isabel and the children couldn't believe it when I arrived home empty handed as it were, and were naturally very upset.

On the second occasion, I again went to Heathrow to meet Jeanie from Brazil. I panicked when she didn't at first appear but, after what seemed like an eternity, she eventually emerged. Her English was confined to the mispronounced expression 'a jood idea', which we sometimes still imitate to this day. I drove her home in unavoidable silence. She was short and fat and developed a particular fondness for Tim whom she called 'Timoty'. Tim reciprocated her fondness by calling her 'fat bum' and once, to my knowledge, anticipated his sporting prowess by scoring a direct hit on the said part of her anatomy with his right foot, which only served to enhance her fondness for him. Sadly, it soon became apparent that she was very unhappy. She burst into tears at frequent intervals, obviously desperately homesick. We comforted her as best we could, taking turns to embrace her, but after a few weeks made arrangements for her to return to Brazil. I hope things worked out for her. She was such a dear person.

Less warm-hearted and lasting for even less time was a French girl, whose name I can't now remember. Being a bright sort of girl, it took her only a few days to work out that the night life of Granborough didn't exactly live up to that of Paris. The lights of the metropolis beckoned and, after a few weeks, she left to take up a similar job with a family in London.

Feeling that we were jinxed, we gave up the unequal struggle and fell back on the part-time help of Rosemary, a nice girl who lived in the village. Caroline, being five years older than Tim, sensitively observing the pressures on her mum, was remarkably good at helping to look after her three younger siblings.

My professional life filled an important gap in my experience, my main responsibilities relating to the Planning and Highways Committees. Buckinghamshire was a long, narrow county stretching from the boundary of Greater London in the south and covering part of the Metropolitan Green Belt, the Chilterns, the Vale of Aylesbury and the farming areas in the north. I represented the County Council at literally hundreds of public inquiries about refusals of planning permission and some concerning the compulsory purchase of land for new roads. The last public inquiry at which I represented the County Council concerned the proposed establishment of an 'over-spill' new town to be based on a village called Milton Keynes. Mistakes though I must have made in my constant advice to the Planning and Highways departments, I recall none that were so embarrassing as to be of any particular interest.

After a year or so, I was appointed a Deputy Clerk of the Peace, in which capacity I sat intermittently as Clerk to one of the Courts of the Buckinghamshire Quarter Sessions. I had to buy a wig, which, being as white as only brand-new wigs can be, made my inexperience plain for all the world to see. In actual fact, I felt a complete prat wearing it until I got used to the idea. Some of the trials were extremely interesting and it was fascinating first-hand experience of our legal system in operation. The Assizes were held in the same Court, which was in the same building as my office. The most famous trial held there was that of some of the perpetrators of 'the Great Train Robbery'. On the first day of the trial, I walked into my office to be greeted by two enormous dogs sniffing round my desk, attached, I was relieved to see, to leads firmly grasped by two burly policemen.

In what turned out to be an important milestone in my career, I attended a three months management course for senior local government officers

Deputy Clerk of the Peace for Buckinghamshire.

at Birmingham University. This was the time when thought began to be given to the extent to which the modern management techniques – including computerization, then in its infancy – being introduced in the commercial world, could be applied to the non-profit making public service. Some of the techniques then currently mooted seemed somewhat fanciful so far as their application to local government might be concerned and I recalled more than once Mr Wheatley's advice not to overlook 'plain horse sense'.

I was intrigued by computers. At the end of each of the first few sessions on the subject, I asked the lecturer several questions about how they worked. On about the third or fourth occasion, the lecturer asked me whether I had a telephone at home. I said, 'Yes'. 'Do you know how to use it, Mr Elton?' Again I replied, 'Yes'. 'Do you know how it works?' This time I was obliged to say, 'No'. 'Then why don't you shut up?' was his terse and telling response, well making the point that senior managers need not, indeed should not, get bogged down in technicalities but should understand enough about the potential of computers to be able to assess the 'pros' and 'cons' of their possible applications.

It was the sessions about personnel management that I found by far the most interesting: we were, after all, discussing people in the flesh rather than machines and techniques in the abstract. I well remember the lecturer on the subject giving a real-life example of a woman, one of whose jobs had been to clean the toilets in the executive suite of a major company. Having long, loyally and efficiently carried out this most unpleasant of tasks, she was rewarded by promotion to a less demeaning position. Not only, however, was she not grateful and pleased but was positively resentful because, when she had been cleaning the toilets, she used to overhear top managers discussing important, private issues concerning the company and its employees, which in turn had made her feel important – much more so than she felt in her new position. How well this example illustrated the pitfalls into which the ways of personnel managers, however well paved with good intentions, can so easily lead.

We were warned that one of the sessions on personnel management could be very upsetting, so much so that a psychologist of some kind would be present. We all entered the classroom full of curious concern about the unknown trauma that awaited us. The lecturer happened to start by pointing at me and asking me how I felt on my first day in my present job. Without turning a hair, I said I felt scared stiff, worried whether I could cope with new and important areas of local government with which I was unfamiliar and anxious lest councillors, chief officers and the staff at large wouldn't like and respect me. The lecturer then asked the others in turn to say how they reacted to what I'd said. Almost, but not quite, to a man, they said things like: 'I didn't think *you* would have felt like that'. One, I remember, mysteriously said 'you *of all people*'. They nearly all 'confessed' (one of them actually using that word) to having the same or similar feelings. I remain astounded to this day that my answer was apparently untypical and that usually the first person to be asked put on a brave face and expressed at least a degree of bravado, ashamed to give the game away and admit the unsurprising truth until probed and probed by the lecturer. I had apparently broken the ice and released the tension that usually prevailed. I had not previously realized the extent to which so many Englishmen felt the need to keep a stiff upper lip lest they betray their natural human emotions. Perhaps things have since changed for the better. I hope so.

Discussion at seminars became quite heated when it revolved around what were called the 'Theory X' and 'Theory Y' styles of management. Theory X meant that, as the boss, you were tough and uncompromising, not unduly sensitive to treading on people's toes or obsessed with 'participative' consensus or seeking compromise in the office politics so as to minimize offence to people's sensibilities. Theory Y, taken to the other extreme, implied being hyper-sensitive to people's feelings, consulting them about management structure and everything else under the sun, ever striving to keep everyone happy and not to put their noses out of joint. I was a strong advocate of Theory Y, arguing that if people liked you and understood that you understood *their* problems they would respond by supporting you and following your lead, even when it went against the grain to do so. One of the main criticisms of Theory Y, which I hadn't thought of but – when pointed out – I instantly recognized as being all too true, was that it imposed much greater stress on a manager and squandered far more of his or her emotional energy than did Theory X – energy which advocates of Theory X argued could and should be better spent in other ways.

I returned to what had by then become the routine of office work, filled with enthusiasm to put into practice such of the techniques I had learnt as I felt were practical in the real world of local government. My enthusiasm was matched only by my naivety. It would have required strong drive and direction from the top to bring about any significant changes in the administration of the County Council which, such drive and direction being lacking, soldiered on regardless. I had been in my job for five years and, having long got to grips with it, felt increasingly frustrated. I began to look around for jobs elsewhere, both within and without local government.

———

It was during my time in Buckinghamshire that a visit to my parents' home in Winchester became imprinted in my mind. My mother and Isabel were out shopping with the children when the telephone rang. I happened to be in the hall on the way to the loo and so picked up the phone and said, 'Hello'. A female voice said, 'Hello, darling'. Taken aback, I said it was Michael speaking. Obviously flustered, the lady asked if she could speak to my father, who was sitting in the piano-less lounge reading the newspaper. I told him the call was for him, whereupon he went to the phone and I to the loo. I returned to my chair in the lounge where I had been sitting, reading. After several minutes, he returned and sat down, flushed and breathing heavily. In the meantime, I had worked out that, because my voice was very similar to my father's – particularly, people said, on the telephone – it had been a case of mistaken identity. We both said nothing but pretended to continue with our reading.

It transpired that he had long since fallen deeply in love with a gentle, warm lady we knew of and she with him. I came to realize the fuller implications of the occasion in Surrey when I had driven him through the suburban rain and his 'rainy eyes' had revealed such deep distress, torn as he was, and as I now could see, between the pull of his deep love and the exigencies of married life, a tug of internal war that had reduced him to breaking point. Such was his guilt, such were then the pressures of society that he had decided to do 'the right thing' and at whatever personal cost not in his last years to break the bonds of his marriage.

———

Reverting to my frustration at work, amongst the jobs I had the cheek to apply for was that of Chief Executive of the English Tourist Board, which was then (in 1970) being established. The consultants acting for the Board replied that, as they had received over 600 applications from people with experience of tourism, they were sure I would understand that they couldn't look outside the tourist industry.

About three months later, I opened a letter while eating my breakfast. It was from the same consultants. They said that I would remember that they had had to disappoint me about my previous application, but they had now been consulted by a well-known trade association which was also looking for a new Chief Executive. If I was interested, would I give them a ring? I did so as soon as I got to the office, and learnt that their client was the Association of British Travel Agents (ABTA). I said I would like to discuss the matter and made an appointment to do so. Not without hesitation, I said I would be interested in pursuing the matter further and was invited to an interview with the full ABTA Council. I was acutely embarrassed, but hardly surprised, to be asked whether I had much experience of travelling abroad. The only time I had been abroad was when I went to Rome as a pilgrim in Holy Year exactly twenty years previously. Thinking that this would not only disqualify me but also be thought by a bunch of hardened travel agents to be positively peculiar, with nothing to lose I replied that I had once been to the Isle of Wight, which gave rise to hoots of spontaneous laughter round the boardroom table. Having apparently irredeemably blotted my copy book, I was surprised to be granted a second interview: even more so to receive a telephone call the following morning and to be offered the job.

That ABTA had engaged the same head-hunters as had acted for the English Tourist Board was one of those remarkable coincidences in life that so often shape one's destiny, whether for good or for ill. Which of the two it was to be, I could not then know. I could only wonder.

CHAPTER 6

The Travel World

O N THE FIRST DAY in my new office in Newman Street, which leads north from Oxford Street, the cultural shock of my change from the public service to the commercial world revealed itself in a minor way. My Chairman, whom I automatically addressed as 'sir', told me to call him by his Christian name, whereas in local government even the County Clerk traditionally called the Chairman of the County Council 'sir'. When a little later a junior member of the staff called me 'Michael', I knew that things were different, but none the worse for that. I soon came to realize that respect and authority did not depend on the trappings of hierarchy.

The fundamental cultural shock did not take more than a few weeks to sink in: the harsh fact that in the commercial world the bottom line is the bottom line: that capitalism is the price of freedom. With notable exceptions, scarcely anything was said by a Council or Committee member that, however it might appear on the surface, was not underscored by the actual or perceived commercial interests of his or her company or firm. That this made the evolution of a coherent policy for the travel industry as a whole difficult is to put it mildly.

This was particularly true for an association that had only been founded in 1950. One can only wonder whether its founders could have foreseen the developments in the travel industry which had occurred in the intervening twenty years. These included the improving economic circumstances of the mass of the population of the United Kingdom in those post-war years; the commercial use of the jet-engine; and the entrepreneurial flair of the British travel industry, resulting in the emergence of tour operators as wholesalers as distinct from retail travel agents.

These factors had combined to bring foreign holidays within the reach of millions of people for whom until then travel in foreign lands had been little more than a dream. The 'package holiday' explosion had become one of the most remarkable social phenomena of the second half of the twentieth century. Indeed, in world-wide terms, international tourism, based to a large extent on package tours, had become what was probably the greatest single global growth industry.

In the United Kingdom, no less than elsewhere, this phenomenal growth had brought its attendant problems. Apart from the very pace of that growth, these problems stemmed partly from the unusually difficult position of the tour operator and partly from the unique position of the customer. The former was the seller and co-ordinator of the different elements that made up the product and was largely dependent on services provided by sub-contractors over whom he might well have little direct control. The latter paid *in advance* for what, even in that increasingly sophisticated day and age, still frequently amounted to the fulfilment of a dream. Paying in advance for a dream was fundamentally different from buying a pullover off the peg at Marks and Spencer: paying for it *after* you have inspected it or even tried it on.

It was because of such special factors as these that the financial failure of, or inadequate performance by, tour operators and travel agents caused unacceptable social problems and enormous damage to the reputation of the travel trade as a whole. This in turn is why ABTA had begun the uphill task of developing into a trade association concerned – apart from such an association's normal commercial functions – to solve these problems or at least to mitigate their consequences. I am bound to say that, in seeking to contribute to this uphill task during my sixteen years as ABTA's Chief Executive (from 1970 to 1986), I not infrequently felt like the legendary Sisyphus, condemned to the eternal task of rolling a large rock up a hill down which it invariably rolled back, ever threatening to crush him beneath its weight. I had often to pull out all the stops of determination and to 'screw my courage to the sticking place' if I were not to be overwhelmed by the conflicting commercial undercurrents and strong personality clashes of tougher men than I had previously encountered. I felt buffeted from pillar to post: I was 'the piggy in the middle', caught in the cross-fire between the external pressures of consumerism and the media on the one hand and the internal pressures of commercialism on the other. I had constantly to fight for survival, psychological and otherwise.

My appointment was met with barely concealed disdain by sections of the media, notably the trade press, particularly the Travel Trade Gazette. I recall words like, 'what was the good of an obscure solicitor from Aylesbury?' This was particularly hard for someone like myself, unused to the rough and tumble of so ruthless a world and ever anxious to be popular. All I could do was to grin and bear it, though the grinning part of this equation was sometimes well nigh impossible to maintain, try as I did to keep up appearances.

All this was exacerbated by a process of internal reorganization involving the complex political and administrative establishment of two Councils, representing tour operators and retail travel agents respectively. The Tour Operators' Council and the Travel Agents' Council, each with its own complicated constitution designed to reflect the various interests within their own ranks, appointed its Chairman and Vice-Chairman and three other members to an 'umbrella' National Council, which in turn appointed the President of the Association. All three Councils appointed their own Committees which, in the case of the Tour Operators' and Travel Agents' Councils, included a Code of Conduct Committee whose remit was to enforce what were now their own separate Codes of Conduct. Politically desirable though these changes were (perhaps essential if the Association were not to split in half or disintegrate altogether), it is hard to imagine a structure which could have been a worse nightmare both to introduce and to administer on an ongoing basis.

A unique peculiarity of ABTA was a mutual trading agreement between ABTA tour operators and ABTA travel agents. By virtue of a longstanding rule in the Association's constitution, an ABTA tour operator could only sell its foreign inclusive holidays ('package holidays') – if not directly to the public – through an ABTA travel agent. Conversely, an ABTA travel agent could only sell the foreign inclusive holidays of an ABTA tour operator. Because this rule, which came to be known as 'Stabiliser', meant that nearly all tour operators and travel agents had to belong to ABTA if they were to trade with each other, the scope of the Association's Codes of Conduct, and particularly its financial safeguards for the travelling public in the event of a member's financial failure, was pretty well all-embracing. As such, our legal advice was that, although a restrictive practice, Stabiliser was – quite exceptionally – legally valid under the Common Law on the grounds that it was overridingly in the public interest. This had an unexpected significance when things came to a head in 1972, which I have ever since called 'the year of the unfinished hotels'.

The package tour being in its infancy, many tour operators produced brochures containing 'artists' impressions' of hotels still in the course of construction in the hope that they would be up and running by the time their first customers were due to arrive. All too often, however, these hopes were unrealized and people found themselves conveyed to hotels other than those they had booked and which they took every opportunity to complain were inferior in one way or another – no 'sea view', for example. They became skilfully innovative at complaining, fairly or otherwise, and, if a ping-pong table mentioned in the brochure was missing, the whole point of their holiday suddenly became their overwhelming wish to play ping-pong from morn to night. I remember one such complaint about a hotel in Spain referred to 'the Donkey Hotee' hotel, an inspirational variant on 'Don Quixote' which would no doubt have had Cervantes turning in his grave. The weight and intensity of criticism about the misleading impressions given by artists' impressions in the written and broadcast media washed off on ABTA itself, which seemed impotent to do anything about it.

In many cases, this practice meant that the tour operators concerned were in breach of the Tour Operators' Code of Conduct. The system for enforcing the Codes of Conduct was more sophisticated than ABTA was (then, at least) given credit for. In order to separate the functions of judge and prosecutor, it was for the Secretariat – which meant myself in major cases – to institute disciplinary proceedings for breaches of the Codes, and for the appropriate Code of Conduct Committee to decide at formal hearings whether the alleged breaches were proven and, if so, to reprimand, fine or – in extreme cases – expel the members concerned which would, as a result of Stabiliser, virtually put them out of business because they could no longer trade with other ABTA members. Importantly, there was an independent Appeal Board to which a member who was penalized could appeal.

Observing that one of the Association's fundamental objectives as set out in its Memorandum of Association was 'to do all such things as may be deemed necessary to raise the prestige and status of members of the Association', I decided – after much agonizing – that ABTA would become nothing less than a farcical non-entity if I did not commence disciplinary proceedings against all the tour operators whom I felt were in breach of their Code of Conduct. I acted accordingly.

All hell was let loose. In particular, some directors of some of the major tour operators – including a Council member – made remarks to me like, 'Don't forget you have a wife and children. You'll be out of a job if we all leave ABTA.' I realized, as it was their intention I should, that they were so powerful commercially that, if they carried out their threat to leave ABTA, whatever the technical legal niceties, there would in practice be no way that I or anyone else could stop them continuing to trade with ABTA travel agents. The practical consequences would therefore be the demise of Stabiliser, the very foundation of ABTA's existence. The lawyer in me began to wonder if it was legal to threaten me in so blatant a fashion. I decided to seek Counsel's advice, which I found interesting. It was to the effect that it is not *per se* illegal to make threats of almost any kind, however dire the consequences would be to those on the receiving end if the threats were carried out. There was, however, one exception. It *was* illegal if the threats involved doing something that was itself illegal. Because Stabiliser was legal under the Common Law, a threat to breach it *was* a threat to do something illegal. I could, therefore, take out an injunction in the High Court if the threats continued.

Needless to say, the threat was repeated by the Council member. I quietly said that I had taken Counsel's advice and proposed to take out an injunction against him and his company (one of the largest tour operators in the country) restraining him and it from continuing to threaten me and, by necessary implication, my wife and children (by referring to whom – with an eye for the main chance and its dramatic effect – I was mischievously adding my own gloss on my legal advice).

That was the first – but by no means last – time during my time at ABTA that I learnt the truth of the statement that bullies are cowards. My comments must have spread like wildfire. I was never so threatened again. In the event, it was beyond my control that the political powers-that-be reached a political compromise, whereby representatives of the tour operators concerned appeared before the Tour Operators' Council, formally apologized and gave appropriate undertakings as to their future conduct. At least that was a step in the right direction and it was always a comfort to me to keep my legal advice tucked away in the back of my mind.

———

It was in that same year (1972) that we moved from Granborough back to our roots in Winchester. My parents had decided to move from their house in Bereweeke Close to a flat in Christchurch Road. As Bereweeke Close was near Peter Symonds, which was now a distinguished Sixth Form College, and the comprehensive Henry Beaufort School, we bought their house and so I literally returned home. Both Henry

Beaufort School and Peter Symonds were in a 'good' catchment area. (When we say we are not being snobbish, we usually mean that we are.) It was not much further to commute from Winchester to Waterloo than it had been to do so from Bletchley to Euston, as I had done for two years since joining ABTA. But whereas I had had to drive from Granborough to Bletchley station and back again every day, Winchester station was only ten minutes walk from Bereweeke Close.

It was a strange feeling to go back to the home where I had lived since soon after the war until I got married, except during term time at Oxford. We built an extension over the garage comprising our own bedroom with an en-suite bathroom, which helped us to feel the house was our own, and I rearranged the garden for the same psychological reason. I didn't want to feel I was still a boy living in 'mum and dad's house'. It is quite difficult enough to grow up at the best of times.

Winchester itself had changed. It was no longer the stuffy place we perceived it to be as adolescents. In those days, broadly speaking, you belonged to the closed community of the Winchester College/Cathedral set *or* to the professional and City/County Council set ('the Castle' being the offices of the Hampshire County Council) *or* to the social 'also-rans'. I distinctly remember that just as we at Peter Symonds regarded the boys who went to 'the other school at Winchester' as posh snobs and, on the rare occasions when some of them were actually sighted trespassing outside their hallowed precincts, poked fun at them as such, so too those who went to the secondary modern schools poked fun at us 'toffee-nosed' grammar school types, particularly when we wore straw hats called 'boaters' during the summer terms. This three-tier class division was set in the firmest of concrete.

Now the concrete was at least a little softer and occasionally even crumbled at the edges. The introduction of comprehensive education was a major factor. There was also a much larger and more disparate middle class emanating, for example, from the arrival of IBM at the nearby village of Hursley. Whereas, too, in my youth a trip to London was something of an event, now Winchester had become commuter country. Indeed, the morning trains to London were already quite full of commuters from Southampton, the New Forest or even as far as Bournemouth, though I regarded Winchester as the outer limit of sanity for the daily drudgery of the journey to and from Waterloo. By the time I retired, my younger son, Mark, worked out on his calculator that I had been as far as the moon on British Rail (as it was then). The obvious difference was that they got to the moon on time. But it wasn't wasted time. You can get a lot of work done going by train from Winchester to the moon. Another influence on the changing social pattern was that the Art School and King Alfred's Teachers Training College were already on their way to becoming amongst the larger of their kinds in the country. The night life of Winchester – if not exactly spectacular – could even then be more than a little lively on Fridays and Saturdays in term time.

We were happy to be living in Winchester. I needed roots and we felt at home there. Isabel had a full social life as did I so far as time permitted. Amongst other things, we joined the tennis club onto which the garden of what was now our own house in Bereweeke Close backed and where we had spent happy times in our youth; we joined the Winchester Music Club, which performed choral works to a high standard twice a year, usually in the Cathedral; and we played bridge within an increasing circle of good friends.

Back at ABTA, the episode of being threatened with the loss of my job paled into insignificance compared with the dramatic events that ensued in the latter part of 1974.

The background to these events was two-fold. Firstly, every ABTA tour operator was required to provide a bond whereby a third party, such as a bank or insurance company, guaranteed to pay the Association a certain amount of money if the tour operator went bankrupt. The tour operator had to pay the guarantor a premium for the privilege.

Secondly, I had long been concerned that in some cases the amount of money available under the bonds might be insufficient both to mount a 'rescue operation' to bring back the holidaymakers who were still on holiday at the time of the tour operator's bankruptcy and to reimburse those whose holidays had not yet commenced. Fearing that this might one day happen, I had submitted a report to the Tour Operators' Council suggesting that this problem should be addressed and resolved by a compromise between the (desirable) principle of individualism and the (undesirable) principle of collectivism (collective cross-subsidy). Each tour operator should continue to stand on its own individual bonding feet as the first line of defence, but a collective fund should be set up as a second line of defence, to which all tour operators should be required to contribute amounts relative to their turnover and on which ABTA could draw if a bond were ever inadequate to fulfil its twin aims of rescue and reimbursement. I could not recommend that the amount of the bonds be increased to cover every eventuality because, if a tour operator's financial position was a little shaky, the premium for its bond would have had to be correspondingly greater proportionate to the increased risk to the guarantor. This could itself have caused the very problem we were seeking to solve by forcing tour operators into liquidation. It could also be unfair because, for example, British Airways had not then been privatized and so its tour operating subsidiaries couldn't go bust. They could therefore have provided bonds of greater amounts without paying the much higher premiums that would have been required of their purely commercial rivals.

The Tour Operators' Council did not accept my recommendation, a director of Clarksons – one of the very biggest ABTA tour operators – complaining that there was no reason why efficient companies like his should subsidize inefficient companies that went bankrupt by contributing to a collective fund, albeit only a second line of defence. Those words came flooding back to me in the days following 15 August 1974.

That was the day on which, about 4 o'clock in the afternoon, the 'Court Line crash' was announced. The Court Line group of companies had been forced into liquidation. This included some ABTA tour operators, including Clarksons! In what turned out to be a crucial factor in the drama that ensued, the Labour government had earlier that summer taken over parts of the Court Line Group (including its tour operators) and Tony Benn, the Secretary of State for Industry, had said in the House of Commons that this '*should* secure' the holidays of the Group's tour operating companies for the rest of the summer.

It was immediately apparent that the amount of money available to ABTA under the bonds of these companies, including Clarksons, was sufficient to mount a huge rescue operation to bring home some 35,000 customers who were abroad at the time of the collapse. But it was also only too clear that there was not enough money to reimburse some 100,000 customers whose holidays had not yet commenced. Day after day there were headlines on the front pages of nearly all the newspapers referring to this 'scandal' and the plight of the Court Line 'victims'.

An emergency meeting of the Tour Operators' Council was held that evening, concerned mainly with the immediate practicalities of the situation. I retired to a small hotel near the office in the small hours, my head reeling as the implications of the shortfall in the money available from the Clarksons' bond sank in. 100,000 people who had relied on the supposed security of the ABTA symbol would lose both their holidays and the money they had paid for them. I had always tried hard to ensure that the public relations department did not go over the top – tempting though it was in public relations terms – by implying that the ABTA symbol was an absolute guarantee. Nevertheless, this was the impression left in the minds of the public at large. My legal mind conjured up the vision of a 'class action' against ABTA on behalf of those who had lost their money. Even for my innumerate self, it didn't take many seconds to work out that if 100,000 people had paid only £100 for their lost holidays, the total sum involved would be £10,000,000. ABTA faced not only the certainty of the shameful destruction of its reputation, but also the distinct possibility of total extinction.

A temporary reprieve was secured because the media had cottoned on to Tony Benn's statement in the House of Commons. There was a general election approaching and it suited the Conservative opposition to turn what I thought was a molehill into a mountain. Nevertheless, I was shameless in not restraining the public relations department from adding fuel to the fire and fanning the flames of criticism in the direction of the Secretary of State for Industry.

At the end of August, I was due to go on holiday in the West Country. We drove down on the Saturday. As soon as we arrived, I shut myself away in the hotel and spent the rest of that day and most of the Sunday drafting a report recommending a solution to the apparently intractable problem facing ABTA. Desperation concentrates the mind wonderfully. In brief, I reiterated my earlier proposal that a fund should be set up to act as a second line of defence if a bond ever again proved to be inadequate, and that ABTA should approach the government requesting it to make an interest-free advance to the fund of the amount needed to reimburse the customers of Clarksons and other tour operators in the Court Line Group. I realized that it would be difficult for the government to accede to such a request but clung on to the remote hope that the widespread criticism of Tony Benn's statement in the House of Commons and the impending General Election might tip the scales in favour of a solution on these lines. Moreover, there was hardly a constituency in the country whose Member of Parliament hadn't been flooded with complaints by would-be holidaymakers who had been affected by the Court Line crash. Few things are as emotive as the combination of a lost holiday and lost money.

I returned to London by train first thing on the Monday morning. My report divided the ABTA Councils. Generalizing, travel agents applauded it to the heights: they wouldn't have to contribute to the reserve fund and, being at the sharp end, would be able to cope with their customers who were banging on their doors and counters. Most, but not all, tour operators opposed my recommendations, still arguing against the principle of a collective fund and more interested in picking up the bookings from customers who could no longer travel with Clarksons. They also feared that, as they would have to pass on to their customers the extra cost of their contributions to the reserve fund, their future sales in an acutely price-sensitive industry would be reduced. It was, nevertheless, agreed that we should ask to meet Peter Shore, the Secretary of State for Trade, within whose ambit the problem lay, and put my proposal to him.

My President was then George Skelton, he and I sometimes being referred to as 'the Skelton/Elton axis'. He was the boss of the whole of Pickfords, including its chain of travel agencies. He was enthusiastic about my proposal. Early in September he had written a letter to Peter Shore requesting a further meeting to discuss the situation. I say a *further* meeting because we had already discussed the crisis with him several times, driving backwards and forwards between the Department of Trade's offices in Victoria Street and the ABTA office in George's chauffeur-driven car.

By Friday, 13 September, he had not received a reply from Peter Shore, opining that he (Peter Shore) was giving us 'the bum's rush'. What he didn't know I will now record, having placed myself under a self-imposed '30-year rule' of secrecy, though I have told a few close friends.

The person then responsible for public relations in my office was one George Mathews who had made useful contacts in Government, including a close one in the Department of Trade. He knew that I knew this and one day walked into my office to discuss the crisis. In the course of our discussion he mentioned this again and asked me whether I thought he should 'go for a walk'. I knew exactly what he meant: should he give a copy of my report to his buddy in the Department of Trade? I suggested that some fresh air would do him good. He returned after about an hour and said 'mission accomplished'. I knew for sure that my report, with its proposed solution to the crisis, would reach the eyes of Peter Shore.

I could count on the fingers of one hand the number of people who knew something else. After one meeting with officials of the Department of Trade, three of us – Norman Hunter, ABTA's Financial Controller (responsible among other things for the administration of the bonding system), a member of the Travel Agents' Council who was a bit of a wild card and I – had met for a drink in a pub near the Department of Trade's office. To my astonishment, Norman said that at the meeting he had been sitting next to a senior civil servant who had opened a green file marked 'confidential'. He (Norman) had glanced at the document on top of the file. It was a memorandum to the Secretary of State for Trade from the Attorney General. It briefly stated his (the Attorney General's) opinion that, in view of the statement by the Secretary of State for Industry in the House of Commons, 'Her Majesty's Government might well be legally liable for the losses incurred by the customers of tour operators within the Court Line Group'. Norman had written a precise note of the material words, unobserved by the civil servant. He had even made a note of the reference number of the file in question.

I have myself always thought that this was a surprising piece of advice – at the very least surprisingly positive – as Tony Benn had only said that the taking over of part of the Court Line Group *'should'* – not 'would' or 'will' – secure the holidays of the Group's tour operators – the sort of fine but important distinction beloved of lawyers and the Courts. What more carefully chosen word could he have used?

But who am I to question the legal advice of the Attorney General? I kept my thoughts to myself, unlike the madcap Council member who went berserk. He was proposing to stand as a Liberal candidate at the forthcoming election and said he would blow the gaff and – because the Government had not revealed the Attorney General's advice – call the whole affair 'a Watergate cover-up'! I thought it was a ridiculous idea and assumed that he must have been joking.

For all that, it was an intriguing piece of information. As I said earlier, by Friday, 13 September, George Skelton had received no reply to his request for a meeting with Peter Shore. The chaos at ABTA was exacerbated by a widespread advertising campaign by Thomas Cook on television and in the newspapers on the lines that, if in future a tour operator went bust, customers would get their money back within 24 hours *only* if they had booked their holidays with Thomas Cook. This was clearly designed to cash in on the prevailing public atmosphere and persuade people to book their holidays at one of the many Thomas Cook retail outlets. All the other travel agencies, but especially the small independent agencies, were distraught at the likely loss of business that would ensue. Many of them thought that the advertisement gave the impression that, if you booked with any travel agent other than Thomas Cook, you would not get your money back at all: it did not make it clear that you *would* do so but in more than 24 hours. Indeed, friends of mine said things like, 'I thought the protection of your bonding system applied whatever ABTA travel agent you booked with'. Arguably, it was a subtly misleading advertisement and therefore a breach of the Travel Agents' Code of Conduct. More pertinently, however, one small travel agent amidst the hundreds who wrote or phoned complaining about the advertisement provided me with clear evidence that he too was offering 'a 24 hour money back guarantee'. It is profoundly unwise to risk using the word 'only' in any advertisement.

Amongst everything else that preyed on my mind on that fateful 'Friday the Thirteenth', what to do about this also occupied my shattered thoughts. Suddenly, like an automaton, I picked up my phone and dialled the number of Peter Shore's private office. I heard myself saying that I had some important information that it was essential that The Secretary of State should know as a matter of the greatest urgency. Ten minutes later, his private secretary rang back to say that Peter Shore would see me at 5.00 p.m. that evening. I sat in a daze and left my office early enough to find myself in a waiting room well before 5 o'clock. Eventually, his private secretary emerged and ushered me in to Peter Shore's now familiar room. He was sitting at the head of his large conference table accompanied by two of his Junior Ministers, the head of his Department (Sir Peter Thornton) and other civil servants including an Under Secretary, Mary Lackey. He invited me to take a seat, looked at me carefully and said he understood that I had some information I thought he should know about.

Words on the following lines found their way out of my mouth: 'I think it is my duty to tell you, Secretary of State, that it is within my knowledge that there is a memorandum from the Attorney General on confidential file number xyz advising you that, because of the Secretary of State for Industry's statement in the House of Commons, the Government might well be liable for losses incurred by customers of tour operators in the Court Line Group. Unfortunately, this is also known to one of my Council members who is proposing to stand as a Liberal candidate in the forthcoming General Election. He intends to reveal this advice and condemn the whole affair as a Watergate cover-up'.

I can hear the ensuing silence as I write. I can hear the clock ticking on the grand mantelpiece. You've got to hand it to these politicians. On the surface, at any rate, Peter Shore didn't bat an eyelid. After a long pause, he calmly said – his head nodding and his famous quiff of hair bobbing up and down: 'I appreciate why you felt it was your duty to tell me this, Mr Elton. I am most grateful. Is there anything else you would like to add?' I replied in the negative, whereupon he personally and courteously conducted me to the door and shook me by the hand.

Outside in Victoria Street it was a warm autumn evening. I walked up to Westminster Cathedral and sat down on a seat, my main thought being that I must be stark, staring bonkers. After a few minutes, I walked slowly across Westminster Bridge to Waterloo, where I caught the first available train home.

I felt increasingly foolish as the weekend progressed, conscious of the absurdity of the charade that Peter Shore and I had played in talking about my duty to inform the Government, when we all knew perfectly well that all I had done was to make a pathetic attempt to blackmail Her Majesty's Government in all its might. I felt sure they must have thought I was a stupid little squirt. The weekend newspapers were plastered with the Thomas Cook advertisement.

At about 7 o'clock on the Sunday evening the telephone rang. It was George Skelton. He apologized for not having got in touch with me earlier. Peter Shore had rung him at home at about 6.30 on Friday evening – an hour and a quarter after I had left his office – saying that he would like to meet us at 10.00 a.m. on Monday morning. George said that he was pleased that his 'rather good' letter to Peter Shore requesting a meeting had produced results and I duly congratulated him. He asked me if I could meet him and several Council members he'd been in touch with at Peter Shore's office in the morning at 9.30 so that we could discuss tactics before the meeting. In case there were delays, I got an early train to Waterloo and retraced my steps across Westminster Bridge. Basically, we agreed that George should present the case for the solution in my report which I, but not the others, knew that Peter Shore had already seen.

We were invited into a conference room. After a few moments, Peter Shore and his entourage entered and sat facing us. He asked George, as President of ABTA, to open the proceedings. He presented our case very well. When he had finished, Peter Shore said that people who knew him well knew that he could think very fast if he had a recess. Would we forgive him if he retired with his colleagues to consider what George had said?

No more than ten minutes had passed before they all traipsed back in. Peter Shore said they had drafted a press statement during the recess which he proposed to issue immediately but, as a matter of courtesy, he would like to read it to us first. Dated 16 September, 1974, it contained words to the effect that the Government had considered representations from ABTA about the unfortunate consequences of the Court Line crash and had agreed to introduce early legislation authorizing a new Air Travel Reserve Fund Agency to impose levies on organizers of package holidays by air. Such levies would be paid into an 'air travel reserve fund', which would be administered by the new Agency and would be used to reimburse customers of failed tour operators if the money available from their bonds were ever again insufficient to do so. As requested by ABTA, the Government would in the exceptional circumstances make an initial advance to the fund of an amount sufficient to cover the losses incurred by the customers of the tour operating companies in the Court Line Group. The advance would be repayable over time as the fund was built up from the levies and would be interest-free.

George Skelton was plainly bowled over and thanked Peter Shore profusely. As we left, Peter Shore stood by the door and shook us all by the hand. As he shook mine, he looked me straight in the eye with an expression that spoke volumes. I had no doubt that civil servants had drafted the press release late on the Friday evening or during the weekend. When we separated, I returned to the office light of heart and foot. I was cock-a-hoop. I felt an enormous burden had been lifted from my shoulders. For once, I felt confident that I had done the right thing: that the interests of the vast majority of my members had been well served, that public confidence in ABTA members and the travel industry as a whole would be restored, and that ABTA itself had been saved from a fate worse than death. When I returned to the office, the news had already reached George Mathews via his friend in the Department of Trade. We embraced each other. In the wake of these events, ABTA introduced its own reserve fund covering package holidays by land and sea.

Mary Lackey, to whom I referred earlier, was the classic Under Secretary of those days, Oxford educated and highly intelligent, well able to dissect the falsities of false arguments. She was splendidly articulate and sometimes used Latin phrases, like 'desiderata' (the things desired to be achieved), which amused Council members no end, some of whom for months afterwards introduced 'desiderata' into discussions at Council meetings and became adept at imitating her posh voice to the amusement of all. But they liked and respected her. She was a great character whom I got to know well.

It was one evening several years after everything settled down that I walked into the dining room at the United Oxford and Cambridge Club in Pall Mall. Mary was sitting at one of the tables and caught my eye. I hadn't seen her there before, nor she me. We exchanged pleasantries about each of us not knowing the other was a member, the state of the weather, and so on. After a while, she paused and said: 'Michael, how *did* you know about that memorandum from the Attorney General?' With an attempted twinkle in my eye, I suggested that she should instruct all her staff that they should not open confidential files at meetings if they were sitting next to people who were not members of her Department. She was visibly shaken but soon reverted to her amusing intellectual style of conversation.

Such, I suppose, was my closest acquaintance with the world of realpolitik. The strangest, and in a way the saddest, part of it all was that, whereas I feared that I must have ruined my reputation in the eyes of Government, I later learnt that, on the contrary, my reputation had soared. Presumably, the politicians recognized and respected the political game I had played for what it was. I was speaking their own language.

At the General Election that was held on 10 October 1974 – just over three weeks after Peter Shore issued his press statement on 16 September – the Labour Government was relieved to be returned to power with a small overall majority.

—————

While all this was going on, two other matters occupied my mind. The first was that I felt I had no choice but to institute disciplinary proceedings against Thomas Cook on the grounds that their '24 hour money back guarantee' was a misleading advertisement, not so much because of the ambiguity in its wording but more because of the strong complaint by the small travel agent who had offered a similar guarantee. Thomas Cook had recently been privatized and the advertisement was a consequence of its new-found commercial aggression. Although no threats of any kind were made against me, I felt reassured by the Counsel's advice I had received in the year of the unfinished hotels. I did, however, have to endure a lunch with the new high-powered Chief Executive, to which I was pointlessly, but hardly coincidentally, invited. Thomas Cook naturally argued that it was stretching things to suggest that their advertisement would be taken as meaning that customers of other travel agencies would not get their money back at all: it only meant that they would not get it back within 24 hours, and they had acted in good faith in using the words '*only* at Thomas Cook'. Strangely enough, I do not recall the formal outcome of my case against them, perhaps because the important thing was that they stopped advertising in this way, much to the relief of all the other ABTA travel agents.

The second matter that occupied my mind during those difficult days was an article that appeared in the *Daily Mail* the day after the Court Line Crash. It was written by the *Daily Mail*'s influential travel correspondent, Jill Crawshaw, and began something like this: 'On this shameful day when hundreds of thousands of holidaymakers have lost millions of pounds, I have one message for the leaders of ABTA, *including the paid leadership* (my italics): they should resign'. I had got reasonably hardened to carping criticism in the travel press, but this pointed attack in a popular national newspaper was something else again. I tried to ignore it but, in those first days following the Court Line crash, however well my personal assistant tried to protect me from telephone calls from angry would-be holidaymakers, she couldn't avoid letting some of them get through to me. The first thing they usually said was that I should resign, as Jill Crawshaw had demanded, because it was my fault that they had lost the money they had paid for their holidays. There were several variations but the theme was the same.

As a lawyer, I had already worked out that Jill Crawshaw's article was a serious libel of myself. She had specifically picked on me and identified me, if not by name. As the Chief Executive, I was clearly and unambiguously 'the paid leadership', as well she knew. What she did not know was that I had previously recommended the establishment of a reserve fund and that my recommendation had not been accepted by my political masters. My report and the relevant Council minutes were on the record. To suggest by necessary implication that a solicitor in what was then a very high-profile position had failed in his duty and that his negligence had caused so many thousands of people to lose so many millions of pounds was a serious libel by any standards. Her accusation was entirely unjustified and she had pointedly singled me out for special mention.

I let things drift on, mainly because I was working round the clock coping with the aftermath of the Court Line debacle. Things finally came to a head when George Mathews (the head of the public relations department whom I mentioned earlier) told me that Jill Crawshaw had told him she was willing to write a nice article praising ABTA for its recent introduction of an independent, low-cost arbitration scheme whereby customers of ABTA members could easily and cheaply resolve their complaints. Rightly or wrongly, I felt there was a subtle implication that I would be mentioned favourably somewhere along the line. Perhaps it was rather childish on my part, but this infuriated me. Having written a preliminary letter to the *Daily Mail* complaining that the article was libellous, I knew blackmail, though of a negative kind, when I saw it. It also made me realize that Jill Crawshaw and the *Daily Mail* recognized they would have no defence to a libel action. I was told of a firm of solicitors which specialized in libel cases and offered any potential plaintiff one free consultation. I took up this offer. The solicitor I met agreed that the article was libellous and could see no defence in all the circumstance I recounted. He asked me why I wanted to sue. I replied that I wanted to vindicate myself and restore my professional reputation. I remember his exact cynical words in response, which brought me down to earth with a bump: 'Bollocks! There is only one respectable reason for suing for libel and that is to make some money.' This pricked the bubble of my pomposity. He advised me to think it over and get in touch if I decided to proceed.

His comments gave me much food for thought. Our finances, as usual, were fully stretched, and we could have done with some extra money. On the other hand, I was extremely worried that, if I sued and, for some unknown reason, lost my case, I was putting my house and everything else on the line, because I would have to pay the *Daily Mail*'s costs as well as my own. (Legal Aid is not available for libel actions.) Furthermore, I had no money to pay a solicitor anything up-front. I explained my dilemma to a solicitor friend who lived in Granborough, David Morris. He kindly agreed to act for me on the basis that it was a clear-cut case and he would take the risk of recovering his costs from the *Daily Mail* at the end of the day, an act of faith for which I have always been grateful. We commenced proceedings accordingly.

It was only slowly that the full implications dawned on me. The Counsel whom David briefed pointed out that it was always a worrying thing to sue for libel. The defence have only to find something remotely relevant to hold against you. 'Every time you walk into your office, you'll wonder whether you've tied up your shoelaces properly.' Worse still, I came to realize that I should have to say in open court that it wasn't my fault that so many people would lose so much money: rather it was the fault of my employers in the shape of the Tour Operators' Council and, ultimately, of the National Council, for not accepting my recommendation to set up a reserve fund in the first place. How on earth could I do that and retain my position as ABTA's Chief Executive? Ironically, would I have to resign for suing Jill Crawshaw on the grounds that she had said – albeit for different reasons – that I should?

The months dragged by until more than a year later David rang me to say the case had been scheduled to start the following week, but that the *Daily Mail* had offered £500 in damages, a public apology and full settlement of my costs. Although £500 was then more than it now sounds, my reaction was that such a paltry offer only added insult to injury. For all that, faced with my anxieties and the harsh realities of the situation, I asked David to say I would accept £1,000. As I expected, he phoned back ten minutes later to say that they were prepared to offer £750. In all the circumstances, half reluctantly but half relieved, I accepted. There was a remarkably prominent apology in the *Daily Mail* a few days later saying that they had paid me substantial damages! Council members and many others besides thought I must have made a small fortune but I kept my silence, leaving them to think what they liked. Amongst other things, we bought a much-needed new washing-up machine which we nick-named 'Jilly'. Even now, when we put the crockery into our dishwasher after a meal, we sometime say, 'Let's stuff Jilly'.

In the light of this experience, I hold little truck with the view of most journalists that the libel laws in this country are unduly restrictive of their right to criticize people without fear or favour. In broad terms, they are entitled to express critical opinions about people in public life – however outrageous those opinions may be – so long as there is at least a germ of truth in the facts they allege and their criticisms relate to that germ of truth. Moreover, it is virtually impossible for individuals who are not wealthy to pit themselves against the financial muscle of a national newspaper, which can try to frighten you off by taking you right up to the door of the Court, even if, unbeknown to you, they intend to cave in at the eleventh hour.

In the spring of 1976, my father had quite a severe stroke, one of the initial consequences of which was that he frequently wept uncontrollably. For several months my mother nursed him with patient concern and affection, eventually having to feed him with a teaspoon. His condition slowly deteriorated to the point of his having to be admitted to the Royal Hampshire Hospital, where my mother had nearly died of 'yellow jaundice' before the war and where, early in the war, I had heard the soldiers groaning and had been glad dad hadn't had to have his arms or legs cut off. Here, in the same place, he was now approaching death. I visited him every day and John came down as often as he could from Hemel Hempstead where he lived. It goes without saying that mum visited him at least once every day. Towards the end, he became barely conscious.

That summer of 1976 was long, hot and sunny. An official drought had been declared and sprinklers banned. Everyone's lawns had become parched and brown. This had upset dad when he had been fully conscious at home in his flat, able only to sit and gaze at the lawn through the French windows with impatient frustration, regretting its fading greenness. I described earlier how much it had always meant to him to keep the lawns at Bereweeke Close in perfect condition.

One evening, when I visited him in hospital, the drought suddenly broke and it poured with torrents of teeming rain. By then, dad could hardly understand anything anyone said. At one point, in desperation, I said, 'It's pouring with rain, dad. The grass will soon turn green again.' He made a grunting, gurgling noise in his throat, which somehow managed to convey understanding and pleasure. That was the last thing I, or anyone else, said to him that he understood.

After a couple of hours or so of silence, a kindly doctor said that dad would never again regain consciousness but might survive in that state for several days: I might as well go home and get some sleep. Acting on his advice, I drove home.

I had only been home for a few minutes when the phone rang. That same doctor said he was sorry to have to tell me that my father had just passed peacefully away. I thanked him for ringing and for his kindness in dad's last hours. I wished I had stayed with him a little longer.

I experienced a feeling-less numbness, as if I was somehow abstracted from myself. Although it was already after 11 o'clock, I phoned mum with whom her sister, Jane, was staying to comfort her. Jane answered and I told her dad had just died. She wept and said she would tell mum herself. I told Isabel who had gone to bed: she had already guessed why the telephone had rung so late. Then I rang John, who had had temporarily to return home. Although he didn't cry, I could hear his grief.

I sat in my armchair until well into the small hours, thinking about dad's life. I remembered the happy times he had had: his love for mum, John and me during our family holidays at Southbourne before the war; the fulfilment he found as a much respected Major in charge of his own Company during the war; his delight in our musical evenings before the war and his acting with the dramatic society afterwards; his inordinate pride that both his sons had gone to Oxford and done well there; his modest pride in his own work, with regard to which I recalled for the first time that he had once said that new roads didn't have to be ugly – they could be 'like rivers rolling through a valley' – and that well-designed bridges could be works of art; and the comfort he received from his new-found Catholic faith in the earlier part of his adulthood and marriage. Although for many years he and mum had stopped going to mass, a few weeks before he died he had asked to see a Catholic priest and Father (now Canon) Mullarkey had spent some time with him: I hoped that this had been of comfort to him when death was staring him in the face. I thought again of my Oxford days: how he had thoughtfully recognized and understood my mental condition. I wondered how, without his help and advice, I could have survived. I had never thanked him but now wished I had. I was comforted that his last awareness had been that the greenness of life would soon return to the arid grass.

After such thoughts as these had whirled around in my mind for a long time, I thought about his self-thwarted love for the gentle lady who had mistaken me for him on the telephone all those years ago. I sensed his profound, all-pervading grief that, united though they had been in the depth of their mutual love, they had not been able to spend the end of their lives together. I felt that they had suffered as only good people can: that, at the age of 73, dad had died too young of a broken heart. With that thought my numbness evaporated and allowed emotion to fill the void. At last I wept quietly until emotion drained away, in its turn suddenly to be replaced by a pellucid certainty that at least he was now incapable of further suffering, mingled with a misted wondering whether it could somehow be that he was in some sense beyond my understanding at conscious peace with and within himself and would remain so until 'the last syllable of recorded time'. I remembered his love of Shakespeare. I envisaged long-deserted, moss-encrusted tombstones overshadowed by ancient, black-seeming yew trees in small country churchyards and inscribed with the no-longer impersonal, unmeaningful words: 'Peace at last'. Whereupon I found peace enough to snatch a few hours sleep.

John came down to Winchester immediately and arranged for the funeral service to be held at the St Peter's Catholic Church of old, to be followed by cremation at the Southampton Crematorium. Many people attended the requiem mass, people from all the walks of life in which dad had been respected with such affection. Canon Mullarkey conducted the requiem mass. As we left the church, he shook me warmly by the hand and expressed his condolences and the hope that all was otherwise well with me.

Among the scores of flowers laid out in the gardens of the Crematorium was an unmarked wreath.

———•———

Back at ABTA things progressed more positively. Many of the idiosyncratic characters were pleasant and always made life interesting and sometimes great fun.

ABTA held a major conference abroad every year, as did the Universal Federation of Travel Agents' Associations (UFTAA) to which ABTA belonged. To start with, therefore, during my sixteen years with ABTA, I visited thirty-two of the major tourist destinations of the world (usually accompanied by Isabel), ranging from Athens to Acapulco, Cannes to Cuba, Lisbon to Los Angeles, and Majorca to Miami Beach, to name but a few. The ABTA conferences were attended by some three to four thousand delegates comprising representatives both of ABTA members and of companies which were anxious to attract their business, such as the major airlines, cruise companies and car-hire companies. In their efforts to seduce ABTA travel agents, these 'principals' vied with each other to throw bigger and better parties. It must be true of ABTA conferences that never in the field of human imbibulation has so much alcohol been poured down the throats of so many by so few. Many delegates competed to secure accommodation in bigger and better suites in bigger and better hotels. A travel agent once said to me – somewhat unkindly – that the size of a man's suite at an ABTA conference was in inverse proportion to the size of his brain.

Despite the responsibility that often weighed heavily on my shoulders, Isabel and I were able to join in the fun which was for me a welcome release from the administrative pressure. Sometimes even the parties were too much of a good thing. I remember that we walked into the Casino in Cannes for a party thrown by our generous French hosts for approaching three thousand delegates. We were accompanied by a charming travel agent from Northern Ireland who, as we entered, opined that it was worse than Dante's Inferno. We retired and had a quiet drink together. Sometimes, there were posh dinners for a smallish group of VIPs. At one such, though I can't remember at which conference, I heard the snobbish remark to beat all snobbish remarks. The table plan was such that husbands sat opposite wives. One of the husbands was a little late and tendered appropriate apologies. Then he said to his wife in the poshest voice you ever heard, 'I say, darling, I've just rung home. It's pouring with rain there'. To which his wife replied, 'How spiffing, daarling. That will help to top up the moat!'

Some things, perhaps, are amusing only for those within the travel trade. When we had meetings abroad, the local tourist office invariably arranged for us to have an official tour of whatever town we were in so that we could visit whatever fascinating buildings were supposed to excite our intellectual interest. Once, when the Travel Agents' Council met in Madeira, a less traditional coach tour of the remote parts of the island was arranged. After a while, our guide thoughtfully asked the driver to stop so that we could have 'a comfort break' at a spot where there were some loos sited at the back of beyond by a tourist office which fortunately understood the demands of nature. When one of the travel agents on the Council, one Ron Booth, who was ever something of a wag, disembarked, he asked in a loud voice, 'Where's the museum?' Even now, when we are on holiday and stop in places off the beaten track, Isabel or I invariably say, 'Where's the museum?'

Inevitably, there was an association consisting of the travel agents' associations of countries within the European Community whose function was to try to forestall the wilder excesses of an idealistic bureaucracy insofar as they might affect the real world of the travel trade. Brussels became the milk run and Brussels airport my second home. We also took turns to meet in our respective countries and I became familiar with all the capitals and many of the largest cities in the member countries of the Community.

One of the best clubs in the world must surely be that which comprises the people in similar positions to myself throughout the world. Under the auspices of UFTAA, we held an annual meeting of all the Chief Executives, Managing Directors, Secretary Generals (or is it

Secretaries General?) or just plain Secretaries (a rose by any other name would smell as sweet). These were not just 'jollies', though we made sure they were jolly good fun. Apart from discussing the issues facing our respective associations and exchanging useful information and ideas, we were all in the same boat – or at least in similar boats – with regard to the conflicting pressures to which we were daily subjected back in our offices. For those of us, like myself, who did not have the luxury of having developed a skin as thick as that enjoyed by your average rhinoceros, metaphorically to cry on each others' shoulders helped us to keep what was left of our sanity more or less intact. We learnt much from each other.

There was also the practical advantage that, whichever country we went to on holiday, there was always a host or hostess who could help with our travel arrangements and make us feel at home. The deep friendships I enjoyed with many of my opposite numbers was the most rewarding aspect of my time at ABTA.

I made some trips to countries behind the Iron Curtain, which had not then fallen. Places that come to mind are Warsaw, Sofia, Prague and Moscow. In the latter case, Isabel accompanied me. As guests of Intourist, I had to sing for my supper by having a meeting with the President of Intourist in his office overlooking Red Square. His main theme was that he wanted me to see for myself how the Western media misrepresented the Soviet Union, presumably suffering from the delusion that my conversion would increase tourism to Russia in particular. I felt it would be impolite and impolitic to say that, from what I had so far been allowed to see, the impression held by those in the West was absolutely right. A trivial example was that, on the bedside table of our room in our huge hotel, the best one in Moscow, there was a customer survey, which we were asked to complete. The first question was, 'Do you regard the hotel as satisfactory, good or very good?' So much for the joys of freedom of speech. I didn't like to say under 'Other Comments' that we were forbidden to have a second cup of coffee at breakfast, even one being regarded as the ultimate luxury. For all that, we had a charming young lady as a personal guide and took the train to St Petersburg (then still Leningrad), surely one of the great cities of the world, quite apart from the splendours of the Hermitage museum and the Summer Palace. After ten days in Russia, seeing innumerable statues of Lenin, monuments to his memory, huge portraits of him, Lenin museums and Lenin parks began to make me feel almost physically sick. I am reminded of this because I am writing this passage during the war in Iraq (in April 2003) and the pictures and statues of Saddam Hussein constantly appearing on our television screens have the same nauseous effect on me.

One morning in Moscow, I looked out of the window of our bedroom which was towards the top of our tall hotel. Looking down, I saw cars halting at some traffic lights four or five abreast. They were like Dinky toys which, with a few exceptions, all looked exactly the same except that they were of three or four different colours. It seemed that if you wanted to buy a car you simply had to select one of those colours.

Soon after we returned home, a senior Intourist official paid a reciprocal visit to London. As a matter of courtesy, I felt obliged at least to meet him for coffee at his hotel. His main reaction to London was to feel overwhelmed and psychologically 'stressed out' by the endless advertisements on television advocating the subtle, comparative advantages of many different makes of car, as well as by the vast array of choices in all the shops in Oxford Street. He could hardly wait to get back to Moscow, where, if nothing else, everyday life was at least much simpler and so much less stressful.

Whenever I went by air, I nearly always travelled first class. I have never wanted to live in a mansion or own a Rolls Royce but the one real extravagance I would indulge in if I were rich would be to continue to fly first class, especially on long-haul flights. To do so made a huge physical and psychological difference to an experience that – blasé though it may sound – had become tedious in the extreme. (My definition of a hardened travel agent was 'someone who doesn't look out of the window when crossing the Alps'.)

I still savour an incident that occurred when my President, Eric Sutherland, and I were flying to Madrid for an audience with King Carlos. We were planning to hold our 1983 conference in Majorca and wanted to invite the King's son to open the conference as part of a grand opening ceremony in Palma Cathedral. The Spanish Tourist Office had advised us that the correct etiquette was to put our request personally to the King and had arranged an audience and our flights with their national carrier. We were to collect our flight tickets at the Iberia desk at Heathrow. By some mistake, they were tickets for economy class and Eric, suitably affronted, asked if we could be upgraded: after all, we were the President and Chief Executive of the Association of British Travel Agents. Unconvinced of the phenomenal importance of our respective offices, a flustered young Spanish lady behind the desk asked who we

Myself with King Juan Carlos of Spain, planning Palma '83 Conference.

would be visiting in Spain. With barely concealed triumph, Eric handed her our invitation and proclaimed, 'your King!' Pandemonium ensued. Senior managers were summoned. Profuse apologies were offered all round. It must have been the quickest upgrading in history.

King Carlos lived up to his reputation for charm and courtesy. We waited with various officials in an elegant room, which he entered right on cue. He shook us all by the hand and engaged in some small talk designed to put us at ease. When Eric put the formal request to him (which, of course, he knew was coming), he replied, presumably as a let-out, 'I shall have to consult the Queen. We always do it together.' His English may not have been perfect but it was quite good enough for him instantly to recognize the double entendre. He roared with laughter and we all joined in, the ice well and truly broken. In the event, our invitation was declined and the Minister for Tourism was given the task.

I have lost count of the Prime Ministers of host countries who opened ABTA'S or UFTAA's conferences. The main problem in organizing opening ceremonies was that the etiquette varied widely from country to country. In a different context, I recall that one year the late Princess Margaret was our guest of honour at our annual banquet and ball at the

HRH Princess Margaret is welcomed to ABTA's 25th Anniversary Ball by
President George Skelton and myself in March 1975.

Grosvenor House. The main instruction about etiquette from her private office was that our President should propose the loyal toast after the first course so that she could start smoking at the earliest opportunity.

I was lucky to work under four Presidents – George Skelton, Margaret Hook, Ivor Elms and Eric Sutherland – and, for my last few months, under Jack Smith – with each of whom I developed a good working and personal relationship: a close enough relationship to recognize – better, possibly, than most – the positive qualities that each in his or her own quite different way brought to the office of President. Furthermore, at any one time over the years, there were enough members of the three Councils who were big enough to help to hold the tiller with a steady enough hand to steer ABTA through its stormier seas and to rise above the ultimately self-defeating short-termism of internal commercial or personal power politics. The Councils apart, many of the members gave their time and expertise unsparingly to the work of the committees both in London and in the various regions across the United Kingdom.

Quite often I had to undergo the new and daunting experience of giving interviews on radio and television. ABTA wisely arranged for me to go on a training course for such interviews, which was not just invaluable but indispensable. Apart from obvious (once you know) tips like sitting upright with your bottom pressed against the back of your chair, not wriggling about but keeping still and looking the interviewer in the eyes, making sure your tie is straight and at all costs resisting the temptation to drink alcohol before an interview in order to acquire Dutch courage, I learnt some fundamental techniques – particularly with regard to 'confrontational' as opposed to 'information seeking' interviews. This was well-judged because most interviews about the travel industry, especially in my early days, were consumer oriented.

The main technique for a confrontational interview on which you were likely to be on a sticky wicket was to think up in advance three plus points in your favour and to make these points whatever fast balls or googlies the interviewer might bowl at you, however irrelevant your plus points may be to the interviewer's questions. You have only to watch politicians being interviewed on television to realize that they have been on similar training courses. Another technique relevant to group interviews is to shake your head if one of the other speakers is saying something your disagree with. Your hope is that the producer will press a button so that the viewers catch a glimpse of your doing this and implying quite effectively that the other speaker is talking rubbish. You can see this technique being adopted on programmes like Question Time.

One technique, to be used only as a last, desperate resort, was to counter-attack and ask the interviewer a question in the hope of catching him off his guard, hitting him for six (to pursue my cricketing analogy) and generally flummoxing him. I employed this technique in one of the more impossible, though – as it turned out – better, interviews I gave on television. The interview was about the practice adopted by tour operators of excluding themselves from liability in small print in their brochures in circumstances where the consumer suffered as a result of the negligence of one of their sub-contractors. One simple example would be if the waiter in your hotel, which was not owned by the tour operator but with which he had contracted to reserve x number of beds, spilled soup all over your best suit. The consumerist view was that, as your contract was with the tour operator, you should be able to sue him in England and not have to sue the hotel in a foreign jurisdiction. If ever there was a case in which I was on a loser, this was it. The BBC as usual sent a taxi to pick me up and take me to the studio. As we drove along, the thought suddenly, and thankfully, occurred to me that, if the taxi driver were to drive negligently and I were to suffer injuries from a crash caused by his negligence, the BBC would be astonished if I were to sue it for damages, rather than the taxi-driver's firm which it had contracted to pick me up. When the going got really rough, I asked the interviewer whether, in such circumstances, the BBC should be liable to compensate me for my injuries. This had the desired effect in spades, as they say. The interviewer was put on the defensive and was completely lost for an answer. It didn't occur to him – as it didn't to me until afterwards – that this was a false analogy because I was not paying the BBC for the privilege of being interviewed: on the contrary the BBC were paying me their standard fee.

People sometimes ask me what is the most memorable of all the sights I saw throughout the world during my sixteen years with ABTA. There were always 'post-conference tours' at bargain prices after ABTA and UFTAA conferences, which Isabel and I had to miss because I had to return to my desk. There was one exception. At an UFTAA conference in Buenos Aires before the Falklands War, we noticed that there was a short weekend tour to the Iguaçu Waterfalls, of which I had never heard, as surprisingly many people still seem not to have. For once we took the opportunity to go on the tour, especially as waterfalls had always held a fascination for me. It was entirely fortuitous that of all the great sights I have seen – the Grand Canyon, the Norwegian fjords, the Victoria Falls, the Parthenon and the Taj Mahal spring to mind – the Iguaçu Waterfalls remain for me and for Isabel the most hauntingly memorable. They are separated by hundreds of forested miles from any trace of civilization and straddle the boundaries of Argentina, Brazil and Paraguay.

There is a small monument nearby marking the spot where, if you had three legs, you could stand with one foot in each of these countries. There are 275 magnificent waterfalls, of varying heights and widths covering several kilometres. We walked for ages along a narrow wooden gangway that crossed the tops of some of them at the point where the massive never-ending torrents of brownish, silty water rushed close beneath our feet and plunged headlong to the steamy depths below whence the River Plate begins its long journey, eventually to flow into the Atlantic Ocean between Argentina and Uruguay. The Niagara Falls, apart from the handicap of their artificial, commercialized environs, pale into insignificance compared with the awesome scale of the Iguaçu Falls, surrounded by the vastness of seemingly ageless forest as yet unravaged by man. Even the towering height and mighty force of the Victoria Falls is less sharply etched in my memory and imagination.

I must resist the strong temptation to turn my memoirs into a travelogue. How far I had come since my first interview for my position as Chief Executive when I said I had only been to the Isle of Wight. This is well illustrated by one of my first visits abroad when I had to go to Los Angeles, whose supposed delights we were destined to enjoy because ABTA in its wisdom was planning to hold one of its conferences there and some preliminary planning was required. On the first jet-lagged morning, I woke up in room 2063 in the downtown Bonaventure Hotel, whose lobby seemed as big as a football pitch and whose many lifts somehow managed to cling to the exterior of the building and, from a distance, resembled bottle-flies crawling up the kitchen wall (except that it doesn't require an act of faith to assume that bottle-flies don't fall off kitchen walls). I managed to plough my way though the technology beside my bed, in which half a dozen other adults could comfortably have joined me – a thought at which the mind boggles – and eventually found room service. Determined to show – as befitted the new Chief Executive of ABTA – that I was no little-Englander, I announced with all the aplomb I could command that I would like to have a continental breakfast sent to my room. In three words, which have already passed into the annals of the Elton dynasty, a lady with the broadest of Californian accents replied, 'Gee, which continent?'

Finally, I must briefly recount the last strategic development in which I was closely involved at ABTA.

Early in 1976, the scope of the legislation relating to restrictive practices was extended from the supply of goods to embrace the provision of services. As a result, the travel industry was caught within the net of what was then the Restrictive Trade Practices Act of 1956 (in its present reincarnation the Act of 1976).

It followed as night follows day that the Director General of the Office of Fair Trading, Gordon Borrie (later Sir Gordon, later Lord Borrie) referred ABTA to the Restrictive Practices Court, as he was legally obliged to. The main point at issue was Stabiliser, the mutual trading agreement between ABTA tour operators and ABTA travel agents. The law naturally assumed that such an agreement – or, more emotively, 'closed shop' – was contrary to the public interest unless ABTA could prove otherwise. Indeed, in the eyes of a Court whose concern was to eliminate undesirable restrictive practices, the very idea of a commercial closed shop embracing a whole vast industry was – on the face of it – anathema.

After years of preliminary proceedings, our case came to Court in the summer of 1982. ABTA briefed Anthony Graham-Dixon, QC, who was the leading Counsel in the field of restrictive practices. It was a hectic business because I had to keep my eye on things at the office as well as attending the Court every day for three weeks. My long-standing personal assistant, Ann Cooper Reeve, held the fort for me at the office and came round to the Court at the end of each day's session, telling me of anything that required my attention and bringing with her any important letters which had to be dealt with. I sat with her dictating notes to the staff and replies to letters for as long as it took, sometimes well into the evening.

I was the first witness to be called – on a Friday morning – to give evidence on behalf of ABTA. In a nutshell, I was able to swear on oath that, since the introduction of Stabiliser, no member of the travelling public had ever lost money as a result of the financial failure of an ABTA tour operator or travel agent. I expressed the fear that if Stabiliser had to be abandoned there was a distinct risk that, at best, some members would leave ABTA and their customers would no longer be protected by its financial safeguards and, at worst, the Association would fall to pieces.

The irony, which had quietly amused me over the preceding years, was that some powerful maverick members kept publicly expressing the view that Stabiliser should be rescinded so that they could be free to trade as they liked or form separate associations which would put them in a stronger negotiating position. Some even gave evidence to the Court on these broad lines. They were blithely unaware that, in pushing these lines of argument before and during the Court proceedings, they were immeasurably strengthening the case for maintaining Stabiliser. This was not only for the obvious reason of the increased financial risk to the travelling public that would probably ensue if ABTA were to disintegrate. It was also because I could not recall a single example of the increased commercial advantages supposedly to be enjoyed by various groups within the membership if they were to become independent of ABTA that would not itself be a blatant restrictive practice for which there was no conceivable public interest justification. A typical example was the argument often touted by some travel agents that, if they could form their own separate association, they could all agree to boycott tour operators who didn't pay them enough commission, thereby forcing up their commission levels. Nothing I could say over the years could ever persuade them that this was wishful thinking.

I hated being cross-examined by the Queen's Counsel who acted for the Office of Fair Trading. Perhaps it was worse for me as a lawyer to be cross-examined because I couldn't help wondering what trap I was falling into or what the questions would be down the line. I felt I was making a complete mess of things: that I was hesitant and unconvincing. What was worse was that, having gone into the witness box just before lunch that Friday, I went to join our legal team in the expectation that we would have our usual light lunch at a restaurant in Chancery Lane, just round the corner from the Law Courts – lunch, I might add, that was always alcohol-free at the understandable insistence of Anthony Graham-Dixon. When I walked up to join Anthony, he immediately said I couldn't have lunch with them. Once a witness has started giving evidence, he is forbidden to speak to his lawyers. I hadn't realized this, though the point of it was instantly clear to me. It would obviously be wrong for my legal team to discuss with me how my evidence was going, to suggest how it might be better to adopt a different tack after lunch or to influence me in any way. As my cross-examination hadn't been completed by the time the Court adjourned that Friday evening, I spent the loneliest weekend of my life wondering what sort of idiot I had made of myself and endlessly rehearsing in my mind possible answers to possible lines of cross-examination when the Court reconvened on the Monday morning. The only thing Anthony did feel free to say to me after my cross-examination on the Friday was, 'Don't worry, Michael. Any half-decent QC can make a witness look a fool.' I could see that this was intended to cheer me up but it only confirmed my worst fears that I had indeed made a fool of myself. I did not do any better when I was further cross-examined for the whole of the Monday and part of the Tuesday morning. I was emotionally drained but could now relax while the other ABTA witnesses gave their evidence, in many cases rather impressively.

When all the evidence on both sides had been given and Counsel had completed their final submissions, the Court adjourned to consider its findings. We would be told in due course when the Court was ready to hand down its judgement. I should have said that the President of the Court was Mr Justice Anthony Lincoln, who was accompanied by two lay assessors.

In its Judgement of 20 December 1982, the Court made judicial history by upholding Stabiliser on the grounds that it was – quite exceptionally – in the public interest. I was absolutely astonished to hear Mr Justice Anthony Lincoln say early in his delivery of the Court's Judgement that 'Mr Elton was a balanced and temperate witness who knows his members'. Apparently relying in part on my knowledge of ABTA members, he went on to say that the Court was satisfied that ABTA was 'fissiparous' – a word of which I hadn't heard but, when I looked it up in the dictionary at the first opportunity, was exactly right – 'inclined to undergo division into separate parts or groups'.

Although ABTA had to abolish Stabiliser in October 1993 because an EC directive made financial protection of package holidays a legal requirement, it remains one of the more remarkable coincidences in my life that I had occasion to reflect on the reasons for the Court's decision when I became the Director General of the National Association of Pension Funds – 'Plus ça change, plus c'est la même chose.' The greater the change, the more it is the same thing.

CHAPTER 7

The Pensions World

ONE FRIDAY afternoon in the summer of 1986, my office phone rang. A head-hunter announced that he had been commissioned by the National Association of Pension Funds (NAPF) to find a new Director General. Knowing that Gordon Borrie, still the Director General of the Office of Fair Trading, had had close contacts with many Trade Associations, he had sounded him out. Gordon had suggested that he approach me.

My reaction was that pensions sounded a dreadfully dull subject compared with the travel industry and, never having even heard of the NAPF, I said I wasn't interested in taking the matter further. The next day I had to drive my elder son, Tim, all the way up to Hull for the start of his new term at Hull University. At one point during this long journey, I happened to mention that I had been approached about a job in the pensions world but had declined to pursue the opportunity because it sounded so boring. Tim, who was reading economics, said that actually pensions was likely to become one of the most important economic, social and political topics of the twenty-first century. (How prescient he was is already evident as I write in 2003.) I mulled over his comments during the tedious drive back to Winchester and decided to enquire further about the potential of the job as Director General of NAPF, bearing in mind that, as usual, we were financially over-stretched. First thing on Monday morning, I rang the head-hunter back and said that, on reflection over the weekend, I might be interested in the job after all.

At the ensuing interview with the top brass of the pensions world, I was asked how much I knew about pensions. I replied, 'As much as I knew about the travel industry when I was appointed Chief Executive of ABTA: in other words, nothing.' A member of the interviewing panel said that at least it was better to come clean and confess my ignorance than to waffle and flannel. The end result was that I was no less astounded to be offered the job than I had been to be appointed Chief Executive of ABTA sixteen years previously.

It was thought wise that, for a couple of months, I should overlap with my distinguished predecessor, Henry James, who, amongst his other achievements, had been Chief Press Secretary to the Prime Minister, Margaret Thatcher. I was fearful of following in the footsteps of so well known a communicator with such vast experience of relations with the media at the highest levels of government.

Early in 1987, I walked into the NAPF's smart offices in Grosvenor Gardens, full of trepidation. Henry was unstinting in his help and advice until he left and I formally succeeded him.

The contrast with ABTA was marked from the word go. The members of the NAPF's Council and Committees were all professional people of one kind or another, including the highly paid managers of the largest pension funds in the country, investment managers from an esoteric place called 'the City', solicitors specializing in pensions law and last, but definitely not least, that strange evolutionary aberration, *homo super sapiens*, otherwise known as actuaries, before whose peculiar mathematical prowess the rest of humanity could only stand in awe.

The oldest joke in the book about actuaries is that they are people who found accountancy too exciting. Less old is a joke that reflects their innate characteristic of targeting their forecasts within parameters that were wide enough for them never to be proved wrong. Two actuaries were out hunting deer. When one appeared, they both took aim and fired their guns. One of the bullets just missed the deer's nose and the other just missed its tail. They immediately shook hands and simultaneously and excitedly shouted, 'Got him!' The one I like best is in the form of a question and answer. Question: 'What is the difference between an English actuary and a Sicilian actuary?' Answer: 'An English actuary can tell you how many people will die in the next five years. A Sicilian one can tell you their names and addresses.' Amusingly, actuaries in England are members of the Institute of Actuaries and invariably graduates as well, with the result that the letters after their names are often 'MA, FIA'.

I had hardly got my feet under my desk when I had to entertain a group of Japanese men who were involved with pensions in Japan and were accompanied by an interpreter. We had visitors from countries far and wide because our funded occupational pension schemes were the envy of the world. After much bowing (not to say scraping), they settled round my conference table. I thought I would start with a brilliantly lucid summary of the pensions system in the United Kingdom. Pausing at suitable intervals for the translator to translate my words of wisdom into Japanese, I started by saying, 'There are three main systems of pensions in the United Kingdom (pause for translation). Firstly, there are pensions schemes provided by employers (pause for translation). Secondly, there are pensions provided by the Government (pause for translation). Thirdly, there are now personal pensions which individuals provide for themselves (pause for translation).' Before I could elaborate further, one of my visitors raised his hand and jabbered away in the by now familiar, if incomprehensible, Japanese gobbledegook. When he had finished, I looked enquiringly at the interpreter, who said, 'Can you explain the details of small-company contracted-out, money-purchase, occupational pension schemes?' This has always reminded me of the 'Gee, which continent?' incident in my early days at ABTA. Will I never learn? For all that, with their usual courtesy, they presented me with a gift before they left, as did subsequent groups from Japan. By the time I retired, I had a drawer so full of fans that, had I thought, I should have donated them to Covent Garden for its next production of *Madam Butterfly*.

At least in major conferences – with one exception, which I mention later – I never forgot my dressing down by the Chief Constable of Cumberland for talking down to his sergeants. I was asked to address my first Annual Conference on the nature and role of the NAPF. I sought the views of many people within and without the Secretariat. If there had been different views about the nature and role of ABTA, that was nothing compared with the range of quite disparate opinions people held about the NAPF, amongst them that it was a professional institute, a commercially-oriented association of pension scheme advisers and a consumer-oriented association of trustees of pensions funds. A few thought it was an association of employers who ran pension schemes. Not a few thought it was a mish-mash of two or more of the above.

Since ABTA members often challenged the Council's right to do this, that or the other, I had become all too familiar with the need to go back to base and study its 'Mem and Arts' (the Memorandum and Articles of Association) in great detail. It was, therefore, second nature to look up what NAPF's 'Mem and Arts' had to say on the subject. In non-legalize summary, I found that there were two categories of members, namely 'Fund Members' and 'Other Members'. The former comprised companies, firms, local authorities or other organizations which provided pensions for their employees and/or the corporate trustee bodies (as opposed to individual trustees) which employers created to run their pension schemes on their behalf. The latter – the 'Other Members' – comprised companies or firms providing professional services to pension funds, such as consultancy, actuarial, legal, administration or investment services. If these competing interests were to be reconciled, it seemed clear to me that, in the final analysis, NAPF was in essence an association of employers. After all, it was they who appointed the corporate trustees to run their pension schemes on their behalf, conceptually, if not legally, as their agents. I was also conscious from my experience in local government that local authorities did not appoint trustees but ran their pension schemes – amongst the largest in the country – themselves. In a nutshell, if employers didn't run pension schemes, there would be no corporate trustee bodies, the fund managers would be out of a job and the professional advisers – the 'Other' Members – would lose a significant proportion of their commercial business – a common interest if ever there was. Furthermore, the employers were the only class of members who contributed to their pension funds. Put another way, he – the employer – who pays the piper, calls the tune.

As I was determined to avoid the error of 'talking down' to such a high-powered audience at the most prestigious event in the UK pensions calendar, I did not think it wise to argue my viewpoint in too elementary a way. I also expressed my views on other matters, particularly about relationships with government. I suggested that it was a fundamental mistake to criticize almost everything governments did in the pensions arena: far better to be objective, even-handed and professional in our approach, thereby gaining the respect of Ministers and Civil Servants and getting them 'on side' when we *did* have a good case to make. Perpetual government bashing was counter-productive.

Although there were some rumblings about my analysis of the nature of the Association, on the whole my speech seemed – on the surface, at any rate – to be received well enough. Indeed, it received a rave review in one of the leading financial magazines.

In other ways, too, my honeymoon with NAPF was a happy one. I said at the end of my previous chapter that the decision of the Restrictive Practices Court in the ABTA case was relevant to pensions. As I believe a Director General worth his salt should, I thought deeply about the underlying philosophy of the new world into which I had entered, particularly in the wake of the Conservative Government's recent introduction of personal pensions, which employees were now free to take out instead of having to remain in their occupational pension schemes – a major threat to occupational pensions whose well-being it was NAPF's raison d'être to promote.

My supportive Chairman, Charles Woodward, agreed that I should publish a short pamphlet outlining my views. I entitled it 'Travelling to Retirement', with its subtle double entendre of moving from the travel to the pensions world, and added the sub-title, 'Plus ça change, plus c'est la même chose.'

In order to make the comparison between travel and pensions, I had first to refer back to my experience at ABTA, particularly with regard to the Court Line crash and ABTA's success in upholding Stabiliser – the mutual trading agreement – in the Restrictive Practices Court. With regard to the latter I briefly explained that the reasons for the Court's decision were basically threefold. First, it was exceptional in our society that the consumer should have to pay for a service before he received it. Second, there was a risk that, having paid for his holiday abroad in advance, he would lose both his money and his holiday because of the bankruptcy of the tour operator. Third, that risk was a 'latent' one in the sense that, when he paid his money, the consumer had no way of ascertaining whether or not the tour operator would subsequently go bankrupt.

I then pursued the analogy in the following terms:

> In the travel industry, therefore, we see a situation where the instinct of society at large, reflected by the reaction of the media and of politicians to the Court Line crash in 1974 and by the more detached analysis of the Restrictive Practices Court in 1982, is one of revulsion where customers pay money in advance for package holidays abroad and are either stranded in foreign lands or deprived of their holiday altogether.
>
> I now know, however, that the evidence I gave to the Restrictive Practices Court was mistaken in one material respect. I was wrong to suggest that the foreign package holiday was the only important example in our society where the customer pays for a service in advance.
>
> Pensions also involve payment in advance. But here the consumer is not making a one-off payment of a few hundred pounds but regular payments throughout his working life amounting to many thousands of pounds. He is not paying a few days, weeks or months in advance but twenty, thirty or even forty years in advance. And he is not paying for a fortnight's holiday but for his well-being throughout what is increasingly likely to be as much as a quarter, or even a third, of his life on this planet.

That being so, it is pertinent to consider whether the two other key elements underlying ABTA's successful defence of its mutual trading agreement in the Restrictive Practices Court – namely risk and 'latency' of risk – also apply to the provision of pensions. This is most sharply focused by comparing a personal pension with a 'final salary' occupational scheme.

The distinguishing feature of final salary schemes, to which the vast majority of employees in occupational schemes belong, is that the employer promises to provide each employee with a pension based on his or her earnings at or close to retirement. The actual proportion of those earnings, which – importantly – are likely to have kept up with inflation, depends on the length of time the employee has worked for the employer. The essential principle is that, even if things go wrong – say, with the investments comprising the corporate pension fund to which the employer and, in most cases, the employees make regular contributions – the employer must still keep his promise to the employee, who is secure in that knowledge.

In clear contrast, someone with a personal pension – particularly one of the unit-linked type – faces a substantial degree of risk. Such is the name of the game (not to say gamble) that – as a general proposition – the greater the chance of doing better than a final salary scheme, the greater the risk of doing worse. There could, for instance, be an untimely crash on the Stock Exchange, depreciating at a stroke the value of the individual's personal fund and so reducing the amount of money available to buy the annuity which provides the retirement income. Annuity rates themselves – being peculiarly sensitive to changes in the interest rates in the financial market – might be low at the time of retirement. And the possibility of the recurrence of high inflation, substantially reducing the value of the pension in real terms, cannot be ruled out. If any one of these phenomena – let alone all three – were to occur, a person's standard of living throughout old age could drop significantly, even disastrously. Undoubtedly, therefore, the element of risk applies to personal pensions – the risk of consequences infinitely more critical, distressing and prolonged than the loss of a holiday.

Undoubtedly, too, the risk is 'latent' in the sense I have described. The consumer can no more tell whether there will be a crash on the Stock Exchange just before he retires, what annuity rates will be in the first quarter of the twenty first century or whether the plague of high inflation will return in the longer term than he can tell whether a particular tour operator will go bankrupt within a few months.

Next I went right to the heart of my philosophy, not forgetting that Thatcherite 'individualism' was the flavour of the month and 'collectivism' was widely regarded as a dirty word.

Personal pensions, as I have already suggested, are based on the principles of competition, freedom of choice and 'caveat emptor': in a word 'individualism'. The corollary is a degree of risk.

The price of the relative security of final salary occupational schemes, where both the employers' and the employees' contributions are 'pooled' in the pension funds, is an element of cross-subsidy between various groups of employees, just as the price of the financial security of customers of the British travel industry is the element of cross-subsidy inherent in the reserve funds in which the tour operators' contributions are similarly 'pooled'. The nature of the cross-subsidy may be different in each case, but the principle of 'collectivism' is exactly the same.

Whenever it has come to the crunch in the travel industry, the public interest has not demanded that this price was too high to pay. The trouble is that the real crunch in the pensions industry, if it comes, will not occur until well into the twenty first century, so recent is the introduction of personal pensions and so distant the prospect and actuality of retirement for those who choose them.

It is all too easy, therefore – particularly for theoreticians who base unqualified praise of personal pensions on the concept of 'individualism' and condemn final salary schemes for their 'collectivism' (and, when short of rational argument, 'centralism', paternalism' and any other '-ism' which suits their preconceived conclusion) – to ignore the prospect of events which in their practical consequences could be far more devastating for millions of people in old age than those which, in the absence of financial safeguards, would have faced thousands of holiday makers in 1974 and on many occasions since. I, for one, would not be so sanguine as to assert that it is impossible, or even improbable, that the chickens will one day come home to roost.

From all of which, I concluded that there was a powerful case to be made for the long-term well-being of final salary pensions schemes.

My conclusion is that in a free society it is in the public interest that 'individualism' should play a dominant – even predominant – role, but that a degree of 'collectivism' is sometimes unavoidable if other goals which are equally in the public interest are to be achieved: specifically – in the context of this paper – the financial security of the travelling public and, more fundamentally, of those in retirement.

It can be no bad thing to test theory against reality and – by tempering dogma – to forge a temperate view. In the travel industry I could not escape that discipline.

Looking back at 1974 through the mists of time, I remember to this day the deep human distress in the distraught eyes of an elderly couple in the crowded and angry reception area of my office – two old age pensioners who for years had struggled to save up for their one foreign holiday of a lifetime, only to find their departure aircraft impounded by the Court Line receivers at Luton Airport whence they had come. I remember the insistent clattering of a telex late that night from a hotel in Portugal threatening to turn away the transfer coach on the point of arrival with a special party of disabled people – a threat only withdrawn when I replied guaranteeing the money paid by them to the bankrupt tour operator but not passed on to the hotel. And I remember the countless sad scenes – sometimes even the violent scenes – in travel agencies throughout the length and breadth of the land.

I doubt whether in these situations a lecture about 'individualism' or 'caveat emptor' would have been thought to be of much relevance or felt to be of much comfort. How much more – immeasurably more – would that be true in the different but comparable situations which I have suggested could sooner or later occur against the back-drop of the new pensions scenario – the introduction of personal pensions – where the potential cost in human terms beggars the imagination.

It is strange how things so often go round in full circle. The Government has now produced a draft Pensions Bill which includes a proposal to set up a 'Pensions Protection Fund', designed to compensate people in final salary schemes where their employers go bankrupt with insufficient money in their pension funds to meet their obligations to existing and/or future pensioners. The fund is to be built up by levies on employers who run final salary schemes. What, I suggest, the above extracts from my pamphlet show is that there is a stronger philosophical and social case for such a fund in the case of pensions than in the case of foreign holidays.

Sadly for some 60,000 people who have already lost their pensions as a result of their employers' bankruptcy, the proposed legislation will not be retrospective. Presumably the representatives of these unfortunate people do not have a trump card up their sleeves such as I was able to play following the Court Line crash when I persuaded the Government to allow the Air Travel Reserve Fund to operate retrospectively and so reimburse the Court Line victims. The principle is the same, but the politics are different.

———

I embarked on two other enterprises, one on my own initiative, the other at the suggestion of our then public relations consultants, Shandwick.

My own idea was that NAPF should publish its own book about the new choice to leave occupational schemes and take out personal pensions instead. The main part of the book was a series of 'twenty questions', accompanied by objective comments highlighting the issues raised. For commercial reasons, it was published in co-operation with and in the name of Gyles Brandreth (the well-known broadcaster amongst much else). Gyles thought up a title with a brilliant double entendre – 'Future Perfect'. Being up against a tight deadline, I and two of my colleagues in the Secretariat worked round the clock to produce a final draft. The help and enthusiasm of Richard Fairclough, the NAPF Secretary, in terms of clear exposition, and of Colin Steward, our pensions lawyer, with regard to the legal technicalities, was second to none. I say that Colin was a pensions lawyer when in fact, though highly respected throughout the pensions world, he was not a qualified solicitor. He had a suitably dry, self-deprecating sense of humour (as befitted someone who spent his life studying interminable Social Security legislation and enthralling statutory instruments) and took positive pleasure in proffering his business card which, at the behest of the Law Society, included the prominent words 'Not a Solicitor'.

Despite a review in the *Financial Times* which described it as the best book so far written on the subject, it was not a commercial success. Apart from the general malaise about the contemplation of retirement in the dim and distant future, there was much competition in the form of 'freebies' published mainly by the right-wing press who jumped on the bandwagon of personal pensions with less than perfect objectivity.

Shandwick's initiative was to produce a video starring Lenny Henry. It was hard-hitting about the risks of personal pensions, for example showing a weeping widow sitting beside Lenny Henry in his coffin – weeping because Lenny had not taken out any life insurance, such usually being part and parcel of the overall package of occupational pensions. Another scene ridiculed what would be a new breed of grasping salesmen selling personal pensions. The video was a commercial success, though not favoured by the more traditionally staid pensions managers. After it was shown at one of our conferences, one member complained to me that it was 'ungentlemanly'. I thought to myself that the last thing the impending commercial battle was likely to be was 'gentlemanly'.

I cannot claim to have anticipated just how ungentlemanly it would turn out to be. As history now records only too clearly, the mis-selling of personal pensions became one of the biggest commercial scams of all time, involving the improper receipt by unscrupulous salesmen of goodness knows how many millions, if not billions, of pounds – salesmen who unashamedly cashed in on people's unsurprising ignorance of the complexities of the issues at stake. It is not good public relations to crow and say, 'I told you so'. Never mind. NAPF's work was done for it, even the right-wing press rapidly changing its tune and warning of the disadvantages for most people of leaving good occupational pension schemes. Better, I suppose, late than never.

Particularly shameful was the Government's role. We were, for instance, summoned to a press conference at which the Department of Social Security, whose Secretary of State was Norman (now Lord) Fowler, was to give an advance showing of its proposed advertising campaign about the introduction of personal pensions. It simply showed a man unravelling himself from the chains which had bound him to his occupational pension scheme and from which he was now free to escape. Was this not aiding and abetting the potentially fraudulent selling of personal pensions?

———

So far so reasonably good. But then a quite astonishing event upset the apple-cart. I have agonized much over whether to include it in my memoirs, but felt free to do so since it happened so long ago that to recount it now would not undermine NAPF's current standing. I would certainly not have done so had I thought otherwise.

Tucked away towards the end of Nigel (now Lord) Lawson's budget speech as Chancellor of the Exchequer early in 1989 came his apparently innocuous announcement that tax relief for employees' contributions to occupational pension schemes and for the pension funds themselves would no longer be granted insofar as they related to annual earnings above £60,000. He added: 'I have deliberately set the ceiling [of £60,000] at a level which *will leave the vast majority of employees unaffected* and it will be subject to an annual up-rating in line with inflation.'

In simple terms, the position till then had been that your tax relief on contributions to occupational pensions was limited to 15% of your annual salary. What the Chancellor's proposal appeared to mean was that, if your annual salary was, say, £80,000, tax relief would be limited to contributions of 15% of £60,000. Your eventual pension would, therefore, be smaller than it would otherwise have been. Since in 1989 £60,000 was by most people's standards a huge annual salary, this didn't seem to be the end of the world.

Within twenty four hours I learnt that it was not as simple as that (nothing ever is where pensions are concerned). Actuaries soon worked out the long-term effect of linking future increases in the 'earnings ceiling' to price inflation. (The earnings ceiling came to be known as the 'earnings cap', which is the expression I shall use from now on.)

The short point was that, since – based on the experience of the last ten years – average earnings were projected to outstrip price inflation by an average of 2.5% a year, in thirty years' time some 40% of the younger people at work would be affected by the earnings cap by the time they retired. The number of people affected would thereafter increase further and, the differential percentage of 2.5% a year being compounded, at an ever-increasing rate. It was therefore untrue to say that the cap would not affect the vast majority of employees.

What particularly riled the actuaries (and others in the pensions world as the news of this analysis spread) was something I didn't know. In his budget speech in 1985, Nigel Lawson had given an undertaking to the House of Commons that he would not make any fundamental change to the pensions tax regime without first publishing a consultative Green Paper. The strong and overwhelming view took hold that Nigel Lawson was in breach of this undertaking because the long-term effect of the earnings cap represented a fundamental change in the taxation of pensions. I was swept along by a tide of emotion, the like of which I had come to expect at ABTA but had certainly not expected to find amongst coldly-calculating actuaries.

Recognizing that there was no chance of Nigel Lawson backing down altogether by removing the offending clause from the pending Finance Bill, the NAPF Council rightly felt that the only hope was to try to persuade him to modify his proposal by linking the earnings cap to increases in average earnings rather than to price inflation. This would mean that the number of people affected in the long term would remain roughly the same.

Soon after Nigel Lawson's budget speech came our Annual Conference. My Chairman, Charles Woodward, wisely felt that in his opening address to the NAPF members he could hardly refrain from criticizing the proposed earnings cap for the reasons I have explained, but that he should do so in moderate language, bearing in mind that our intention was to propose that the cap be linked to earnings rather than inflation. It would be counter-productive to upset the Chancellor unnecessarily.

By a most unfortunate coincidence, later on the same day that Charles delivered his opening address, a well-known actuary made a speech in which he tabled the issue in far from moderate language, openly accusing Nigel Lawson of behaving dishonourably on the grounds that he had breached his undertaking to the House of Commons to publish a Green Paper before making a fundamental change to the pensions tax regime.

The next day, *The Times* reported both speeches, the actuary's under a heading which made it clear that the Chancellor had been accused of dishonourable conduct. The tragedy was that the reports did not specifically make the distinction between Charles' official line as Chairman of NAPF and the personal slant taken by the actuary at the subsequent session.

My feedback from the treasury on my return from the Conference to my office fulfilled my worst fears. Having seen *The Times*, Nigel Lawson was hopping mad and Norman (later Lord) Lamont, then Chief Secretary to the Treasury, was positively apoplectic with fury, his boss – and by implication himself – having been so publicly and deliberately accused of dishonourable conduct by, as they saw it, the NAPF as such. Such chance as there may have been of negotiating a linkage of the cap to earnings rather than inflation had gone by the board. The pass had been well and truly sold – to mix my metaphors – down the river.

For all that, the pressures from some quarters of the membership (egged on by the actuary's speech at the Conference) for NAPF to do something about it rose to a crescendo and approached fever pitch.

It was clear to me that there wasn't a snowball's chance in hell of reaching a negotiated solution. There was now no way in which Nigel Lawson could possibly climb down without appearing to admit a charge of dishonourable behaviour, involving of all things a breach of an undertaking to the House of Commons. It was no less clear that we either had to incur the wrath of many members by doing nothing for reasons we could hardly explain or we had to turn the knife in the Chancellor's back in the hope, if a forlorn one, that to cause a public scandal by bringing the whole thing out into the open might force the issue. Wisely or unwisely, but certainly against my normal policy of avoiding Government bashing, I drafted a pamphlet clearly explaining the rationale for the accusation of dishonourable conduct by the Chancellor and reinforcing that criticism in the strongest terms. I circulated my draft to the 'the officers' who, from memory, comprised my new Chairman, Peter Stirrup (who had succeeded Charles Woodward at the conclusion of the recent Conference), the two Vice-Presidents (the office of President having been left vacant since the appointment of my predecessor, Henry James, as NAPF's first Director General), the Vice Chairman and the Honorary Treasurer. Peter Stirrup was away on holiday but, to a man, the others enthusiastically endorsed the draft and authorized me to have it printed and sent to a wide range of Members of Parliament and, for information, to our members. Peter Stirrup gave his retrospective endorsement of my action on his return from holiday.

On the very day that the posting of the pamphlet with suitable covering letters was being completed (having started the previous day), my phone rang. It was Nigel Lawson's private secretary, who said she was about to see the Chancellor to discuss the pamphlet, a copy of which had just been drawn to their attention. She thought it courteous to ask for my comments. There followed a long and technical discussion which I will try to reduce to its bare bones.

She asked, much to my astonishment, whether I realized that the way the proposed cap would work in practice would be to withdraw tax relief only insofar as contributions would produce pensions of more than £40,000 and not insofar as they related to earnings of more than £60,000 a year: in other words it was, in effect, a pensions cap and not an earnings cap. She reminded me that the legal maximum for pensions was two thirds of final salary, £40,000 being two thirds of £60,000. The Government estimated that, in practice, as few as 1% of people actually achieved pensions of two thirds of their final salary, from which it followed that my pamphlet had grossly over-estimated the number of people likely to be affected by the Chancellor's proposal – possibly by as much as 99%! At the conclusion of our discussion, all I could think of saying on the spur of the moment was that she could hardly be right because the actuarial profession as a whole had advised differently.

The second we finished our conversation, I rang one of the actuaries who had advised me and told him of my conversation. I have recorded many of the precise words said to or by me in the course of these memoirs, but I remember none more clearly than his comment and my reply. His comment was, 'That's a bit below the belt.' My reply was, 'It may be below the belt, but is it true?' He said he thought not but would ring me back as soon as possible, which he did after the longest half an hour of my life. Being as nice, as decent and as honest a person as you could wish to meet, he was clearly in great distress when he said he was afraid she *was* right.

I had had some bad moments in my professional career but none anywhere near as awful as that one. I felt faint. As the full implications permeated my brain, I felt worse and worse. NAPF had made a complete fool of itself in the eyes of the Government, as had I of me. The thought that we had accused the Chancellor of the Exchequer of dishonourable conduct on the basis of almost entirely false projections cut me to the quick.

The whole thing was surreal. All I could do was to contact those who had authorized me to publish the pamphlet. They were duly horrified but, understanding my own distress, supported me as best they could and, big men that they were, did not disassociate themselves from blame.

We had no choice but to try and bluff it out and cover up our mistake as best we could. At least it never emerged into the full light of the public arena. Opinions about the leaflet varied from high praise ('not before time' was an expression used more than once) to strong condemnation for criticizing Nigel Lawson so strongly instead of negotiating with him. The critics did not realize that negotiation was a lost cause for the reasons I have explained. It was ironic – and just as well – that they were not aware of the real grounds for criticism. I had then to endure weeks of receiving from Members of Parliament copies of letters that Norman Lamont had written to them in which he took undisguised delight in pointing out that the author of the pamphlet did not understand how the earnings cap would operate, which sadly I had reason to know to be only too true.

All this took its toll on my physical and mental health. It had already begun to do so when Peter Stirrup, who – as I said earlier – succeeded Charles Woodward as Chairman at the conclusion of that fateful Conference, came into my office early one morning at the beginning of August and bravely got straight to the difficult point of saying that members of the Council had noticed that I seemed to be uninterested in my work and generally apathetic. He himself was understanding of my position and recognized my distressed mental state. He thoughtfully suggested that I might like to take the rest of August off so as to recover my strength and energy. I declined his kind offer because I thought that it would only make things worse were I to sit at home worrying about everything. I realized that I had to pull out all the stops of my determination which, when push came to shove – an appropriate expression in the circumstances – could be very strong indeed. As tennis commentators say, I 'dug deep' and 'regrouped' (though how an individual, as opposed to a number of people, can 'regroup' has always eluded me). I was able to galvanize sufficient energy to show a brave face to the world, though underneath the stuffing had been knocked out of me. I became increasingly depressed.

I fear that this may appear to have been a rather whining account of this remarkable event, though I have tried objectively to explain what happened and the reasons – whether sound or unsound – for my own part in the fiasco. Strange but true to say, I did not feel critical of the actuarial profession. On the contrary, I felt sympathetic. All professional people, as I know myself, are bound sometimes to make mistakes. My main reaction, however, was and remains utter bewilderment and mystification that this distinguished and elite profession should have made so untypical a collective misjudgement. Time and again, I have tried to understand how it could possibly have occurred. I suppose that the very fact that in his budget speech Nigel Lawson called the cap an 'earnings ceiling' of £60,000 was enough to put anyone off the scent; that there had been a failure in communication between the actuaries and the pensions practitioners who did not work out how the cap would operate until the die was irretrievably cast (failure in communication being the classic cause of errors in complex areas of business and public life); and that the power of 'group psychology' can all too easily become overwhelming, particularly when underlaid by insecurity and downright fear about the perceived threat to final salary occupational pensions, which constituted a significant proportion of their professional work. More immediately, actuaries of all people were more likely than most to be affected straight away by an earnings cap – if such it had been – of £60,000 a year.

Finally, to have omitted this event from my memoirs would have left a gaping hole because of its significant influence on other aspects of my life, some positive and some negative.

———

I came to see in retrospect that one of the consequences of my depressive state was the emergence from deep inside me of a strong yearning to express myself in some emotional artistic way: to seek some psychological escape into, and to find solace in, 'eine bessre Welt' – the 'better world' of

Schubert's 'An die Musik' ('To Music'), words which had sprung to my mind when I had glanced at Father Mullarkey in St Peter's in Rome all those years ago and imagined him to be transported to the better world of his Heaven above. My life-long love of lieder began to dominate my mind. I felt I had the feeling and intellect to appreciate the combination of great music and great poetry that is the essence of lieder. I desperately, if doubtfully, wanted to see if I could translate this into practice.

After much hesitation and procrastination, one evening I found myself pacing nervously up and down outside the house of Mark's (my younger son) piano teacher, Jean Ball, trying to pluck up the courage to knock on her door and ask if she would accompany me on the piano. Eventually, I did so. Jean thoughtfully suggested that I should contact someone with much more experience in accompanying singers, one David Naysmith, who was a pro/am (partly professional/partly amateur) accompanist. After further mental 'to-ing and fro-ing', I phoned David who agreed to have a trial run one evening. I took along the only book of lieder I had. It was a volume containing some of the best known of Schubert's more than 600 songs, a relic of 'the olden days' of musical evenings I had so enjoyed over forty years ago. (In passing, it is beyond my comprehension how one human being in a short lifetime of 31 years could have written – amongst everything else – so many songs, so many of which were masterpieces. His great successor, Hugo Wolf, is supposed to have said of Schubert that, if you gave him the menu in a restaurant, he could write a good tune about it.)

In his house in Winchester, David and his wife, Virginia, had a fine music room containing two grand pianos. At our first meeting, I had a nervous shot at Schubert's famous 'Serenade' and, for all my imperfections, was immediately uplifted by a sense of 'oneness' between David and myself. I think David genuinely felt that my singing was not beyond hope. At any rate, he was kind enough to compliment me on my German pronunciation and said that it was not always that he accompanied singers who didn't just 'bash it out' but had a feeling for the words and music. So encouraged, I went round to his house most Wednesday evenings. So began a rewarding journey into the unknown, throughout which David, as well as Virginia (herself a sensitive soprano soloist) never failed to give me their full support.

As time passed, I extended my repertoire to the other great lieder composers, namely Schumann, Brahms and Hugo Wolf, and to English songs, such as those written by Roger Quilter, Michael Head and Gerald

Finzi. David even persuaded me to dip into the French repertoire, mainly the songs of Fauré and Debussy, though my French pronunciation fell far short of my German. Of course, we tried some Italian songs but, although I could do a passable imitation of a Neapolitan tenor, I always felt, for reasons I couldn't explain, that I was doing just that – 'imitating.' I felt entirely comfortable with German lieder, presumably because of my Anglo Saxon roots. More surprisingly, I also felt at ease with French mélodies, though, come to think of it, I probably have some Norman and Frankish blood in my veins, the Normans having been partly of Flemish origins and the Franks having been of Germanic origin. While that may be complete hogwash, it is incontrovertible that, to have any chance of being any good, a singer must feel on the same psychological wavelength as both poet and composer.

David was incredibly patient during a long process of trial and error on my part. Having tried and erred, I have gained a heightened appreciation of the technique of the great singers, an insight which has been worthwhile for its own sake. Golf may seem an improbable analogy but my problem with both golf and singing is the inherent contradiction in my mind between total concentration on the one hand and full relaxation on the other. I had picked up some basic hints from the conductors of the choral societies we had belonged to over the years. After much experimentation, I found that tightening my stomach in order to support my breath – apart from doing just that – took tension and tightness away from my throat which I should have thought is the most important single technical requirement, indeed the *sine qua non*, of good singing. I just *couldn't* be tense in two parts of my body at the same time.

After a year or so, my singing improved considerably. I began to wonder whether to make a recording of some kind or other and developed a deep need to try to create a half-decent piece of art that would survive me. By a great stroke of luck, I came across Rob Aubrey, who was a professional in recording what I called 'pop music', my dislike for which was matched only by Rob's dislike of 'classical music'. We had great fun teasing each other and he, David and I became the best of friends. Rob's ear for rhythm and tuning was second to none.

We had about a dozen recording sessions in David's music room, from which we all learned as we went along. There is something utterly unforgiving about a recording of one's singing. I had not only to sing in the middle of every note but what I came to call the middle of the middle. The most fractional deviation towards being sharp or flat showed up in a quite ruthless way, as did the slightest squeak from the pedals of David's piano which he constantly oiled. I was particularly concerned that my words could be heard, it being a not uncommon defect that they can't. But if I over-emphasized, say, a 'p' at the end of a word like 'hope', it sounded like a pistol shot. The telephone ringing in the hall sabotaged the whole thing, so David turned the phone off when we were recording. David or I turning over the pages of our music made an awful crackling noise, with the result that David used scissors and yards of sellotape so that he never had to turn over, while I learnt my songs by heart and dispensed with the written scores altogether. Knowing the songs by heart had the important added advantage that there was one thing less to worry about. I could concentrate on the meaning of the words rather than struggle to remember what they were.

Another of the most fundamental techniques I learnt the hard way was never, never to try to be too clever by half. Until David pointed out the error of my ways, I tried *artificially* to emphasize the feeling underlying *all* the words by a suitably expressive tone of voice. This was thoroughly counter-productive. Emphasizing them all meant that all emphasis flew out of the window, leaving behind a meaningless jumble. I learnt to emphasize only the few words which it came *naturally* to emphasize, thereby losing neither the essential meaning of the poems nor the flow of the music. I learnt that technique for its own sake can, if we are not careful, become an unwarranted straight-jacket, casting freedom of expression to the winds.

At our very first recording session, I was comforted and, in my ignorance, astounded to learn about the potentiality of 'editing'. I sang a song twice and was happy enough about the second version, except that one of the notes wasn't perfectly in tune. Rob Aubrey said, 'Don't worry, Michael. That note was in tune the first time and we can transfer it to the second version.' The result was that I spent several days with him obsessively selecting the best extracts from several versions of a song and stringing them together. Apparently, this has long been commonplace in many recordings of both classical and pop music. A friend of Rob's who loaned him the necessary editing equipment showed me in confidence the score of a piece of music performed by a well-known string quartet on which the places where he had been instructed to switch from one version to another were marked with red crosses. The score was littered with red crosses, which made me feel less of a fraud.

Rob arranged for a hundred compact discs to be made comprising twenty songs in which, as a result of the editing, every note of my singing was in tune to my satisfaction and, more importantly, to his.

The whole process had been a thoroughly satisfying experience of mutual understanding between David, Rob and myself. For me, it was especially emotionally rewarding when I passed the stage of singing as I thought fit and leaving David – as the *accompanist* – to follow whatever took my fancy in terms of speed, pauses and so on. Until then, I had been only half-consciously aware that a lieder recital was a *duet* between voice and piano, between singer and *pianist*, the part played by each being of equal importance. While it remains true that it is largely up to the pianist to follow the singer's lead, it is not a one-sided affair. Eventually, I came to enjoy *listening to,* not just hearing, David's sympathetic and sensitive playing and mentally to *feel* our mutual togetherness and even to contribute to it in a subtly slight way. Only then did the feeling that we were in complete musical, intellectual and emotional harmony with each other show through in the recordings and become one of the most fulfilling experiences of my life. Whatever other qualities the compact disc may or may not have, I like to think that a sensitive listener can actually *hear* – and so *share* – the 'oneness' that is the hallmark of lieder and other songs for voice and piano.

It was also rewarding to create my own song cycle, though agonizing to select only twenty contrasting songs from the vast repertoire of German lieder, French mélodies and English songs. Nor was it easy to put them into a meaningful sequence that expressed the contrasting feelings I wanted to get across to the listener and out of my system, while at the same time avoiding undue clashes between the keys of successive songs. I entitled the cycle 'Poetry in Music', reflecting the unity between words and music. It gave me particular pleasure to include two poems by W.B. Yeats, the music for which was written by my brother, John. It is not everyone who could compose songs that are not out of place in such eminent company.

Appendix 1 comprises a list of the songs I selected and a brief explanation of the structure of the cycle. You will see that I included 'An die Musik'.

———◦•◦———

Although this intensive extra-curricular musical activity successfully supplanted my depression while it was going on, it did not lead me to the 'better world' I had hoped it would. My internal depression remained and exacerbated all my worries, which otherwise I might well have taken in my stride, in a remorseless vicious circle. I had to fight on regardless.

Things came to a head when I had to step in at the last minute and fill a gap in the programme for the next Annual Conference. Amongst other things, I developed my theme about NAPF being essentially an association of employers by examining the nature of the interest of employers that it followed should be the Association's primary concern. I suggested that the employers' interest was that their pension schemes should be cost-effective and our strategic efforts should therefore be directed towards creating a climate of public and political opinion and an economic environment that would be helpful to employers in this regard.

The pity of it was that I made by far the worst speech of the many I had made during my whole working life, particularly at ABTA conferences. My depression made me feel inwardly defensive, verging on the paranoid. I clung hard to what had on that occasion became a complex: not to 'talk down' to an audience of such intellectual calibre. I over-reacted and realized as I was speaking that I must be sounding over-assertive to the point of dogmatism. But I was helpless to do anything about it. In the following days, subject as I was to entirely justified criticism, I became as close to complete breakdown as I had been since my unhappy summer term at Oxford. Severe depression is almost synonymous with a loss of self-esteem. Of self-esteem I had none.

It was not, I think, that I was wrong in substance. Looking at the Association's Year Book for 1997, which I happen to have to hand, I read the usual insertion: 'The NAPF's mission is to foster an environment in which employer-sponsored pension and benefit provision can flourish.' That this is absolutely fundamental can sadly be seen as I write in 2003, when some experts estimate that British companies face a £300 billion shortfall in their final salary pension schemes as a consequence, amongst other things, of the disastrous fall in the value of shares in which pension funds are mainly invested and Gordon Brown's decision as Chancellor of the Exchequer to stop a valuable tax relief on dividends. It has been estimated that many companies are reducing the benefits for employees who already belong to final salary schemes, 63% of which are being closed to new entrants and in many cases replaced by money-purchase schemes. These carry the same risks as personal pensions whose disadvantages I touched on in the extracts from 'Travelling to Retirement' that I quoted earlier. One such was that the annuity rates might be low at the time of retirement. It is a tragedy that this possibility has already become a reality. Since my own retirement annuity rates have plummeted – due largely to falling interest rates and improving mortality rates.

Thankfully, circumstances now forced me to come to terms with my mental illness. I traced via Yellow Pages, and made an appointment to see, a Dr Sutton, a leading psychiatrist in Harley Street. He had recently retired from running one of the largest mental hospitals in London. He was a delightful old Jewish chap with whom I struck up an immediate rapport, as I did with his wife, who was also a psychiatrist and whom I saw once when her husband was unwell. To cut a long story short, the unsurprising diagnosis was clinical depression and the remedy appropriate medication, which gradually pulled me round. I was able to face up to my problems and began to regain a positive attitude to my work and even my sense of humour, which is always a sign of seeing things in perspective. The only thing I thought was a shame about my experience of meeting Dr Sutton was that, both in Yellow Pages and on the brass plate on the door of his premises in Harley Street, he described himself only as 'Dr Sutton', whereas on his accounts he was 'Dr Isaac Sutton'. My guess was that he felt that, if he included his first name in public announcements, he would be recognizably Jewish and that this might put some people off consulting him. I felt that, if I was right in my surmise, it was infinitely sad that so charming and humane a person at the top of his profession should nowadays have been driven to think on these lines.

That I recovered my mental equilibrium was just as well. A small but powerful element in the NAPF hierarchy mounted a strong attack on my overall analysis of the Association as being an employers' association. It was suggested that I could be forgiven for having thought this when I was a new Director General but, having now been in my job for three years, I should have learnt the error of my ways. I submitted a report to the Council defending my analysis on many grounds. One thing I emphasized was the position of local authorities, which I had mistakenly taken as read. I checked this out with a bridge-playing friend, John Scotford, who happened to be the County Treasurer of Hampshire, so as to be in a position to quote chapter and verse in support of my view that local authorities did not appoint trustees to run their pension funds and could not be members of the NAPF in any other capacity than that of employers. John felt so strongly that he went as far as to say that, if the NAPF regarded local authorities as members in any other (non-existent) capacity, they would all be obliged to resign their membership. As the major local authorities – like the Hampshire County Council – controlled many of the largest pension funds in the country, their exclusion from membership would have decimated the Association and with it its power to influence. I weathered the storm until its force subsided, not least because my critics never suggested an alternative analysis but thought it better to let sleeping dogs lie.

My period of office ended up as happily as it began. During my last few years, further social security legislation partly affecting occupational pensions was wending its weary way through the Palace of Westminster to the Statute Book. Ron Amy, my last Chairman, said more than once that I had given helpful advice about not pursuing suggested amendments which, as he put it, my experience and political instincts showed 'wouldn't fly' but confining ourselves to amendments which had a realistic chance of being adopted. Ron was a far-sighted Chairman and helped me to see the funny side of things, even including the earnings cap disaster.

Once he and I had occasion to meet Michael Portillo, whose charm and charisma lived up to our expectations. He came down to greet us in the waiting room himself, rather than dispatching a civil servant to show us in, as was the case with other Ministers. As we sat down in his office, the band of the Scots Guards struck up within earshot. Having instantly recognized Ron's Scots accent, he said he always liked to make sure his guests received a suitable welcome.

Our discussion touched on final salary schemes, which he condemned as involving an element of cross-subsidy. He was less informed – dare I say ill-informed – about the overriding practical advantages of such schemes, preferring ideology to pragmatism. Throughout a long professional life dealing with politicians of all parties at all levels, I had come to realize that this was a common phenomenon which one had to recognize for what it was and somehow cope with by subtle negotiation rather than by wielding a sledgehammer, except, exceptionally, as a last resort. Ingrained ideology is a hard nut to crack. It is because I have tended to prefer a pragmatic to an ideological approach to political issues that I have always been a floating voter.

My time with NAPF hardly justified my apprehension, when I first put the phone down on the head-hunter, that it would be boring. It was a real eye-opener to discover the vast apparatus and extreme complexity of the world that lay beneath the surface of the deceptively straightforward process whereby our pensions appear in our bank accounts every month. It was, too, a rich and rewarding experience to work closely with men and women of many professions whose expertise never ceased to amaze me. I shall always appreciate the support and encouragement shown by so many of them.

CHAPTER 8

Retirement

I RETIRED FROM NAPF at the end of May 1995, the month of my sixty-third birthday.

I have been happy in my retirement, often profoundly so. I have thoroughly enjoyed the relaxation of playing tennis, golf and bridge; the pleasure of rehearsing with the choir of the Winchester Music Club on Friday evenings without feeling exhausted by a week of work, and of performing in Winchester's great Cathedral or Winchester College's splendid New Hall; and the extra time and energy available to spend with my family, which now includes six grandchildren. We are lucky that the Welsh National Opera comes to the Mayflower Theatre in Southampton twice a year. It is barely half-an-hour's drive from home and the tickets are reasonably priced. We have extended our repertoire beyond the more traditional composers and have become particularly fond of Janáček.

Soon after I retired, I undertook a four year stint as chairman of the Winchester area fund-raising committee for a new children's hospice, Naomi House, at nearby Sutton Scotney. It was a rewarding experience to be associated with a team of helpful and kindly people who were prepared to give so much of their time to so worthwhile a cause. More recently, I began to attend courses on philosophy organized by the Winchester branch of the WEA (Workers Educational Association). Philosophy, by its very nature, is likely to remain of inexhaustible interest and it has been a pleasure to get to know a group of people who are as liberal-minded in their intelligent interest in philosophy as they are diverse in their backgrounds and viewpoints.

About the time I had moved from ABTA to NAPF, we had been constrained to move house. 4 Bereweeke Close had become too expensive to maintain and so, with an eye to my eventual retirement, we moved to a smaller house in Olivers Battery on the south-west outskirts of Winchester. Olivers Battery was so named because Oliver Cromwell's Roundheads sited a battery of guns there during the English Civil War in the seventeenth century. There are only a few houses between ours and open countryside and we overlook the South Winchester Golf Club, of

150

which Isabel and I are both members. Although it was distressing to have to move from Bereweeke Close, as is often the case with what seems like a disaster at the time, it turned out for the best. We are thoroughly content to be living in a smaller house, which is cosier and has calming views across the countryside towards the setting sun.

I took the eleventh commandment of retirement to be: 'Thou shalt go to painting classes.' I signed up for a class run by Mark Flemons and turned up at the first one not knowing the first thing about painting except that I had a clear preference for oils as against watercolour. For some reason, I felt that oil paintings were somehow more 'masculine' – stronger and more powerful: literally less wishy-washy than watercolours. This is not for a moment to suggest that good watercolours cannot aspire to wonderfully gentle and delicate beauty. It is only to rationalize a subjective preference, which in another sense turned out to be just as well. From limited experimentation I found out for myself that watercolour was a more difficult medium to cope with and that it would take even longer to learn the techniques involved. Time was not on my side. I once asked Mark, from whom I picked up many helpful tips, how best to become a good painter, to which he replied: 'Paint every day for forty years.'

Most of the other people in the class had had considerable experience of watercolour and produced some really lovely pictures. After some eighteen months, I managed to paint a couple of landscapes in oils that were adequate enough to have framed.

Then two thoughts coincided and set me on a long and difficult trail. One day, when I was painting a simple landscape, it occurred to me just to paint the sky in three horizontal strips of blue and the fields in two of green, in each case the strips becoming fainter towards the horizon. The result was a semi-abstract painting, which actually looked rather beautiful in its simplicity. I became more and more inclined towards more and more abstract paintings. At the same time, the thought sprang to mind of painting pictures representing the songs on my compact disc.

Most of the songs being love songs, I wondered how to represent the lover and his beloved. For whatever reasons, conscious or more probably unconscious, I decided to represent the lover by a square and his beloved by a circle. My idea was that, set against different patterns and colours, the squares and circles should represent their changing moods and relationships as befitted the poems and music.

Just as I was never much good at choosing the colours with which to paint the kitchen walls but was better at knowing I had chosen wrongly when it was too late, so it was with my paintings. The result was that I had to paint several versions of each until, by my own limited lights, I was satisfied that they were as good as I was likely to be able to make them.

I soon discovered that many of the songs conveyed more than one mood. There might, for instance, be three verses each conveying different emotions and so demanding three different pictures. After a further eighteen months of trial and error, I ended up with forty paintings coincidentally representing twenty songs, though it was not a case of two paintings per song. As, on average, I did about three versions of each, I had had to paint some 120 paintings, of which I consigned about 80 to the dustbin.

The main lesson I learnt for myself was the same one as I had learnt when recording the songs on which my paintings were based – never try to be artificially clever. This was driven home when I painted three pictures representing Fauré's song, 'Les Roses d'Isphahan' (The Roses of Ispahan). In the third verse, the singer hopes that one day his beloved's love will return to his heart like a light butterfly. This phrase is so beautiful in the original French that, after I had finished the picture, I thought up the idea of adding a duly sophisticated butterfly shape. I then showed it to a friend, proud of its masterful symbolism. He immediately said, 'What's that bow tie for?' I chucked it straight into the dustbin and had to repaint it without my precious butterfly – precious in both its senses.

Having completed forty pictures on canvasses measuring 16" x 20", I then had to think how best they could be combined with the music. To my technologically uninformed mind, it seemed the obvious answer was to produce a video, fading the pictures in and out at the appropriate moments in the music.

Through Yellow Pages, I tracked down Graham Nye, who ran Southern Studios in Southampton. I hadn't realized that the first step was to have the pictures photographed. Luckily Paul Clelford, a professional picture restorer, who varnished the paintings for me (but only, on his insistence, after they had been left for six months to dry rock hard), put me in touch with Stephen Skurray, the professional fine art photographer. Every other Saturday, I took ten of the pictures to his home near Tadley, not far from Basingstoke, where he had had a studio designed and built in his garden. He took ten photographs of each with differing exposures and types of film, having made a special frame to hold the pictures in exactly the right position. He then arranged to have them converted into what, as a layman, I call slides. On my next visit, he placed them on a light box so that I could go through the agonizing process of choosing the one I thought most closely matched the original picture or was otherwise the most acceptable. I am bound to say, never having had cause to think about it, that it hadn't registered with me that it was not possible to produce photographs of pictures in which the colours were the same as the originals. Stephen pointed out that this problem was exacerbated in my case because I had selected strong colours at the opposite ends of the spectrum.

The third stage was to have the forty slides I had chosen transferred to Graham Nye's computer by a process of 'digital rephotography', which I did not begin to understand.

Just as I had spent ages with Rob Aubrey editing the songs, so I now spent several long days editing the pictures which, again, I had no idea was possible. Graham was as skilled at this task as Rob was in his own sphere of expertise, and we developed a similar kinship of feeling.

The main problem to be resolved was that, despite the professionalism involved in the previous stages, the colours still varied from the originals when they finally ended up on the screen of Graham's television monitor on which we based our editing decisions. This, apparently, was inevitable. Moreover, when Graham adjusted one colour of a picture, however slightly, it inevitably changed the appearance of the other colours. He and I had to fiddle about for ages to get all the colours acceptable in their own right and in harmony with each other. This could have been worse because I had generally limited the number of colours per picture to three (not counting different shades of the same colour) because I found that more than three colours detracted from the simplicity for which I strove. My brain just couldn't take them all in and became more confused than usual.

Another problem was that, if two pictures had the same basic pattern, however carefully I had measured and drawn the pattern on the canvas before starting to paint, there were fractional differences. These didn't show up when looking at them side by side but became glaringly obvious when one supplanted the other on the screen. Graham painstakingly corrected such imperfections so that they merged with each other perfectly.

There then followed the long process of phasing the pictures in and out so as to coincide with the music.

Having achieved all this, I remained dissatisfied. I felt that the pictures on the computer screen looked better than those on the screen of the television monitor – something to do with the different ways they are lighted. Graham agreed. We therefore embarked upon the further task of attempting to restructure the whole project as a computer presentation in the form of a CD Rom. This involved some re-editing because, as I said earlier, we had based the final colours on the television monitor's screen rather than the computer's.

We then, believe it or not, hit another snag. None of the computer programmes that Graham acquired – including one designed by Microsoft in America – produced a sufficiently smooth method of fading the pictures in and out. Eventually, Macromedia's 'Director' (a complex 'presentation and authoring' programme) became available and Matt Duffield, one of Graham's business associates, worked hard and long to achieve a satisfactory result. Not that I am ever satisfied with my artistic efforts. It is ironic, as Graham said, that I – an ignoramus in things technological if ever there was – should have found myself at the cutting edge of a new technological process. Although all this caused a delay of some eighteen months, we have at last completed the project. Whatever impression it may leave in people's minds, it is at least an original piece of art.

It has been said that 99% of genius is an infinite capacity to take pains. I think I can reasonably claim to have demonstrated that I have that capacity. The shame of it is that, in all my creative endeavours, the vital 1% has been missing.

A number of coincidences led me to embark upon two further art projects. At one of our lessons, Mark Flemons suggested that we try our hands at drawing with black ink, using pens designed for that purpose. After several attempts, I composed a picture which is shown [on the opposite page.]

A few days later I happened to visit a shop which specialized in copying documents, the task in hand being to have my tax return copied for future reference. One might well be forgiven for thinking that, of all documents, none is less likely to inspire artistic creation than one's tax return. Yet glancing round the shop I noticed several packets of A4 cards of various colours. Quick as a flash, I wondered what my drawing would look like if copied on a selection of these cards. On further enquiry, I was surprised to learn that they were available in thirty different colours.

Acting on impulse, I had the picture copied on cards of every colour,

rushed home and spread them out on the floor of the spare room. The colours ranged from delicate, pale shades to strong, deep ones. I was bowled over by the gentle beauty of the former and the dramatic intensity of the latter.

After much thought I divided them into two groups of fifteen, one group comprising the lighter colours, the other the darker colours. I arranged each group into three rows of five, constantly moving them around in an endeavour to ensure that the overall effect was harmonious. It was a stressful process trying to attain the unattainable: the perfect solution for which I strove in vain.

Luckily it was only after I had settled for a reasonably satisfactory compromise for each group that I wondered how many different ways there actually were in which fifteen cards could have been arranged. Remembering how to work out permutations, I amused myself by multiplying 15x14x13x12 and so on. I came up with the staggering total of 1,307,674,368,000! Thank goodness I didn't know this before I started to arrange them. I am quite neurotic enough without wondering which of the one thousand three hundred and seven billion, six hundred and seventy four million, three hundred and sixty eight thousand ways of arranging each group of fifteen cards would be the best!

As to mounting and framing each group, Stephen Skurrey, who had photographed the pictures on which my CD Rom was based, suggested that I should approach Hazel MacDonald, a professional framer, who runs a firm called Fine Framing based in Alton.

After some discussion, I agreed to have both groups framed in black and mounted on a black background. Since variety of colour was of the essence, I agreed that the pictures should be covered in 'museum' glass, which, I was fascinated to learn, not only minimizes the reflection of light, but also maximizes the retention of colour by filtering out at least 97% of ultraviolet radiation.

The result is two rather striking pieces of artwork, each measuring 4 feet 2 inches by 3 feet 9 inches. I feel strangely comforted that this pair of artistic oddities will long survive me relatively undiminished in the impact of their colours.

I entitled the dark group 'The darkest hour is just before the dawn' (an anonymous proverb of the mid-seventeenth century) and the lighter group 'Hail, gentle Dawn!' (William Somerville, The Chase).

The second project resulted from just one coincidence and was, thankfully, virtually effortless on my part.

One Saturday evening we visited our friends, Tom and Pat Mounsey, at their home in Winchester for one of our regular bridge sessions. Before starting to play bridge we wandered into their back garden where they had had a new patio laid. It was made of some kind of Indian stone. On several of the slabs were some fossils of plants which had survived for goodness knows how many million years.

The thin stems of the plants and the tiny leaves looked just like trees in the distance. I doubt whether, in our comparatively short existence on this planet, the human hand has drawn or painted trees with greater delicacy. I was moved to silent tears by this beauty and antiquity.

Tom and Pat agreed that I could ask Stephen Skurrey to photograph them for me. Stephen came with me to look at them and was no less intrigued. He agreed to photograph them but waited for a day and time of day when the light was at its best for the purpose.

The result is three square photographs, each measuring 10x10 inches and two extracts from another, each measuring 10x4 inches. I arranged for Hazel MacDonald to mount them on a speckled golden frame which is 'old looking' and measures 37x28 inches. The cibachrome process which Stephen used to make the photographs has made them 'colour stable' and will ensure that they will remain in pristine condition for many a long year.

I have entitled the larger ones 'Storm over distant hills', 'Lull and light between storms' and 'Three stars at twilight' (there being three small blobs that, with a little imagination, resemble stars).

One of the greatest joys of retirement has been to go on holiday without having to clear up my desk beforehand and afterwards to face the pile that has accumulated in the meanwhile. We have particularly enjoyed river cruises and musical holidays and, above all, a combination of the two. Thus, we recently had a cruise on the Danube from Vienna to Budapest, enjoying at the start a peerless performance of Bellini's La Sonnambula' given by the Vienna State Opera and, to finish with, a moving performance of Prokoviev's ballet Romeo and Juliet at the opera house in Budapest. There were other fine concerts, including one in Bratislava. The opera house in Budapest felt like home because a couple of years ago we enjoyed there an excellent production of the whole of Wagner's Ring Cycle.

We have now virtually exhausted the possibilities of European rivers, having also cruised on the Rhine, the Rhone (from Lyon to Marseilles), the Douro in Portugal (ending up with a trip to Salamanca in Spain) and the Po (starting with a tour of the less familiar parts of Venice, visiting the artistic treasures within range of the river and flying home from Milan). We also plugged some of the major gaps in our experience of travel when I was with ABTA, such as a trip through the Canadian Rockies ending up in Vancouver and making the beautiful crossing to Vancouver Island; a journey by one of the magnificent trains run by Rovos Rail from the Victoria Falls to Cape Town, thence to a cruise on Lake Kariba where we had close-up views of prides of lions from a launch that ventured up various creeks, and thence on the way back to the Victoria Falls to a game park where we saw elephants galore; and a coach trip embracing Boston, New York, Washington, the Amish country, Gettysburg and Williamsburg, where they have attempted to put the clock back by banning cars, preserving the old buildings and dressing in clothes of the eighteenth century.

Following my father's premature death in 1973, my mother, having come to terms with her bereavement, enjoyed a fulfilling widowhood. She had retained many friends from her days with the operatic and dramatic societies and played bridge with a wide circle of other friends. She also retained her engaging, flirtatious personality, which continued to endear her to so many people.

Soon after I retired, it became clear that she was no longer capable of living on her own. She was beginning to show the first signs of senile dementia. John and I were lucky to find a wonderful residential home run by Siobhan Shine, a delightful, positive character with a great sense of fun. She has made Otterbourne Grange a place where old people are treated by all her staff with rare humanity, care and humour. Mother is completely happy there and – at the age of 94 – physically still very strong, though her dementia has become slowly but perceptibly worse. In her more lucid moments, her favourite saying is that the world is a wonderful place in which everyone is kind. Suffering from such an enviable delusion, there is no reason why she shouldn't live to be at least a hundred years old. Siobhan shares John's and my view that she almost certainly will.

I leave my deepest reflections about life until the last two parts of my book. Thinking here about my life, a number of random and disconnected thoughts occur to me.

I remember, for instance, the hundreds of staff at all levels in local government, at ABTA and at NAPF – including the staff of various public relations consultants – who gave me their loyal support, sometimes, in the case of ABTA and NAPF, in circumstances when it cannot have been easy for them to do so. I owe them more than I can ever say.

My family apart, a fundamental value in my life has been music, thanks to my upbringing, and literature, thanks to Oofie Priestland, Bill Sykes and Perdy Cooksey, whose contrasting styles of teaching at Peter Symonds I briefly described in Chapter 3. I also mentioned my last lesson when we had been reading some Homer with Perdy and he expressed the hope that he had taught me something that would stay with me until the end. How right he was. Homer has surely been one of my abiding values. Passages of Homer that would sound trite if written now are not trite – on the contrary, they are touching – because he wrote them getting on for three thousand years ago. Such a case in the Odyssey is where he describes Odysseus's return home from his adventures after 20 years and how his old dog sees him, wags his tails and then dies. Such a passage in the Iliad that lives and breathes our common humanity is where Hector is leaving home to fight the Greeks in the Trojan Wars. He takes his baby in his arms so as to bid him farewell and smiles fondly when the baby, frightened by the plumes on his helmet, starts to cry.

So, too, with individual words. The adjective ῥοδοδακτυλος ('rosy fingered'), which he used to describe the dawn, having been written at the dawn of western civilization itself, remains beautiful in its simplicity and unsullied freshness. I particularly love his expression επι οινοπα ποντον ('on the wine-dark sea'). Wine-dark is a wonderful description – uniquely evocative and adaptable to the changing colours of the Mediterranean Sea in certain lights and moods.

Apart from Homer, it means so much to me that I cannot resist the self-indulgence of recording in my memoirs the following passage from Sophocles' Antigone, which I still remember by heart. King Creon has decreed that Antigone's brother may not be buried within the city walls. She objects to his decision in the following words:

οὐ γαρ τι μοι Zeus ἠν δ κγρυξας ταδε,
οὐδ' ἡ ξυνοικος των κατω θεων Δικη

τοιους ἐν ἀνθρωποισιν ὡρισεν νομους,
οὐδε σθενειν τοσουτον ὡομην τα σα
κηρυγμαθ' ὡστ' ἀγραπτα κ'ἀσφαλη θεων
νομιμα δυνασθαι θνητον ὀντ υπερδραμειν.

I believe someone once said – and if they didn't they should have – that poetry is what is missing when it is translated. In the original Greek, this passage is as simple and sublime as the greatest passages of Shakespeare, with its relentless but gentle undertow of Shakespearian rhythm.

I would not insult Sophocles by trying to translate this passage in a pseudo-poetic form. For what it is worth, it means in prose:

> For it was not Zeus (the head of the Gods) who made such rules as these, nor did Justice, which dwells with the Gods above, promulgate such commands amongst mankind. Nor did I think that the laws of yourself, a mortal, had such power as to override the unwritten and safe laws of the Gods.

As a footnote, I would add that 'safe' is a literal translation of ἀσφάλη which in its context has the connotations of 'sure', 'certain' and even 'eternal' – in contrast to mortal: a good illustration of the sheer impossibility of translation in general and the tawdriness of mine in this particular instance.

Soon after my Aunty Jane died, her daughter (my cousin), Ann, found amongst her belongings a short piece of writing by our Grampa Gray. It so briefly and beautifully encapsulates the essence of his life and humanity that even people who never knew him and to whom I have shown it have been moved. It is wonderfully literate, especially for an almost entirely self-educated person. I attach a copy of 'I am sixty years old' as a second Appendix.

The two grandchildren he mentions are John and myself. His reference to having to answer innumerable questions reminds me of the story he used to tell of an occasion when John had kept on and on at him with one question after another until he (Grampa) was so weary that, in reply to John's umpteenth question, and in a desperate attempt to bring the discussion to a close without offence, he said, 'Really, John, I'm afraid I just don't know.' Whereupon, John said, 'Why don't you know, Grampa?'

My final thought is about the part that pure chance has so often played in shaping my life, as it does everyone's. What would have happened to me if Mrs Fillery had *not* gone away (as I explained she had in my very first words)? What further suffering would I have had to endure if I had had to stay at the Lion School rather than go to the Western School, where I was happy? Would I have gone to Peter Symonds when I was nine if Miss Scott hadn't suggested I should instead of somehow marking time until I was eleven? If Cuzzy hadn't told me I had to change to Classics because John had done well at them, would I have for every been deprived of the supreme value of Homer's great epic poems, of the *Antigone* and the other plays of Sophocles, of the plays of the other great Greek tragedians, and of Greek and Roman literature generally? Would I have appreciated Shakespeare if Oofie hadn't opened my eyes to his genius? Would I have survived Oxford if I hadn't had a father who understood and helped me in my hour of need? Would I have become a solicitor and enjoyed the rewards of my first career in Local Government if my father hadn't been the Deputy County Surveyor of Hampshire? If he hadn't been respected by Mr Wheatley, would he (Mr Wheatley) have agreed to consider taking me on as an articled clerk? If not, would we otherwise have got to know so well the loveliness of the Lake District? How different would my career have been – and would I have seen so much of the world – if I hadn't been on the books of the head hunter whom ABTA asked to find a Chief Executive? Would I have become Director General of NAPF if I hadn't had dealings with Gordon Borrie during ABTA's fight to retain Stabiliser and if the head hunter hadn't thought to consult him?

Would I have married the best of wives if I hadn't happened to stop opposite Isabel in the lottery of that 'Paul Jones' at the Cadena Café when I was sixteen years old?

Such, off the top of my head, are some of the main coincidences in my life as I have so far recounted it. I am luckier than many, if not most, that they were all coincidences whose consequences were fortunate indeed.

There is, however, one coincidence that I have not so far mentioned. How would I have survived to tell my tale if one day towards the end of 1957 it hadn't so happened that I had to wait to have my hair cut and, to while away the time, picked up a certain tabloid newspaper and opened it at a certain page?

Part II

CHAPTER 9

The Unconscious Mind

WHEN I GOT MARRIED after I had completed my first year as an articled clerk and obtained my postgraduate degree, I had emotional problems in the physical expression of my love for Isabel. My own frustration apart, I found it hard to bear causing Isabel such stress and distress. The external pressures of my life were quite bad enough and it needed all my willpower to soldier on without breaking down completely.

After I passed my solicitors' final exams, there were only a few months to go before I was due to start my national service, the 'medical' for which I had passed without any reservations. This meant I would soon have to be separated from Isabel for two years except for short periods of leave. My despair was close to intolerable.

As fate would have it, I was at the barber's one morning and, while waiting to have my hair cut, picked up a popular newspaper (I forget which) and, quite by chance, it contained a column by what we would now call an 'agony aunt'. Her column was about my condition and she invited men who suffered from it to write to her so that she could advise them. In desperation I wrote to her and, impressively, she replied by return advising me to get in touch with a doctor in Harley Street. I immediately made an appointment to see him. After a long examination, he said there was absolutely nothing wrong with me physically and recommended that I should see a psychoanalyst who specialized in this field and whose address and telephone number he gave me.

So it was that at twelve noon the following Saturday I found myself sitting in the consulting room of the late Dr Wilfred Lester in his apartment on the top floor of Harley House in Marylebone Road. Dr Lester not only cured my condition, or, as he would have preferred me to say, helped me to cure myself, but became the most important influence on my adult life.

He was sitting behind a large desk. He wasn't good looking or suave but had an unobtrusive and strangely down-to-earth charm and spoke in a quiet, matter-of-fact way and with a socially neutral accent. He was clearly Jewish with a sallow complexion and thinning black hair swept straight back over his head. I rapidly came to appreciate that he had a profound understanding of human nature in general and my condition in particular, was very intelligent and, more importantly perhaps, remarkably wise, straightforward and practical in his professional approach.

He asked me to tell him as briefly as I could about my childhood, my family background and my life in general. Sometimes he asked questions as I went along. When I had finished after about three quarters of an hour, he put his hands together under his chin, paused for several seconds, and then came straight to the point in what I came to know was his own inimitably direct way.

He said that the root of my problems was that I was emotionally insecure. I had a remarkably powerful 'life force' but however powerful a person's life force may be, it was always limited. I had used up far too much of my life force in overcompensating for my emotional insecurity (to take a recent example, by my compulsion to achieve academic distinction) with the result that far too little of my life force had been available to allow me to grow emotionally. My emotional development had therefore been stunted and my personality was out of kilter and immature.

To digress for a moment, I sometimes recall this even now when I'm pruning my roses. They, too, have a limited life force. If you don't prune them evenly down to the same level, some branches shoot up far too strongly leaving the others to become weak and eventually wither and die.

He went on to say that the 'blockages' that had distorted my emotional development were largely unconscious. His professional view was that they needed to be brought out into my conscious mind if my life force was to be released and redirected into its proper channels, thereby enabling me to harness it to grow emotionally and recover from my condition.

None of this offended me in the slightest, partly because of the matter-of-fact way he said it and partly because I understood very clearly not only what he had said but also that he was absolutely right.

He said I should see him every Saturday morning. He would make a 'frontal assault on my psyche' (which alarmed me more than a little) and would give me injections to help me relax, speak freely and gain insight into my unconscious mind. He asked me to try hard to remember any dreams I might have in the meantime.

I kept my appointment for the following Saturday with some trepidation. He asked me to take off my jacket, roll up my left shirtsleeve and lie on the couch. He went behind a screen and emerged with a syringe and injected a drug into the artery on the inside of my left arm. My recollection is that he said that the drug was methadrine.

Within seconds I felt 'woozy' and said I felt like crying. He said 'Let the tears flow, Mr Elton'. And flow they did. I talked without interruption for nearly an hour. I said nothing of any depth but just got off my chest the external stresses and strains of recent years. He sat at his desk so that he could write as quickly as possible and record as much as he could of what I was saying. I imagine his experience told him that there would be an exceptional outpouring of words following my first injection. In subsequent sessions he sat in an armchair behind my head in the traditional way.

At the conclusion of this torrent of words and tears he asked me if I had remembered any dreams. I said I'd had one last night and could remember it exactly – as I can to this day. I have drawn it below because it is the easiest and clearest way to describe it. I've only omitted one thing because I couldn't fit it in. The engine driver was shovelling coal from the coal tender behind him into the boiler inside the back of the engine. The little lines coming out from the boiler are meant to illustrate the glow coming out of the boiler where the coal was burning fiercely.

He asked me to describe the dream in detail. He made sure he'd written down every detail accurately and painstakingly checked it with me several times to ensure I hadn't left anything out. Then he reminded me that he'd asked me to remember any dreams and asked why I hadn't bothered to tell him about it until he asked me. I said it was because it was a silly dream and so not worth mentioning. He asked me why I thought it was silly. I can remember my reply word for word. 'Because the engine driver was wearing a skirt and if I wanted to go on holiday by train, the last place I'd go to was Leicester.'

He responded by saying that it wasn't at all silly but, in fact, an extremely important dream which we'd often come back to in future sessions. For the moment he'd just make two observations about it. Firstly, when I had described it to him, I hadn't mentioned that the engine driver was wearing a skirt but had accidentally let it slip only when I was 'off my guard' and answering his question spontaneously without thinking about it. Secondly, I dreamt I was going to Leicester last night because I was coming to see him, Dr Lester, in the morning! Since then, I have always called this my 'Dr Leicester' dream and found this play on words rather hilarious.

I mention his two observations at this stage because they well illustrate important unconscious mental processes. Even though 'Lester' and 'Leicester' are pronounced in exactly the same way, the self-critical, guilt-inducing and civilizing part of my unconscious mind (the 'superego') changed the spelling because it was trying to put me off the scent and prevent me from consciously recognizing two things: firstly, that another part of my unconscious mind (the 'id') contained primitive, uncivilized and socially unacceptable impulses and, secondly, that I was directing those impulses towards him ('transference'). Furthermore, I had only let slip that the engine drive was wearing a skirt when I was 'off my guard' because this was the only part of the dream that wasn't a symbol for something else and was recognizable for what it was – a skirt is a skirt. So my superego tried to stop me even from remembering it lest it gave the game away about the meaning of the dream. Of course my superego would have succeeded in its subterfuge if it hadn't been foiled by the expertise of a psychoanalyst who recognized that 'Leicester' was 'Lester' and remembered that I hadn't mentioned the skirt when I first described the dream. (Although the engine driver's cap was obviously a cap, it wasn't in my conscious mind as unambiguously masculine as his skirt was unambiguously feminine, though I came to realize that in my unconscious mind a peaked cap was a powerful symbol of masculinity.)

The above paragraph also illustrates my 'resistance' to discovering the extremely unpleasant things in my 'id' because I said 'the last place I'd want to go to was Leicester'. In other words, the last thing I wanted to do was visit Dr Leicester again lest he found out what my superego was repressing ('repression') into my unconscious mind. I would rather let sleeping dogs lie. I will explain the meaning of the 'Dr Leicester' dream in some detail in the following pages. For the moment, it is worth quoting what Owen Flanagan says about dreams in his book *The Science of the Mind*: 'During sleep the superego is resting enough to let the unconscious surface, but it is not so off guard that it will let any disturbance through'.

You will see from the rest of this chapter how the more horrifying the feelings within my id were, the more powerful was my superego in repressing them, especially when their emergence into the light of day was not helped by dreams so that my superego wasn't resting but was wide awake – alive and kicking! The pressure was like an irresistible force pushing against an immovable object. Many of those feelings were only dragged to the surface after years of treatment with powerful, insight-inducing drugs.

———

Before proceeding with my account of my psychoanalysis, I should make some other preliminary observations.

On two occasions, Dr Lester injected a different drug that made me virtually fall asleep and talk in my sleep. In each case, at the next session he injected a mild dose of the usual drug and told me from his notes what I'd said at the previous session. I gathered from Dr Lester that the use of both drugs was unusually effective in helping me to gain insight into my unconscious mind.

Whenever I gained an important emotional insight – as opposed to making an intellectual deduction – I always felt a great release of energy from right inside my brain which I can only describe as being like a massive discharge of electricity. This was invariably accompanied by a slowing down of my heartbeat, which I could feel quite clearly. Sometimes I felt Dr Lester gently feeling my pulse. An example of this phenomenon is that, if I had a dream that was hard to interpret, he would make several suggestions as to its possible meaning, which had no such effect unless and until I recognized he'd found the right interpretation. As to dreams generally, I came to appreciate how right Freud was in describing dreams as 'the highroad to the unconscious'.

I have to face the fact that I can't avoid making frequent reference to the erect penis and shit. My feeling is that some readers may find the continual use of these words unduly offensive, even though much of what follows is anyway liable to be quite offensive enough. So the former I will call the 'phallus', which is an easy enough substitute. I found it harder to find an acceptable substitute for the latter, though it was the word Dr Lester and I used. Odd though it may at first strike you, I have decided to call it 'poo', which is the word I used as a child. This is quite appropriate in the context of psychoanalysis: even when I use it in an adult context, I am invariably talking about 'the child within the man'. To save tedious repetition of 'Dr Lester', I will call him 'DL'.

Another textual point is that I will frequently make back references to Part I by inserting a little number in brackets, this being the number of the page on which I recounted the event in my past life to which I am referring. This is as much a matter of intellectual rigour as to suggest that you keep turning back to the relevant pages which would be tedious, though you may occasionally find it helpful to jog your memory.

I should explain that I had close on a hundred sessions with DL over a period of ten years from 1957 to 1967. This was partly due to the practicalities of life, especially the pursuit of my local government career in Cumberland, Surrey and Buckinghamshire. Access to London from Cumberland was particularly impracticable so during my time in Carlisle I had only four or five sessions a year, mainly when I was in Winchester for one reason or another, at Christmas for instance.

Finally, I should say that at the end of one of my first sessions, DL said I needed to remain with my wife and not be parted from her for two years, so shouldn't do my national service. He would write accordingly to the appropriate authorities. Within a week – the day before my next session – I received a brown card in an envelope saying I was exempted from national service on medical grounds. There were four categories with boxes, the fourth of which had been ticked. I was in the worst category.

It would be dishonest to say that I – and Isabel – didn't feel an overwhelming sense of relief, though part of me much regretted that I would miss the experience of being an officer in the Royal Artillery. (I had attended the War Office Selection Board at the end of my time at Oxford and been selected for a Commission.) DL said, since I wore glasses, I should tell people I was exempted because of bad eyesight. I wonder what he told people who didn't wear glasses to say. He was obviously used to getting patients exempted from national service.

I was greatly worried about applying for jobs. I told the lie about bad eyesight to Mr Wheatley and said I found it embarrassing. The great tyrant was helpful to me again and when I applied for my job in Cumberland explained the position to Cyrus Swift on my behalf.[72] But in all the other jobs I applied for, I was – to my eternal relief – never asked about national service: whether for instance I had been commissioned – qualities of leadership and all that. This was particularly remarkable when I got my jobs at ABTA and NAPF because the applications were handled by well-known 'head-hunters', who should have looked into my background more thoroughly. I always felt on the defensive during interviews wondering what to say if the question was put. Would I be able to look people in the eye and tell a bare-faced, however understandable, lie? Would I tell the truth and argue that the result of my psychoanalysis was that I had a mature, well-rounded personality and balanced judgement? I rather think that that would have gone down like a lead balloon and they would have thought I must be nuts!

Luckily, it remained an academic question. And I do actually believe that my psychoanalysis *did* enable me to withstand extreme pressures, particularly at ABTA and NAPF, the strain of which I might well have otherwise been unable to survive.

Overall my conscience is clear. What else could I do? Volunteer information that would in all probability have ruined all prospects of a successful career?

In any event, DL proved to be right. It was during those two years that my condition was cured. My mind boggles at the thought of the alternative.

<hr />

At my third session with DL following the one about my 'Dr Leicester' dream, I recounted the disabling phenomenon I used to experience whereby high-pitched, sentimental, 'Pucciniesque' music played by the string section of an orchestra filled my brain when there was nothing else I had to concentrate on very hard and the feeling that a metal band was wrapped tightly round my forehead.[70] DL quietly said 'sublimated farting'! I replied quite forcibly that I'd never heard anything so ridiculous and disgusting and wasn't going to waste my time and money listening to such complete rubbish. I would go home and never come to see him again. The drug made it impossible for me to get off the couch and so I had to stay there and I talked about other things I can't remember. At the end of the session, DL congratulated me on my forceful response.

I could feel the diminishing effect of the drug for about two days after a session and could hardly sleep at all the first night. During that period my eyes were dilated but fortunately no-one except Isabel seemed to notice this.

Quite by chance, on the evening of the second day after this session I was watching a programme on television in which Jimmy Edwards, a rather coarse but, I thought, funny comedian with a large moustache whom people of my generation may remember, was holding a large, tuba-like brass instrument and from time to time blew 'raspberries' which the studio audience and I thought were like noises made by breaking wind – as we were supposed to think. Every time he did this the audience – and I – roared with laughter.

Suddenly I began to tremble and wanted to do a poo. I went to the loo and sat on it doing a big poo and began to sob and shake. Jimmy Edwards' breaking wind noises gradually changed in my brain to the famous introduction to the third act of Wagner's *Lohengrin*, which is dominated by loud Wagnerian brass instruments. The pitch of this music gradually became higher and higher and slowly changed to the equally famous prelude to the first act, the beginning of which is pitched very high and played by violins – a piece of orchestral music that is probably as sublime as any music ever written.

I returned to my armchair and sat there gradually calming down and experiencing what I described earlier as like a massive discharge of electricity from deep inside my brain. From that moment, I never again – not once – experienced the disabling phenomenon of the sound of violins surging through my brain.

At a session soon after that, very unusually, I said nothing after the injection but just lay there with my head spinning round and round. After an embarrassing silence which seemed to last for ages, DL asked me if I'd ever seen a film that particularly frightened me. I immediately recalled 'The Mummy's Hand'.[11] I began to describe how the horrible mummy had slouched through the muddy underground passages, how the mummy stretched an arm out in front of him, how the mummy… I suddenly stopped and said 'mummy, mummy, mummy…'. I could see right inside my brain that I felt this fearsome creature was indeed my own mother.

In successive sessions, DL brought me back to this film and eventually I came to see with stark clarity what it had meant and why I'd screamed all night after I'd seen it.

In summary, my mother had a large phallus (the mummy's projecting arm) concealed within a nasty muddy passage – her vagina. I was petrified to enter this dangerous passage because the nasty hand at the end of the phallus would strangle me if I did. More specifically, if my phallus entered this passage, the nasty hand would tear it off and castrate me. There was also confusion between my mother's vagina and her anus because her vagina was muddy – in other words 'pooey' (to coin an adjective). The mummy's protruding eye was somehow dangerous too and DL said it was 'the evil eye' which represented the concealed phallus though I couldn't then see what he meant. My ambivalent feeling about my mother's sex – the mummy in the film was male – gave me a first vague glimmer of hitherto unconscious, confused, homosexual feelings. In particular, I could see that fear of entering her dangerous passage, with its concealed castrating phallus, meant that sex with another male would be less dangerous because at least everything would be out in the open! Note that I saw this film and had these unconscious fears and feelings just before the war when I was a boy of only seven.

Let us now go back to my 'Dr Leicester' dream. Combining several sessions together, I came to see why DL originally said it was important. The symbolism of the dream was as follows.

The piston going in and out obviously symbolized sexual intercourse. There were three carriages and the engine and carriages each had three wheels because, DL explained, 'three' symbolizes the male genitals. The long funnel was a phallus, the 'dome' behind it was an amalgam of a phallus and a large breast and nipple and the engine itself, which protruded unnaturally far in front of its wheels, was both a phallus and a breast. The coal was poo, some of which was burning fiercely inside the boiler. When DL asked me where in the boiler it was burning, I replied 'in its rear end' – in other words, the anus. The shovel, which I didn't have room to draw, was a phallus which the engine driver periodically inserted into the anus. I should, incidentally, have mentioned and emphasized before that, apart from drinking milk from the breast, the other main emotional experience of a baby is pooing, as we can be amused to see when, in the process, he or she goes red in the face with physical – and emotional – exertion.

The driver was an amalgam of a man (my father) symbolized by the peaked cap and a woman (my mother) illustrated by her skirt.

My mixed-up feelings towards my parents were directed – 'transferred' – towards DL who – substituted for the engine driver – became partly my father, for whom my feelings were incestuously homosexual, and partly my mother, for whom my feelings were incestuously heterosexual. Not only did the blazing fire represent blazing poo but in turn the blazing poo represented hell-fire, down to which I would be sent as a punishment for the sinful emotions – the mortal sins – symbolized by the dream.

The smoke emitted by the phallus and breast was a mixture of 'good', white, life-enhancing milk and 'bad', dark yellowy-brown, life-destroying urine/poo. But it is not as simple as that: 'good' and 'bad' can be reversed. For example, since I experienced 'oral deprivation' of milk at my mother's breast, seen in that light she was unloving and so her milk was not life-enhancing but life-destroying and so 'bad'. I therefore had to seek the alternatives provided by a loving person and so life-enhancing and 'good' – semen and urine/poo with their homosexual and anal connotations.

The confusion was worse confounded by the fact that these various foods, whether good or bad, were discharged both by my father's phallus and my mother's breast, which were themselves confused with each other because I saw a female element in my father and hence his phallus as a breast and a male element in my mother and hence her breast as a phallus. To take just two of the increasing number of permutations this produced, I could see myself drinking good milk from my father's phallus and, by a process of identification with him and role reversal, feeding him good milk from mine. I could clearly see how these two permutations, when eroticized at puberty, could – if not outgrown or suppressed – lead to a basic sexual practice between two homosexual males. If we analyse all the other possible permutations, including confusion between cavities (mouth, vagina, anus) as well as of protuberances, we can begin to glimpse the wide range of sexual perversions to which an excessively deprived and emotionally distorted childhood environment can give rise. A simple example is where voyeurism becomes a substitute for – as opposed to a stimilant to – the real thing. Voyeurs, being orally deprived at their mothers' breast, need to feast their eyes instead.

All this I could clearly see, generally for myself but sometimes prompted by DL. I remembered the incident where we met my father from the train at Winchester station during the war and I felt so disappointed and unsettled because he was wearing a beret instead of his usual officer's peaked cap, which I felt was much smarter.[36] In fact, it was a potent symbol of masculinity. It is particularly strange and significant that, even as I write, I *know* he wasn't wearing a kilt but my mind still 'sees' him wearing a kilt – the skirt in the dream. I can see that when I remembered this incident on DL's couch, I didn't discharge sufficient 'electricity' to get it, emotionally and physically, out of my system – out of my brain.

I remembered when my mother was ill with gallstones and we visited her in hospital.[7] I felt a conflict between her giving me a sweet (good, life-enhancing milk) and the rain splashing on the roof (bad, life-destroying urine). I could see how deeply I felt my 'oral deprivation' of good milk provided by a loving mother, because her giving me just one sweet had pathetically meant so much to me that I remembered it and needed to mention it.

At a later session, I remembered the time at Oxford when various stresses made it difficult for me to sleep and the dear old woman who was my landlady said that perhaps I suffered from night starvation (she couldn't have chosen a psychologically more pertinent expression) and it would help if I had a mug of Ovaltine last thing at night, which she arranged for me to have.[54] I could see that this light brown drink was good milk/poo provided by a loving mother substitute and that this was why it did the trick. I always slept well after that. I recalled my father once saying that when he was 'desperate' he bought a bar of milk chocolate to eat, which made him feel better. I could see that milk chocolate was good milk/poo.

On another occasion, I remembered that when I was on the verge of a complete nervous breakdown a few days before my solicitors' final examinations, Mr Wheatley advised me to drink Sanatogen, which he said would 'heal my nervous system' and by the time the exam started, because I had been drinking 'Mr Wheatley's medicine', I was perfectly fit to tackle them.[71] The Sanatogen was good semen/milk provided by a powerful father figure in whom – for that moment at least – I saw a loving motherly element. I was drinking it from his phallus, which satisfied unconscious homosexual feelings towards him as well as my desperate need to drink a 'good' substitute for milk from my mother's breast.

I remembered that when I was kneeling at the altar before Father Mullarkey taking Holy Communion from him, my mouth was opposite his phallus/breast and I was sucking in his seeds, some of which were white like the communion bread and some of which were brown like the grains of wheat from which bread is made and which reminded me of the seeds in Granny Gray's seed cake which I liked so much.[14] A father (*Father* Mullarkey)/mother figure was feeding me from his/her phallus/breast with good semen/poo comprising the very seeds of life (his sperms). Here, too, I felt unconscious homosexual feelings towards Father Mullarkey, the unconscious satisfaction of which made me feel calm and peaceful inside. I also felt fulfilment of my need (a 'perverted' substitute need though it may have been) to drink milk from my mother's breast. I should add that in this and other 'religious' examples of what was in my unconscious mind, I retained a feeling of 'spirituality' underlying everything else.

At the beginning of one session, I had an important memory touching the theme of an 'anal' personality. I remembered how, when I was a young boy, I collected pennies and piled them up in a secret place in the cupboard in my bedroom. DL said I wanted 'to make a pile' and be 'stinking rich'. Money represented poo and the unconscious reason why some people were stingy was 'anal retention' based on emotional insecurity. This phenomenon was also one source of an introverted personality. On the way out an hour later, I asked him if I could use his loo before I left. I did so and did a big poo. I felt relieved in more senses than one! And I have been more extrovert ever since. DL said nothing but was no doubt unsurprised and amused that I stayed in the loo longer than I would have if I'd just been urinating. It was the only occasion on which I did this. He just showed me out with his usual quiet courtesy.

Moving on from memories specifically associated with my 'Dr Leicester' dream, at a later session I had a particularly strong injection and almost immediately saw rather vaguely a large balloon close to my face, with the bit tied in a knot to keep the air in pointing towards me. DL asked me how big it was and I said 'about three times as big as my head'. He asked me to try to keep thinking about it. I did but it meant nothing to me and kept appearing and disappearing.

As usual, I got almost no sleep that night with the drug coursing through my veins and brain. There were patches when I felt hungry and others when I felt rather sick. I could see the balloon from time to time and sometimes it changed into something hard like an engine on the wing of a seaplane I'd seen taking off from Southampton Water when I was a boy. Sometimes the seaplane's engine seemed somehow threatening. Eventually, I had the amazing experience of feeling I was reliving being fed at my mother's very large breast (about three times as big as my baby's head). Sometimes it was the balloon, soft and comforting. Sometimes it was the engine of the seaplane, hard and threatening – the knot tied to keep the air in the balloon and pointing towards my face being the breast's nipple. If I chewed it too hard, the balloon might explode and destroy me.

I recounted this to DL at my next session and he asked me why I thought it was the engine of a seaplane. I said I hadn't the faintest idea. DL simply said 'la mer'. After a struggle, I suddenly saw that 'la mer' was 'la mère' – my mother! I instantly remembered a recent dream I had forgotten about (the superego at work), in which I saw the sea when I was on a holiday in Southbourne and imagined that half of it was flat and cold and the other half was stormy. I could see (and, more importantly, feel) that this represented how I saw my mother.

DL asked if I knew how I was fed when I was a baby. I said I remembered my parents talking about how hard it was to leave me screaming when I wanted a feed and turned up the volume of the wireless so they couldn't hear me. They said it was the recognised practice in those days to feed babies every four hours willy-nilly (which was true, so it wasn't their fault). Again, I saw that the night after the previous session I had been reliving being fed at my mother's large breasts. Sometimes I had milk stuffed down my throat when I didn't want it, which made me feel sick, and sometimes, when I was hungry, I was left to scream for my very survival – a matter of life and death. DL said 'exactly so' and asked how, as an adult, I'd like to be force-fed when I wasn't hungry and starved when I was. It would have been much better if I had been 'demand fed' but he agreed that it wasn't my parents' fault because they adopted the conventional wisdom of the time. He said I'd been *exceptionally* emotionally demanding ever since I was born and so had felt correspondingly *exceptional* deprivation if my feeding demands and other emotional demands were frustrated – and so in turn had an *exceptionally* strong need to find alternative foods (semen and urine/poo) and to over-compensate generally. Which takes us back to my first session when DL explained that I was emotionally insecure and had spent too much of my life force in over-compensating.

At one session I recalled that I used to fold the sheets on my parents' bed before it had been made and turned them into what I described as a shape of an igloo. I used to crawl through the long entrance and curl up cosily inside the circular interior of the igloo.[7] I could see that I was returning to the comfort and warmth of my mother's womb via her vagina. I felt safe and secure.

At another session I described a dream I'd had the night before, in which Aunty Phyllis was sitting upright in a chair with a large, fierce lion sitting on her lap. This was quite early on in my analysis and DL said the lion represented a large, dangerous, castrating phallus that had emerged from where it had been concealed in her vagina. I recalled that, in her presence, I always felt I had to be on my best behaviour because she kept going on about having good manners.[12] But I could now see that my feeling of unease was exacerbated by the unconscious fear of her which this dream so unambiguously symbolized. I remembered that at the Lion School I liked wearing my blazer with the lion on my *breast* pocket and my peaked cap with the lion on the front of it[5] – representing female and male aspects of my personality. I wanted my two lions to protect me from a lion emerging from Mrs Fillery's vagina and threatening to bite off my breast/phallus. Aunty *Phylli*s and Mrs *Fill*ery merged into one woman. I remembered that my mother's eyes were blue like my blazer and cap.

I also recalled the incident when the crown was removed from the statue of the Virgin Mary in St Peter's Church and I was strangely disillusioned. I could now see that her round, bald plaster head was the top of a huge phallus inside her.[34] The garment she wore was also blue, which again reminded me of my mother's blue eyes.

At another session when I had run out of words, DL asked me whether, as a child, I had read a book that particularly frightened me. I immediately said that Conan Doyle's *The Hound of the Baskervilles* had been my very favourite story and I had been frightened by the hound baying in the misty darkness of the dramatic, stark scenery of Dartmoor.[40] I had read it several times by borrowing the book from the library, and vividly remembered two pictures in it. One was the hound loping down a low narrow valley of rocks with the phosphorous glowing round his chops and teeth. I could see that this represented the 'vagina dentata', the Oxford dictionary's definition of which is 'the motif of a vagina with teeth, occurring in folklore and fantasy and said to symbolize male fears of sexual intercourse'. The other picture was of the escaped convict, Seldon, raising his dishevelled, sallow face from a dark hole in the rocks holding a lighted candle which he was using to send a signal to his sister, who was the butler's wife in Baskerville Hall and was peeping out of a window looking for her brother's signal in the blackness of night, so that her husband could take him some food. The symbolism was obvious – a man closely associated with his sister (an amalgam of my father and Aunty Phyllis) appearing from a dark hole (an amalgam of his anus and her vagina) and holding a *burning* candle (a dangerous phallus).

'Burning' – not lighted – was the word I used with its connotations of poo, as in the burning coal in my 'Dr Leicester' dream.

The other main thing I remembered with a mixture of morbid pleasure and stark fear was Stapleton, the villain of the story, as he darted from one firm piece of ground to another, losing his foothold and gradually sinking into and drowning in the Grimpen mire. It is interesting that in writing this I couldn't at first remember whether it was called a mire, a marsh, a slough or a swamp. I was groping for another, better word to describe what it was. When I was watching television last night, the word suddenly came to me out of the blue (or should I say my id?). It was 'bog'.

Once when I had dried up, DL asked me if I'd ever run in cross-country races at school. I described the incident when I was for once doing badly in the annual cross-country race and had stopped and sat down feeling ill.[41] I could see my illness was bogus. I couldn't face the humiliation of not winning or coming in the first two or three and preferred to have what I thought people would regard as a legitimate excuse. DL said the race symbolized the 'rat race' of life in which I had a neurotic compulsion to succeed and what I did was probably the first sign of impending mental breakdown. I could see this was the case. We talked more generally about my sporting activities and he said there was no reason why I shouldn't have been just as good at team games but preferred to play individual, isolated games like squash – my best game. Apart from being a team game, in cricket – in which I was far too defensive a batsman – you only had to make one mistake and you were out and had the humiliation of letting the whole team down. Similarly, dropping one catch let the whole team down. These were risks I couldn't bear to take.

On one occasion, I described the incident where my father had taken me to see the guns being fired on St Giles' Hill and had been disappointed that they'd been so small.[8] DL said that I'd been disappointed because I felt my father was taking me to see him display his genitals and I'd wanted to identify with him having big genitals so that I felt I had big genitals too and was completely masculine, with no feminine element in me. He pointed out that I'd planned to do my national service in the Royal Artillery because I had an inferiority complex about this. This was immediately blindingly obvious to me. Just imagine the symbolism of wearing a smart officer's uniform with a peaked cap (like the driver in my 'Dr Leicester' dream) and standing behind a big artillery gun with its appropriately angled barrel and two large wheels.

This is a good example of the constant process of 'rationalization' by the conscious mind. The two reasons I told myself why I wanted to join the artillery were that it would be more interesting and that it would be safer than being in the 'PBI' (the 'poor bloody infantry'). These *are* rational reasons, though the second one is rather cowardly. Rationalizations are by definition rational though sometimes only just rational enough to justify our actions – they can be pretty tortuous. But, even though in this example my rationalizations were sensible enough, I could have made at least as rational a case for applying to join other regiments, for instance, the Intelligence Corps which my brother, John, had joined. The precedent was there, staring me in the face. I was well qualified academically and it would have been extremely interesting and even safer than the artillery. I have no doubt that this is an example of making an important decision for reasons of which I was completely unconscious at the time.

There was one occasion on which DL roared with laughter at something I said. And I don't blame him when I think how ridiculous, if telling, it was. He asked me why I hadn't 'gone all the way' with my wife before we got married.[52] Can you believe what I said? I said 'Thou shalt not commit adultery'! Once his spontaneous laughter had died down – was it partly deliberate to make me 'lighten up'? – it wasn't necessary for him to explain that you could only commit adultery if you were already married. Hilariously stupid though my drug-influenced answer may in one sense have been, it was also profoundly and pathetically sad. So deeply ingrained was my sexual guilt as a result of my Catholic upbringing (superimposed on my pre-existing emotional insecurity) that, taken off my guard, I felt that sexual intercourse was always a mortal sin like adultery was supposed to be and the penalty for which was to spend all eternity in the fires of hell. If I hadn't been emotionally insecure in the first place, I wouldn't have taken the guilt induced by 'mother Church' so much to heart. And insecurity ('mummy doesn't love me') and guilt ('mummy says I'm naughty') are the two sides of the same emotional coin.

When I was working for the Buckinghamshire County Council, I suddenly developed a very severe 'slipped disc' in the lower part of my back. All I could do was lie on my back and I can't imagine worse pain. My doctor made me an appointment to see a consultant in six weeks' time. But I was anxious to return to work quickly, so I 'went private' and a few days later saw a consultant in Oxford, my wife having driven me there lying in agony in the back of our estate car. I was carried into his consulting room on a stretcher on which he examined me. He managed to fit a strong corset with metal ribs round my middle, prescribed Valium and said all I could do was lie on my back till it got better. After six or seven weeks, I could just about hobble about and returned to work with a camp bed in my office, which I had to lie on most of the time. It was a period when I was seeing DL every week and eventually I was able to get on a train and hobble my way to Harley House, though the whole process was still agonizing.

With DL's help and some yells of pain, I managed to scramble onto the couch and he gave me what seemed like the strongest dose of the drug I'd ever had. I had proudly handed him a whole bundle of sheets of paper on which I'd somehow managed to write down scores of vivid dreams I'd had during my six or seven weeks' absence. To my considerable annoyance, DL said he wasn't interested in them. He said I'd only had them to put him off the scent and he wanted to find out the real reason why I'd avoided a continuation of my analysis by having a slipped disc.

This – though perhaps because I could see it was true – made me furious. I said I wanted to bash him on the head and cut it open with a large axe again and again and again, bash, bash, bash. I wanted to bash my father on the head in the same way, cut it open, bash his filthy brains out, bash the filthy poo out of his head. I reverted to DL and wanted to bash his filthy brains out, bash the filthy poo out of his brains and out of his whole body. His sallow complexion was like urine/poo. He was nothing but a filthy Jew full of stinking poo. This shameful tirade went on and on. When I eventually dried up, he quietly said 'congratulations!'

I was able to get off the couch and find my way home more easily with the drug still coursing through my brain. I felt an enormous burden of guilt had been *lifted from my back*. Within two days my slipped disc was completely better and, somewhat to the astonishment of the medical profession, has never returned – except, perhaps, for one incident that occurred many years later, long after I'd finished my analysis. I was in our bedroom at our house in Bereweeke Close and had started making the bed, when I suddenly felt an extremely severe pain in my lower back and had to lie motionless on the floor. I thought I must have twisted my back in some way. My wife rang our doctor who said it so happened that he was about to visit another patient not far from us and he'd call on us within half an hour. He gave me a brief examination as I was lying on the floor and prescribed something like Valium and, I think, pain killers. He helped me to get up and lie on the bed, an absolutely agonizing process.

Almost as soon as he'd gone, I remembered that just before the pain occurred I'd heard the hissing, splashing noise of my wife urinating in our en-suite bathroom, having left the sliding door open. As I lay there, I had one of those 'energy releasing' insights and remembered how I used to say the Iguaçu waterfalls still 'haunted' me.[122] I recalled that the water was a browny, silty colour and when we flushed the loo in our hotel the water was the same colour. I could hear the incredibly loud, splashing noise of the rushing brown, silty water of the many huge waterfalls. I could see that my wife urinating had triggered this insight and that I felt I was being drowned by her urine and that it was uriney/poo. I recalled fantasies I had had as a young child in which I smeared my mother with poo and the last session I've described when I was bashing the poo out of my father's brain and body, and the awful thing I'd said about DL being a filthy Jew. I knew enough about my psyche by then to know and feel that guilt was essentially fear of punishment in kind; that I was guilty about my childhood fantasies and the awful 'filthy Jew' session, and was being punished in kind by my mother drowning and killing me with uriney/poo. I saw my mother as the familiar amalgam of herself and my father and the passage from which she was urinating as a pooey passageway like the one in *The Mummy's Hand*, an amalgam of her/his vagina/anus. I imagined him/her breaking wind from his/her anus and me being gassed to death by the breaking wind, like the Jews in Auschwitz, a punishment in kind for my intolerable guilt. I saw for the first time that being injected by DL was being penetrated by him! All this poured out with a great release of electricity-like energy even though it was many years since I'd had an injection.

Almost immediately, the pain in the bottom of my back – was that a 'Freudian slip' indicating pain in my bottom caused by penetrating injections? – began to ease and within an hour had gone altogether. I could move quite freely. My wife was about to cancel a game of tennis I was due to play that afternoon but I said I thought I could play after all. And so I did. The embarrassing thing was that, by a strange coincidence, my doctor was playing in a four a few courts away and kept looking in my direction. I imagine he could scarcely believe his eyes and have often wondered what on earth he was thinking.

DL's memory seemed remarkable. Somehow, I suppose, he had the trained and experienced gift of remembering things I'd said that were significant to him, if not consciously to me. I could often hear him flicking over the cards on which he presumably wrote down only what he regarded as key points. At the end of my session about the *Hound of the Baskervilles*, he pointed out that I'd described Seldon as having 'sallow' skin and reminded me that I had used the same word – sallow – to describe him when I called him a Jew full of filthy poo. He further reminded me of some things I had mentioned but which I'd completely forgotten I'd ever told him: that I had also described as 'yellowy brown' the man's face peeping round the door at the Lion School[3] and my mother's face when ill in hospital with jaundice[7], and that I'd said that Mr Quin at the Lion School[5] and foxy-face at the Western School[19] had worn brown suits. These, he pointed out, were the only occasions on which I described the colour of people's skins or clothes. These various colours of course represented poo.

I had three major insights long after I'd finished my analysis.

The first was several years later when I was swimming in the sea somewhere abroad, though I can't now remember where. Suddenly, for no apparent reason, I remembered that, in one of my sessions with DL when I had talked about *The Mummy's Hand*, I had mentioned how one of the mummy's eyes had protruded through the strips of rag wound round his head and DL had simply said it was 'the evil eye', which represented the concealed castrating phallus. When I had thought about this before that day, I had thought it was absurd because a phallus looked nothing like an eye. As I was swimming in 'la mer', I suddenly saw that, if you looked at a phallus head on rather than from the side, it was indeed similar to an eye. My superego had been hard at work for years preventing me from seeing this. This revelation stayed on my mind as I was sitting in the sun in a deckchair after my swim. I felt I was a black native somewhere in Africa and a witch doctor was holding an evil eye in front of my face and I was shrivelling up. I felt a complete identity with an African native and a remarkable and moving feeling of complete identity with humanity as a whole. I came to see that the witch doctor was DL and vice-versa. I remembered a film I'd seen many years ago in which a man dressed in a black cloak was holding a small crucifix in his hand and with it was threatening a man who was cowering and shrivelling in fear in the corner of a cell. I remembered the incident when Dr Freeman gave me the cane and was wearing his black gown and I didn't like the eye, which seemed bulging and dominant, staring at me and I felt shrivelled up inside.[33] I also remembered that I had hated hot sunshine ever since my fair skin had been badly burnt as a child and that DL had once said that the sun generally represented the male/father and the moon the female/mother (the Goddess Diana in mythology). I remembered a silly joke that I used to think was very funny. Someone asked an old lady which she thought was the most useful, the sun or the moon, to which she replied 'the moon' because it shone at night when we needed it most because it was dark. I remembered the beam of sunlight shining on the yellowy-brown face of the man peeping round the door at the Lion School and imagined that the specks of dust floating about in it were like little sperms.[3] I felt that the face was my father's pooey face and that the shaft of sunlight was a shaft of his semen that would 'shaft' me and make me shrivel up. I moved into the shade of a tree.

Perhaps the most shattering of all the insights I experienced after I'd finished my psychoanalysis occurred when I was about sixty years old. I was going through something of a spiritual crisis and feeling extremely anxious about things, including my problems at work with the NAPF. Instead of having my usual sandwich at my desk, I went for a walk and wandered into Westminster Cathedral, the modern Catholic Cathedral only a few minutes walk from my office in Grosvenor Gardens. I had looked in once or twice before and had never liked the interior architecture, much preferring the simplicity of the nave of Winchester Cathedral. In particular, I hadn't liked the large crucifix hanging at the far end from where I was sitting at the back. I thought it was 'flashy', overwhelmingly too big, grotesque and in a vague sort of way rather menacing. Then I suddenly recalled the incident I've just described about the man in the black cloak holding a small crucifix which made the man in the corner of the cell cringe with fear and shrivel up, and felt he was like the African witch doctor holding the evil eye. I felt to my horror, amidst mounting inner conflict and tension, that the contrastingly huge crucifix in the Cathedral represented the male genitals and that the three spurts of blood pouring from Christ's hands and feet represented castrated male genitals. I remembered my 'Dr Leicester' dream when DL had said that three represented the male genitals. I thought about the Holy Trinity – God the Father, God the Son and God the Holy Ghost (which was the word I'd been brought up with rather than the more modern and infinitely superior Holy Spirit). Sometimes the crucifix and three spurts of blood were my father's castrated genitals and sometimes mine, his son's. And I remembered how I'd always been frightened of ghosts and how Allie had said that Winchester was like a 'ghost-town' during the black-out in the war.[24] I recalled the incident when I heard the moaning and groaning soldiers and thought they might have to have their arms and legs cut off and was glad my father only had to have his boots cut off.[24] I felt I had castrated my father and was filled with overwhelming guilt about it. He had punished me in kind by castrating me. I could see that my superego had pulled out all the stops to overcompensate and prevent me seeing that, in fact, my id wanted him to be castrated – to have his limb(s), his member(s) cut off.

The whole experience felt like the mighty, moving, climactic dénouement of Wagner's opera *Tristan and Isolde* – the 'Liebestod' (love/death). It was the ultimate combination and consummation of Christ's love and death on the crucifix, the ultimate humanist and religious experience, the ultimate climactic experience in both sexual and spiritual terms. Indeed, the organ was blasting forth huge breakings of wind sublimated in my brain to become one of the most sublime pinnacles of humanity's musical creations – a throwback to my third session with DL.[171] Muddled up with all this, I had the conflicting feeling that I was being gassed to death by the organ's breaking of wind, again like Jews in a gas-chamber, a punishment in kind for my mortal sins. I saw the gas-chamber as the boiler in 'the rear end' of the train engine in my 'Dr Leicester' dream and that I would be punished for my mortal sins in the burning poo of hell.

I was so shaken to my foundations that I could only sit there till all the electricity-like energy had escaped from the deepest depths of my brain. Eventually, I tottered back to my office giving the receptionist a sheepish grin because I was so late.

I have just had a further horrific insight as I am writing this. It was not an intellectual deduction because it was spontaneous and I feel a release of energy and very shaken and disturbed. Christ was King of the Jews.

The last experience I will recount occurred only about four years ago at the time of writing when I was sixty six years old. I suddenly felt my stomach swelling up and that I was like a woman in labour. I felt I was having a 'Caesarian', the surgeon's knife having cut open my stomach with cuts in the shape of a cross. I also felt he had cut off my genitals so that I was a woman able to give birth in the natural way, though I felt I was breaking wind loudly from my vagina. I suddenly felt I was giving birth, not only to my four children, but also to my brother. Having given birth to them all, my stomach remained hugely swollen and turned into a large globe of the world. An umbilical cord joined my stomach/globe to my brain and milk seemed to be flowing round and round, from my brain to my stomach/globe and from that, via the umbilical cord, back to my brain.

I felt as if I had eaten my children and brother as babies and sucked them into my inside and was greatly relieved at having got them all 'out of my system'. I recalled, almost word for word, DL once saying that 'we internalize the objects of our affection so that we can retain them, especially if we are emotionally immature like you, Mr Elton'. I felt I had externalized my children and brother by giving birth to them and pooing them out of me instead of retaining them inside my stomach and bowels. I felt a less self-destructive *over*-identification with them and a less neurotic *over-a*nxiety on their behalf. I kept feeling all this for two or three days and nights.

Remember that, in the long-lasting experience I'm describing, my brain and stomach were joined by an umbilical cord through which milk flowed round and round. I could again see and feel that as a baby the only things that ultimately mattered to me were my stomach craving for milk and my brain craving to stay alive. I could see and feel that craving for milk and craving to stay alive were one and the same thing. I could see and feel that, because these cravings were one and the same thing, so too were my brain and my stomach. I came further to see and feel that the large globe in my stomach was telling me that this one thing, this amalgam of stomach and brain, was my whole world, the ultimate, fundamental essence of my psyche, of my personality, of my whole being. I came further to see and feel that the foundations of my whole world were insecure – the cravings of my brain/stomach had not been satisfied. I could see and feel that the adverse effects of this could have been mitigated, and it would not have mattered so much, if my emotional environment as a child had been conducive to the restoration of my world's insecure foundations and to the achievement of greater emotional maturity and, by definition, better mental health. Sadly, my emotional environment during my childhood was not conducive to the fulfilment of my overwhelming emotional needs.

———◆———

Such, then, are the main insights I gained during and after my psychoanalysis. There were literally hundreds of others which were less significant and sometimes variations on the same themes.

Having glanced through what I have written, I noticed with some amusement three occasions where, despite all my experience of such matters, my unconscious mind still contrived to play tricks on me. The most obvious example was my drawing of my 'Dr Leicester' dream, in which I omitted the spade shovelling coal into the 'rear end' of the engine.[167] I can now see that this was a classic case of resistance, repression and rationalization. Of all the many aspects of that comprehensive dream, this was by far the most unpleasant because it was unusually direct and unambiguous in its symbolism. My superego had, therefore, to go into overdrive to resist the re-emergence of its meaning into the conscious light of day, which was most likely to have been triggered if I had represented it visually. My superego prevented me from drawing the spade by keeping it temporarily repressed in my id and leaving my conscious mind to manufacture some rational explanation for its omission. The best I could do was think up the facile explanation that there wasn't room to draw it.

The second example is more subtle but well illustrates a device which my unconscious mind often adopted in the course of my psychoanalysis. I refer to the unconscious symbolism of the 'beam' of light that shone on the man's face peeping round the door at the Lion School.[3] When I described the meaning of this important memory, I was momentarily caught off my guard and called it a 'shaft' of light.[184] This was a link in my unconscious chain of thought that lead to my automatic use of the expression 'shafting me', which in turn made me confront more forcibly than before the most horrifying aspect of this memory which my superego was particularly anxious to repress and had to an extent been successful in so doing until my mind adopted the subterfuge of what I call 'verbal linkage'. It is no accident and no wonder that the two examples of repression I have given each in its own way – by means of different symbols (the spade and shaft of light) – symbolize my father buggering me and, by a process of role reversal, vice-versa.

The third thing I noticed was that, when I described how I appreciated the subtle beauty of the German language when Ronald Smart sang lieder at our musical evenings, the example I remembered was the beauty of 'flöte' compared with the ugliness of 'flirter'.[43] This was clearly an example of association of ideas and verbal linkage, because I didn't like my mother being a flirter.

As John Locke said as long ago as the seventeenth century, words are signs of ideas in the mind or of relations between ideas. What he could not have realized is the same is true of ideas in the unconscious mind. Hence the well-known 'association of ideas' and 'free association', which are fundamental tools of psychoanalysis in the use of which the unconscious mind has a ruthless vebal logic of its own, verbal and otherwise.

More general questions arise about the validity of Freud's theories as opposed to those of, say, Jung and Adler. In this context, as in most others, I am what I call a 'both/and' person as opposed to an 'either/or' person.

I regard it as a false question to ask someone whether he or she is a Freudian *or* a Jungian *or* an Adlerian. We should therefore consider for a moment Jung's origination of the concept of introvert and extrovert personalities; his disassociation from Freud's preoccupation with infantile sexuality as the sole determinant of personality; his emphasis on intuition and mystical and religious factors in the unconscious mind; and his notion of the 'collective unconscious' as the part of the unconscious mind which is derived from ancestral memory and experience and is common to all humankind. We should also – if only briefly – consider Adler's view that culture and society are significant factors in causing mental illness and his introduction of the concept of the inferiority complex.

Taking Adler first, I found nothing in my experience of 'Freudian' psychoanalysis that was inconsistent with his views. Dr Lester, though essentially a Freudian, explored my Adlerian inferiority complex which, as far as I could see, was quite consistent with my Freudian infantile sexual insecurity. Moreover, the culture and society which comprised my adult environment were certainly significant determinants of my mental illness.

The adverse effect on my mental health of 'culture' is demonstrated by the then guilt-inducing culture of the Catholic church (remembering that, just as guilt and insecurity are two sides of the same emotional coin, so in turn are insecurity and inferiority) and by the intensive academic culture of Oxford (remembering my acute awareness that my academic standard was inferior to that of Maurice Platnauer and my two colleagues from Winchester College, and particularly the demonstration by Jimmy McKie of his supposed intellectual superiority – and by implication my own intellectual inferiority – at my first philosophy tutorial which finally led to my complete mental breakdown[53]).

The adverse effect of 'society' is demonstrated by the 'rat race' which I felt compelled to win by getting to the top of the tree in my professional career (remembering that the first indication of impending mental ill-health was my self-induced illness during the cross-country race – the rat race – at Peter Symonds[41]).

We can see, too, a clear relationship between culture and society. If the culture of the Catholic church and Oxford hadn't played a significant role in inducing my inferiority complex in the first place, I wouldn't then have felt so compulsive a need to over-compensate for it by winning society's rat race.

Turning now to Jung, his theory of introvert and extrovert personalities was entirely consistent with my Freudian anal retention and release.[176] Furthermore, my Adlerian inferiority complex was consistent with Jung's view that my Freudian infantile sexuality was not the sole determinant of my personality.

When I sat down to write this morning, I had no idea that I would include the following paragraphs which record a series of insights that have just poured out of my brain by a process of free association to which I gave free and full rein. Although it is a digression, I have decided to include these insights for reasons I will explain after I have recorded them by copying out the notes I quickly scribbled using a self-made shorthand I haven't used since I took notes at lectures at Oxford. After I had written these passages, I put certain words or parts of words in italics.

I see before me, not – like Hamlet – a dagger with its handle towards my hand, but Cyclops, a fearsome giant with one big eye in the middle of his head like the one in the Odyssey written by Homer thousands of years ago. I see before me an image of an Egyptian god painted on the wall of a temple thousands of years ago. He or she – my father or mother – I don't know which – has a black falcon's head turned to one side revealing one eye and a sharp beak. I see its blackness as death – *destruction* – *castration*. I see before me the mummy's hand in the film that frightened me when I was a child.[10] The mummy is a male mummy, a mixture of my father and mother. It is wrapped in *swaddling* clothes, revealing one of its eyes. It is Egyptian, like the god/goddess with the black falcon's head. I see myself wrapped in *swaddling* clothes like baby Jesus. I see Jesus on the big crucifix in Winchester Cathedral – I mean Westminster Cathedral[184] – and the small crucifix held by the man in black who was the African witch doctor.[183] Jesus was the King of the Jews.[185] I see the small crucifix is the evil eye of the male mummy in the long dark passage in the film which is like the tube from which a torpedo is being fired from a submarine – from under the sea. The submarine is now firing a *ball*istic missile which is blowing my *balls* to smithereens. The submarine is firing the ballistic missile from the depths of the Atlantic Ocean near Cape *Carniverous*. Under the sea is the lost island of Atlantis, which is a warm happy place even though the sea is cold. Electricity is pouring out of my watery brain, my watery grave, pouring out like the rain outside is pouring, *pissing*. It is pissing with *rain*, with 'la *reine*', the Queen, who *rains* over us, the Queen Mother, the rain pissing on the *roof* when I visited my mother in hospital[187], pissing on to the *roof* of my mouth, pissing from 'la mer's' dangerous tube where a dangerous torpedo, a dangerous tool is hidden. The energy still pours out like water and *elec*tricity which is a dangerous mixture which will *elocute* – I mean electrocute – me to death as it is *prone* to do. I feel *prostrate*, pro*strated*, *castrated* by my father's/mother's tool which is giving me *prostrate* cancer, *prostate* cancer. I can't discharge semen. The energy from my brain is now releasing semen from my prostate, discharging my prostate cancer, *churning* it all out like churning milk from a *milk churn, chest, breast*, discharging my piss, my poo, my pains from chains in a dark prison *cell*, in the deep *cells* of my brain, making me *extroverted, extravert, extracted* like a painful tooth, a rotten tooth full of decay, detritus, waste matter in my mouth, shit in my mouth. One of my teeth is hurting now. I am pulling out the teeth of a man in a black *cape* like Dr Freeman caning me wearing his black gown and his sinister (left) eye staring at me[33], pulling out the teeth of a *carniverous* lion like the one on Aunty Phyllis's *lap* in my dream.[177] The dream is reoccurring in *Lap*land in the cold Arctic Circle. I am using Hamlet's dagger with its handle towards my hand to cut out the lion's eye. I feel like a Roman gladiator being torn to pieces and eaten by a lion. I am cutting out the Cyclops' eye, the eye of the black falcon, gouging it and hacking it out by the roots like the roots of my hurting tooth. An eye for an eye, a tooth for a tooth. I am a Jew. I really *feel* all these insights because they are passing the *acid* test of being accompanied by vast discharges of energy. I now feel the rain outside is *acid rain* and see again an image of Queen Elizabeth the Queen Mother, warm and smiling, but it keeps merging and 'de-merging' with an image of Elizabeth I, an '*acid reine*', cold and unsmiling, staring at me with a destructive stare. I need to have a *break*, to *break wind*, to shelter behind a *wind break*, to shelter from the cold wind, Boreas blowing from the cold

North, but the wind blowing from the warm South is warm, like the warm wind blowing from the South at *Southbourne* when I was on holiday as a child.[8] I feel *born* again in the balmy *South*. For the first time in over forty-five years I now recall DL once saying that the cold North symbolized the homosexual element in my personality. (I must have had insights that led him to say this.) I didn't then see what he meant but I suddenly do now because the cold Elizabeth I is castrating me with her evil eye and so making me feel feminine. Aunty Phyllis is cold like Lapland. Not so with the warm Queen Mother. Hence my confused, infantile sexuality, partly warm and heterosexual, partly cold and homosexual.

I have just had a break because I was dying for a cup of coffee, which I noticed was sweet and brown, and a cigar, as is my wont. I had two remarkable insights. I said to myself (which I never had before) that I was smoking a *Hamlet* cigar and then suddenly realized that it was not Hamlet who said: 'Is this a dagger which I see before me, its handle towards my hand? Come, let me clutch thee. I have thee not and yet I see thee still.' I remembered that it was Macbeth, as I know perfectly well, having studied *Macbeth* so thoroughly and memorably with Oofie for my School Certificate. I also said to myself that I had expressed a stream of *unconsciousness* unlike James Joyce when he wrote his famous stream of *consciousness* in his great book *Ulysses*. I then recognized that Ulysses was the Latin name for the Greek Odysseus. I then thought again of the Cyclops in Homer's Odyssey.

Having finished my coffee and cigar, something inside me made me look up 'prone' in a thesaurus I hardly ever use. The second of the seventeen so-called synonyms was – to my conscious surprise – 'prostrate'.

I now feel emotionally a deep sense of peace and spiritual unity with all humanity – specifically with primitive Africans, ancient Egyptians, Greeks and Romans, Laplanders, Jews and Christians.

I am resuming writing on the morning after I wrote the above digression from the mainstream of my thoughts. I was too exhausted and sleepy to write any more yesterday. I have now italicized certain words or parts of words to illustrate what I call 'alliterative verbal linkage' and 'rhyming verbal linkage'. Not forgetting that ideas can only be expressed in words, I have also italicized some examples of 'bridging words' where a word in the chain of linkage has no significance *per se* but is a means whereby the unconscious sometimes gropes to find words (ideas) that *are* significant – for example, the words (ideas) that followed from 'swaddling', 'churning' and 'prone'. I also noticed that, in introducing these insights, I said I had given them full and free *rein*. I wrote the introductory paragraph after I wrote my insights and can now see clearly that 'la reine' was still active somewhere in my brain – another example, like 'la mer', of *'foreign* verbal linkage'! My reference to 'Cape Carniverous' (instead of Cape Canaveral) was a classic Freudian slip of the tongue that gave the game away. And why did the Atlantic Ocean emerge from my unconscious rather than, say, the Pacific Ocean? The answer, I am sure, is that 'Atlantic' was a bridging word that unconsciously led to my reference to Atlantis – a beautiful, legendary island overwhelmed by the sea (which I did not consciously realize I had heard of before). It was a place of warmth and love for which I yearned, hidden deep beneath the cold sea (la mer/mère). Cape Canaveral is, of course, on the Atlantic coast of North America.

Three days later: I dreamt last night that I was stabbing myself in my chest with a dagger. I woke up sweating with fear and terror.

I realized at once that the dream was somehow connected with my false insight that it was Hamlet who saw a dagger before him. I have looked back to see exactly how I had described this incident in the hope that it would help me to interpret the meaning of the dream. In turning back the pages, I noticed that I had said that I was *'dying for'* a cup of coffee and a cigar and recalled that it was while I was drinking my coffee and smoking my cigar that I realized that I had mistakenly referred to Hamlet. When I found the passage in question, I found that I first denied that I saw any dagger at all and then instantly described it as Hamlet's instead of Macbeth's. I realized that this was another classic Freudian slip of the tongue. My id had taken my superego momentarily off guard and made me let slip what I didn't want to know – that *qua* Hamlet I was wondering whether to kill myself ('to be or not to be') as a self-punishment because *qua* Macbeth I had killed Duncan, a King, that most powerful of father-figures (just as the Queen Elizabeths were two aspects of a Queen, that most powerful mother-figure).

For the first time I feel something emotionally that I have long known in the intellectual abstract. Deeply buried in my mind is a Freudian 'death instinct' or 'death wish'.

'Come let me clutch thee' – the dagger that I see before me. 'I have thee not and yet I see thee still.'

One day later: I had a seemingly dreamless sleep last night. I do not 'see thee still'.

Two days later: Another insight emerges into the light of day. I see an image of the Virgin Mary as if I were Bernadette at Lourdes. She is the Queen of Peace. Peace reigns. It is a peaceful *reign* – a warm, soft *rain*. She is a virgin mother. There is no need to kill my father and then myself – no need, like Oedipus, to castrate myself by gouging out my eye*balls* with a dagger. My Oedipus complex feels released, resolved. I feel relaxed and at peace and at one with the whole world and with myself.

I feel no guilt, no need for forgiveness. Such a need falls momentarily away. 'It droppeth as the gentle *rain* from heaven upon the place beneath.'

All these powerful insights occurred when I was intending to consider Jung's ancestral memories in the collective unconscious, his intuition and his mystical and religious elements of the unconscious mind.

One example of the latter is that the discovery of my buried memory of Atlantis was a profoundly mystical experience. Recalling that I described the unconscious Freudian meaning of receiving Holy Communion from Father Mullarkey, I looked back and discovered that I had emphasized that I retained a feeling of spirituality underlying everything else.[175] Freud's unconscious, infantile sexuality and Jung's unconscious mystical and religious feelings are not mutually exclusive.

As to the collective unconscious, I can see clearly that, although my many insights about the evil eye were triggered by events in my own lifetime, such events were not their source. They were, so to speak, already there for the asking – even when I was only seven years old. Seeing the film, *The Mummy's Hand*[10], triggered my insight about the evil eye but was not the source of its presence in my mind. So, too, I did not remember the evil eye from reading about the Cyclops in the Odyssey at Oxford or from seeing the falcon's eye when on holiday on the Nile ten years ago. The Odyssey and the painting of the falcon brought to my consciousness a *pre-existing* memory. As I write, I intuitively feel a profound spiritual identification with Homer and an unknown Egyptian artist, each unconscious of his own ancestral memory, not consciously knowing why he wrote or painted as he did (Homer round about 800 BC and the Egyptian artist in the second or third millennium BC).

The presence of the evil eye in the human mind is interestingly illustrated by the following passage from the Gospel of St Matthew (Chapter 6, verses 22 and 23).

> The lamp of the body is the eye: if therefore thine eye be single, thy whole body shall be full of light. But if thine eye be evil, thy whole body shall be full of darkness. If therefore the light that is in thee be darkness, how great is that darkness!

This is echoed in 'The Book of Mormon', which two Mormons gave me when they recently called at my house. Seeing there was an index, I looked up 'eye', and was hardly surprised to find the writer refers to 'your wickedness and abominations...under the glance of the *piercing eye* of Almighty God'. (Jacob 2: 10)

It is surely no coincidence that we tend to say 'I looked him in the eye' and use the singular – in both senses – expression 'the mind's eye'. The expression 'I'll keep my eye on you' is suitably menacing.

In the context of this chapter, there is another respect in which I take a 'both/and' view of things.

Some psychiatrists who are experts in prescribing medication argue on the lines that their pills do more good in two weeks than psychoanalysis does in two years. They reject the charge that medication only cures the symptoms of mental illness by arguing that the symptoms *are* the illness. Psychoanalysts, on the other hand, are liable to demur: far better, they say, to get to the root of the problem by curing 'the whole person' than merely to tinker with the superficial manifestations of the underlying mental illness.

It seems clear to me that both medication and psychoanalysis have their place. It is a question of horses for courses. That easily said, it can be extremely difficult to know which course is suited to which horse.

DL once said to me that he was interested in curing the whole person. He did not, however, embark upon psychoanalysis willy-nilly. It is, for instance, within my knowledge that he advised a homosexual man (unknown to me) that he could analyse him for five sessions a week for five years at very great cost but the likelihood of 'curing' him was only about ten per cent. He also told my father, whom I referred to him when he was clearly mentally ill during his crisis about separating from my mother, that it was too late in life for psychoanalysis to be worthwhile and prescribed medication to help him through that difficult and distressing period of his life.

For my part, one of the few things in life of which I am reasonably sure is that psychoanalysis assisted by drugs was the right course for me. DL's use of drugs was, however, controversial and tends to be frowned on by 'purists' in the field of psychoanalysis, including the relevant professional bodies.

I am not sure why this should be so. I can only speculate that it would be argued that psychoanalysis without drugs would have been a more 'natural' way for me to explore and express my unconscious thoughts and feelings and would therefore have been a more effective process in the long run. Whether that would have been so, I do not, of course, know. But 'in the long run' are the operative words. I well remember that, at an early session, when I had presumably confessed to some minor sexual peccadillo, DL said that without drugs it would have taken a year 'to drag that out of you' – which I don't doubt for one moment. His methods were nothing if not practical. Perhaps opponents of his use of drugs fear they might lead to addiction. Certainly there were times when I could hardly wait to be injected at my next session but, in a controlled and professional medical environment, there was never any danger of addiction on my part.

I have to say, however, that in my case DL was not completely successful in his unstinting efforts to cure the whole person. Understanding that he could be of no further help, he eventually made this gently but firmly clear. This I understood and discontinued my sessions with him, though he was at polite pains to say that he would be available if I was ever again really desperate.

It is difficult to quantify but I would hazard a guess that he was, say, 70 per cent successful in curing my whole person. Why so? The reason was that after my first session, when I was taken off my guard, I never again cried on the couch. In Freudian terminology, I was incapable of expressing myself or reliving my childhood with sufficient 'affect' (emotion). DL sometimes said when he was injecting me that he wanted me to express my feelings and emotions and not just embark upon an intellectual exploration of my unconscious. I remember that he occasionally tried in vain to make me cry by calling me 'poor little Michael' (instead of the usual 'Mr Elton') at a particularly sensitive moment. His efforts were to no avail because the emotional deprivation suffered by my young, hyper-sensitive brain had been so extreme that the multi-layered barriers (defence mechanisms) built to prevent the floodgates from opening and releasing unbearable emotions in floods of tears were well nigh impregnable.

On one occasion, DL tried to hypnotize me. Having given me a very mild injection, he stood beside me and asked me to look at the top of his pen. He spoke soft words I can't remember and then asked me if I could open my eyes. It took me a while to do so. It was an extraordinary experience to have to use all my strength and will-power to lift up my eyelids. I have often wondered what would have happened if he had been successful in hypnotizing me. Would it have opened the floodgates?

Thankfully, I have become increasingly lachrymose with the passing years, not easily restraining tears when confronted with the evils of the world or the sadness of individual human beings, or when experiencing the sublime beauty of great poetry or painting or especially music. (If I go to an opera, I don't feel I've had my money's worth if I haven't shed a tear!)

This capacity to express my emotions, combined with the powerful insights that, as we have seen, still occasionally emerge – apparently unsolicited – from my unconscious, has further released my life force and so allowed it to direct me further along the difficult and hazardous path leading towards the emotional maturity and mental wellbeing of my whole person. Whether that is a destination at which any of us can ever finally arrive is amongst the questions I discuss in the following chapters.

Part III

Part III

CHAPTER 10

The Material Mind

I DESCRIBED IN THE preceding chapter how, whenever I gained important insights, I felt previously unconscious thoughts and feelings being discharged from the depths of my brain in what felt like waves of electricity. The more I recall and relive these experiences, the more clearly I can see that, just as a transmitter generates and transmits electro-magnetic 'radio waves' carrying unique signals and messages, so my brain was generating and transmitting 'brainwaves' carrying unique thoughts and feelings.

Although any run-of-the-mill physicist presumably has little difficulty in comprehending that words or notes of music which are being broadcast are physical entities somehow attached to radio waves, my unscientific mind boggles at the thought. It does, however, just about enable me to grasp the concept that our thoughts and feelings are also physical entities somehow attached to our brainwaves. After all, the most advanced microscopes can no more identify the words or notes attached to radio waves than the most advanced scanners or encephalograms can identify the thoughts and feelings attached to our brainwaves.

Memories as such are more obviously physical entities stored away somewhere in our brains. This is consistent with Jung's theory that some memories can be physically inherited. In short, I believe that the so-called 'mind' is indistinguishable from the physical brain.

I recognize that in three short paragraphs I have dismissed Cartesian dualism (Descartes' theory that the brain and mind are separate substances) which was one of the most influential milestones in the history and development of philosophical thought. I recognize, too, that I have done so on the basis of subjective, if remarkably strong and clear, personal insights. On the other hand, modern advances in neuro-physiology, based on a scientific study of the brain, support in rapidly increasing detail the view that, for every thought or feeling we experience, there is a correlated physical state of our brains. Indeed, a team of neuroscientists from the Weizmann Institute in Israel now claim to have evidence that it will one day be possible to use a brain scanner to read minds. The material nature of the mind is further evidenced by the following examples arising from my own mental and physical illnesses.

The first example occurred when my complete loss of self esteem triggered the clinical depression diagnosed by Dr Sutton. Clinical depression means that the chemistry of the brain has changed so much that, by definition, even the most strong-minded person can't pull himself together as is sometimes urged by the uncomprehending. You might as well ask a physically handicapped person to run a four-minute mile. I could feel the prescribed anti-depressant changing the chemistry of my brain so that it no longer discharged depressive feelings. I actually experienced a strong 'tingling' feeling in my head and Dr Sutton said he was not surprised that I could 'feel something happening' in my brain.

Although thoughts are not easily distinguishable from feelings, some time ago my doctor, Tim Cotton, asked me if I had 'instant negative thoughts'. I said I did, giving the example that when the phone rang I would immediately fear some bad news, for instance that one of my grandchildren had had an accident. He changed my prescription to a more sophisticated anti-depressant and very soon my instant negative thoughts disappeared. Now when the phone rings, I think, for instance, that it is someone ringing about the arrangements for tennis next Thursday. The chemistry of my brain having changed again, it no longer discharges 'instant negative brainwaves'! Thoughts, like feelings, are physical phenomena generated and transmitted by the brain.

Two main consequences follow from my conclusion that the mind is a material object indistinguishable from the brain, the significance – or even the truth – of which is not as widely or as well recognized as I believe it should be.

The first is that, if you are suffering from a mental illness, there is something physically wrong with your brain, and so with the thoughts and feelings it discharges. To make the usual distinction between a physical illness and a mental illness, though no doubt helpful in most contexts, is therefore to make a distinction without a difference. They are both physical illnesses. So you should not be ashamed of having a mental illness any more than you would be ashamed of having appendicitis (though you should, of course, be ashamed of any anti-social behaviour it may, if severe, cause). By the same token, other people should not stigmatize you as weak or feeble any more than they would if you had cancer.

The second consequence is consistent with this. Since mental illness means that your brain is in some way physically ill, it is not as surprising as so many people still seem to think that, as the powerhouse controlling your body, it can generate and transmit signals that cause other parts of your body to be physically ill. Indeed, your brain may well regard it as the lesser of two evils to cause another part of your body to suffer an illness than to face up to its own illness and particularly the cause of that illness. My own slipped disc was a classic example of this process.[181] My brain preferred to cause excruciating pain in my lower back than to recognize the dreadful thoughts and feelings that were struggling in vain to emerge into the conscious light of day. I am quite sure that it was this mental state of powerful and unresolved unconscious conflicts that caused my slipped disc (which, incidentally, means that a flexible tissue between vertebrae of the spine swells up and presses on nearby nerves and not, as I thought at the time, that one of the vertebrae has slipped out of place). Dr Lester had no doubt that my slipped disc was psychosomatic and the view of the specialist consultant I saw in Oxford was that stress is the cause of most back problems.

About two years' ago at the time of writing, I suddenly had alarming attacks of dizziness. I could hardly stand up. Both Isabel and I noticed that these occurred when I had had long, intensive painting sessions. I felt I had somehow overstrained the part of my brain that has to do with balancing colours and shapes. Dr Cotton diagnosed my complaint as 'labyrinthitis', which is thought to be caused by a virus in the inner ear. He asked me whether I had been under stress. When I mentioned my painting, he said he had two other patients who were painters and suffered from the same complaint. He prescribed not only the usual medication which cures the symptoms of this illness but also tranquillizers to take before future painting sessions. I have never again suffered from labyrinthitis, though I understand that, like a slipped disc, it is liable to recur. The complaint was psychosomatic – 'caused or *aggravated* by the brain'. And let us not forget that the dysfunction that led to my psychoanalysis was psychosomatic.

In summary, not only were the mental and other physical disorders I've described psychosomatic but so, too, were their cures (in which unorthodox context we need to adapt the definition of psychosomatic to 'caused or *facilitated* by the brain'). My brain, having recovered its own health by means of psychoanalysis or medication, was instrumental in healing my disorders. Incidentally, I was interested to read that in his recent book, *Placebo: The Belief Effect*, Dylan Evans offers a convincing and coherent scientific model of the placebo effect as being the result of a direct link between the brain and the immune system. Apparently, the placebo effect works by suppressing 'the acute-phase response' and so is particularly effective in relieving conditions involving that response, such as fever, inflammation and swelling.

More fundamentally, if more subjectively, and at the risk of tempting providence and straining your credulity, I have long felt a strange, subjective sureness – but a sureness nonetheless – that my drug-induced insights have discharged so much 'bad' toxic shit from the innermost fibres of my being and that my whole body has been so completely washed out and 'purified' that consequently I can never suffer from a wide range of physical illnesses and disorders, including cancer.

Most of us understand that a terrible shock can cause people to have a stroke or a heart attack and that profound grief can cause them to die of a 'broken heart' or, at the other extreme, that stress can cause someone to be 'run-down' and so catch a cold or 'flu' they otherwise wouldn't have caught. But over and beyond straightforward examples such as these, the extent and even the meaning of psychosomatic illnesses or disorders are often not appreciated. Nearly everyone (including some doctors) with whom I've discussed it have said that, since a virus is a physical thing, labyrinthitis can't be psychosomatic. (Fortunately for me, Tim Cotton didn't share this view.) I have heard other people say things like 'the pain in my back can't be "psychological" because I'm not imagining it. It really does hurt.' But, as we've seen, the fact that there is something wrong with your back and the pain is real doesn't mean your disorder can't be psychosomatic, to use the correct term. It certainly can be and probably is. Psychosomatic does *not* mean 'imaginary'. (I do not, by the way, underestimate the part played by genetic and other factors in causing physical illnesses, obvious examples of the latter being the links between smoking and cancer of the lung and between unprotected sex and AIDS.)

Although I've given relatively trivial examples taken from my own experience, for nearly forty years I have closely observed the personalities of other people and the circumstances surrounding their illnesses in the light of the insights I gained in the course of my psychoanalysis. I believe that there is a *far* greater psychosomatic element in a *far* wider range of physical illnesses and disorders than is generally recognized by the world in general or than – although there has been considerable progress over recent years – is universally acknowledged by the medical profession.

CHAPTER 11

The Immature Mind

IF A YOUNG ROSE BUSH is firmly rooted in fertile soil, well cultivated in a clement environment and evenly pruned, it grows into a well-shaped, sturdy and mature bush. Not so with us humans. The brain of a young child grows at such an astonishing speed and is so uniquely complex that, even in the best of environments, there is no such thing as perfect parents, able to respond to each and every one of their children's infinite and unique emotional demands with a perfect blend of praise and blame, never implanting too much or too little guilt, always striking a perfect balance between spoiling them by drowning them with *selfish* love and depriving them of *unselfish* love. This, sadly, is why young humans can never grow into perfectly well-rounded, entirely resilient and completely mature adults. Our human condition entails that emotional immaturity is only a question of degree.

We all have our childish foibles. Sometimes their effects can be relatively harmless, taking the form, say, of petty squabbles at golf clubs or between neighbours. Sometimes they can even be positive by contributing to people's personalities a harmless, eccentric charm, thereby increasing the rich diversity of humanity. Sometimes immaturity is a characteristic of great men – great artists or leaders, for example. It was hardly mature of Van Gogh to cut off one of his own ears and Winston Churchill was well known for the babyish traits in his personality.

The trouble is that Hitler, too, was infantile. You have only to see him in films strutting about like a cocky kid, making obscene salutes and generally playing soldiers. Like a cowardly school boy, he provoked pointless punch-ups with those he thought weaker than himself and tried to pinch their sweets, except that their sweets were their countries.

If, as it seems to me, non-genetic mental illnesses – ranging from severe clinical illness to mild neurosis – derive inexorably from emotional immaturity, they are really two sides of the same coin. Van Gogh was obviously 'mad' to cut off his ear and his extreme depression eventually led to his suicide. Churchill, to the extent that he was babyish, was neurotic, and he too suffered from bouts of deep depression which he famously described to his doctor as his 'black dog'. And few would doubt that Hitler was as mad as a hatter.

But if Hitler hadn't existed, Churchill wouldn't have needed to play his matchless role in our history. And you have only to pick up a newspaper or turn on the television to witness almost daily the appalling consequences of the mental illness of immature individuals acting in groups or by themselves. Having just read the paper and seen the news on television, today's main examples of the former are 'tit-for-tat', 'yah-boo' shootings and suicide bombings perpetrated respectively in Northern Ireland and the Middle East by groups of mad and infantile extremists. Today's main examples of the latter are yet another kidnapping and rape of a young, innocent girl and the indescribably awful activities of a paedophile, carried out by individual madmen whose infantile sexuality, though eroticized at puberty, hasn't otherwise matured beyond that stage.

Closer to home, at my first session with Dr Lester he explained very lucidly how my mental illness was the result of my failure to mature emotionally. I recall that, during his period of mental illness, my father was pathetically desperate to gobble milk chocolate like a child. And I have noticed that other people, when going through a patch of mental illness, cling more precariously to such emotional maturity as they may otherwise have achieved.

I realize that I have used the term 'mental illness' more widely than its orthodox use by the medical and legal professions. Nevertheless, I am not ashamed to admit that I was astounded by the remarks made by Mr Justice Curtis when, in December 2001, he rightly sentenced Roy Whiting to life imprisonment for the atrocious kidnapping, sexual assault and murder of Sarah Payne (though it is arguable whether he should never and in no circumstances be released). His Lordship rightly said that Roy Whiting was 'an evil man', but went on to say, apparently on the basis of psychiatric reports (one of which, following a previous offence in 1995, said he was a high-risk repeat offender), that he (Roy Whiting) was 'in no way mentally ill'. I find it astonishing and disturbing that a judge of the High Court should so clearly imply that Roy Whiting was in perfect mental health when he committed so appalling a crime. This implies that no kind of psychiatric treatment, however prolonged, could help him – however slightly – to achieve greater maturity and mental health. For me, this beggars belief. I do not think that people in perfect mental health go around committing such horrific crimes.

I have expressed my views about a complex subject in a highly condensed form in the hope of achieving a measure of clarity. In summary, the limited advantages of the universality of our emotional immaturity are overwhelmingly outweighed by the human suffering caused by its concomitant mental and consequent physical illnesses.

Many unspeakable evils afflict human kind, such as absolute poverty and mass starvation in vast swathes of Africa and elsewhere, to name but two. That said, if we contemplate the essence of the human psyche itself, I believe that emotional immaturity is the fundamental tragedy of our human condition.

CHAPTER 12

The Selfish Mind

A<small>S A RESULT</small> of my insights into my unconscious mind I have been reluctantly driven to reach two other conclusions about the human condition with which few people with whom I have discussed them agree. People of all kinds, ranging from atheists to profoundly religious people, have reacted by dismissing them as shallow, futile, meaningless, immoral, amoral or even dangerous. Sometimes their reactions have been quite emotional. At this stage I would only point out that such reactions do not logically disprove my conclusions.

In brief summary, this chapter deals with my conclusion that ultimately our behaviour is never really motivated by altruism; the next with my conclusion that we do not have free will.

Since reaching these conclusions, I have been attending the philosophy courses organized by the WEA to which I referred in Chapter 8. The prescribed reading for the first course was a book by Mary Warnock entitled *An Intelligent Person's Guide to Ethics* in which, quite coincidentally, altruism and free will are among the issues she discusses. Amongst her other great distinctions, she was a fellow and tutor of philosophy at St Hugh's College, Oxford. She has been described in the Philosopher's Magazine as 'probably the most famous philosopher in Britain'. I was quite prepared for her to persuade me that I was wrong and was not surprised, in the light of other people's reactions, that she holds the opposite view to myself on both counts.

Before elaborating my conclusions and considering the arguments involved, I should make three preliminary comments that are relevant both to this chapter and to the next.

Firstly, I should, perhaps, have made it explicit that in this Part of my memoirs I limit myself to topics which derive directly from my experience of psychoanalysis. In this sense, they constitute a philosophical sequel to my account of my psychoanalysis.

Secondly, since reaching my conclusions about the absence of altruism and free will (the latter of which I now know is called 'determinism'), I have learnt that the issues they address are amongst the oldest chestnuts debated and written about by philosophers and theologians. Free will was, for example, considered by St Thomas Aquinas as long ago as the thirteenth century AD and even earlier by Aristotle in the fourth century BC, at least to the extent of his rather obscure references to fatalism. It may, therefore, seem strange that I confine myself largely – though not exclusively – to a critique of Mary Warnock's book. I do so because it brings the issues into sharp focus and is more successful than any of the other books I have read about altruism and determinism in combining the virtues of being both wide-ranging and lucid. This provides me with a good foundation on which to build a reasonably comprehensive and, I hope, comprehensible analysis of the main arguments involved.

Thirdly, in putting the arguments and counter-arguments, I do so as if Mary Warnock and I were protagonists. I realize that this artificial device produces a fictitious confrontational scenario which may seem somewhat bizarre. On balance, however, I felt it was the best way to highlight and contrast our respective arguments as clearly and concisely as possible. I should add that any italics I use in quotations from here on are mine unless I say otherwise and that I occasionally use square brackets to add my own gloss on what she and others say.

Finally, I have tried, with all the objectivity I can command, to be entirely fair in selecting and explaining Mary Warnock's arguments and not to do so in a way that suits my own case. In any event, her book is in the public domain and well worth reading. It is an important and extremely interesting contribution to a whole range of contemporary moral issues and is well, sometimes movingly, written.

Let me now open up our discussion about altruism by expressing my conclusion more fully in the following terms. Although most of us often behave in an apparently unselfish way, in so doing we are fulfilling an inner need of which we are nearly always largely or wholly unconscious. In the final analysis, therefore, we are never really motivated by altruism, even though we may consciously believe – and like to believe – that we are and what we do may be profoundly altruistic in its effects.

Turning straight to Mary Warnock's book, in her first reference to my conclusion, she says that she must briefly dismiss the view that we never act altruistically because altruism is the key to her account of the ethical. In other words, since she has already reached her conclusion, she need only casually consider any argument that runs counter to it because she intends to dismiss it anyway. This, logically speaking, is to put the cart before the horse. Should she not have considered any such arguments very carefully and with an open mind *before* reaching her conclusion?

If her mind had been entirely open, I don't think she would have used the sort of emotive language she goes on to use. She says, for instance, that my argument against altruism means 'it is simply that some people like to pose as martyrs'. The innuendo is that it follows from my argument that St Francis of Assisi, say, was no more than a 'poseur', the Oxford Dictionary's definition of which is 'a person who acts in an affected manner in order to impress others'.

She goes on to suggest that my argument is difficult to refute head-on because it can – 'uninterestingly' – mean no more than that we do things because we want to. It seems to me less than fair to define my argument in a way that makes it sound trivial, thereby justifying the gratuitous use of the word 'uninterestingly'.

She further alleges that my view 'obviously' means that all our characters are the same. How can she assert this so dogmatically? If in the end analysis, as I argue, St Francis and Adolf Hitler were both motivated by largely unconscious needs within themselves, how can it be said to follow that their characters were the same? After all, their characters had many other fundamental characteristics which were profoundly different from each other's.

Mary Warnock even suggests that the 'point' of my case against the possibility of altruism is to prove that ethics is a delusion. This implies that I first decided that ethics was a delusion and then thought up my case against altruism in order to prove it. I was putting the cart before the horse.

This is not true. I didn't know what my conclusion would be before I reached it let alone what would follow from whatever conclusion I might reach. Nor did I wish to prove that ethics is a delusion. It is ironical that she wrongly accuses me of putting the cart before the horse when, as I pointed out, she herself did so in her first reference to my argument a few sentences earlier.

Next she says: 'If, however, like Aristotle and Kant, we start from where we are, from the phenomena, we find there is a profound difference between the morally good and the morally bad, the ethical and the unethical, the nice person and the nasty person'. This is apparently meant to be a decisive counter to my case against altruism. Unfortunately, I have limited knowledge of the philosophies of Aristotle and Kant. I can only assume that, great philosophers as they were, in the relevant contexts this statement is of important significance. On the face of it, however, it is a statement of the blindingly obvious. *Of course*, to take my earlier example, there was a profound difference between St Francis and Adolf Hitler.

She continues in the same vein three sentences later: 'We simply cannot get on with the proposition that everyone is alike in these respects [morally and ethically]'. *Of course* we can't. To suggest otherwise is to misrepresent and trivialize my argument against altruism.

Let me illustrate my argument by taking a simple example. If I know my wife is tired after playing golf and so do the washing-up after supper, make her coffee and take it to her so she can sit with her feet up, my argument is that I do so because I would feel unbearably guilty if I didn't. My underlying motive is the self-regarding need to avoid an unbearable feeling of guilt. I just *couldn't* sit there and leave her to do the washing up and get me my coffee.

After I had drafted this chapter, I read the book called *What does it all mean?* written by Thomas Nagel, Professor of Philosophy and Law at New York University. I was intrigued by the remarkably similar way in which he expresses this argument: 'On this view, even apparently moral conduct in which one person seems to sacrifice his own interests for the sake of others is really motivated by his concern for himself: he wants to avoid the guilt he'll feel if he doesn't do the "right" thing.'

Having got this far in my thinking, I could see a strong argument against me. It is that you can't feel guilty in the abstract. There is a reason why I would feel guilty if I didn't do the washing-up and make the coffee. That reason is that I have made the moral judgement that it would be right to do so. Therefore my motive was altruistic.

I was equally intrigued to discover that Thomas Nagel also puts this counter-argument in very similar terms: 'You wouldn't feel guilty about doing the wrong thing unless you thought there was some other reason not to do it, besides the fact that it made you feel guilty, something which made it *right* [his italics] to feel guilty.' So, to add my own gloss, your motive was altruistic.

This seemed such a strong argument against me when I first thought of it that I felt inclined to change my mind. On further reflection, however, I could see it wasn't as simple as that. Let me explain by taking a further example.

A year or so ago, someone rang me up and asked whether I would help a charity by doing a house-to-house collection in the road where I live. First I would have to deliver envelopes to some sixty houses and then collect them a few days later, hopefully with some money in them. If there was no-one in, I should return within another few days at a different time. I felt uncomfortable at the prospect of getting money from 'captive audiences' and it all sounded quite time-consuming. To my shame, I made a feeble excuse about being too busy.

Strangely enough, a few months later another charity rang me with exactly the same request. (Why pick on me?!) Having refused to help on the previous occasion, this time I felt I should agree and so I did.

My point is that in both cases I knew it would have been right to put myself to some inconvenience and do the house-to-house collections. The moral argument was exactly the same. But I made different decisions because I felt different levels of guilt. The inner need to avoid an unbearable feeling of guilt the second time round was the *decisive* cause of my decision to do the collection. Put another way, it was 'the immediate link in the causative chain'. The first time I was asked, this link was missing.

It is interesting at this point to return to Mary Warnock's book. Her 'central point' is that the real source of ethics is not the avoidance of guilt but sympathetic concern for other people.

I entirely agree that sympathy is the *source* of ethics. In the examples I have given, sympathy was the source of my moral actions – sympathy for my wife when I did the washing-up and got her coffee, and for the beneficiaries of the charity when I did the house-to-house collection on the second occasion. The potential guilt, which was the decisive and immediate cause of my actions, *flowed from that source*.

Mary Warnock goes on to say that it follows from my argument against altruism that there is no place for morality and ethics. Apart from pointing out that, even if this were true, it wouldn't logically disprove my argument, I don't think it *is* true. I should have thought it would still be the legitimate concern of moral philosophers to consider the source of morality and ethics (sympathy); in what situations it would, as Thomas Nagel put it, be *right* to feel guilty; whether people's characters are good or bad (bearing in mind what I said earlier about my argument not meaning that the characters of St Francis and Adolf Hitler were the same); and whether people's actions are good or bad in themselves irrespective of their motives and characters. Overall, I hardly think that my argument puts moral philosophers out of business!

Furthermore, I should re-emphasize that the self-regarding mental processes which flow from sympathy are often unconscious processes. When people act altruistically, they tend to resist recognition of their self-regarding motivation. It is only someone like me who, having been psychoanalysed and having explained my views to my wife more than once, would, as I recently did, make what was supposed to be a joke by saying after supper 'Now I'm going to be selfish and do the washing-up and get your coffee'.

If you have not been psychoanalysed and your self-regarding need when you do something apparently altruistic is repressed into your unconscious mind, is it right or fair to judge you by reference to your unconscious non-altruistic motivation? In philosophical terms, would it not be right and fair to judge you by reference to your conscious altruistic motivation? It seems to me that it would. Psychoanalysis of the unconscious mind can easily be used – or misused – to destroy anyone's character. If you judged my own character by reference to the session when I called Dr Lester a filthy Jew, a feeling that was only dragged to the surface after years of in-depth psychoanalysis and with the aid of powerful, insight-inducing drugs, you might well be forgiven for thinking I was a Nazi, whereas the fact of the matter is that I regard racism in whatever guise as among the most loathsome of evils. Nor, for the record, have I ever been a practising homosexual which you might also mistakenly deduce from parts of my account of my psychoanalysis.

On her way to reaching her conclusion that sympathy is the source of morality, Mary Warnock says that altruism requires an '*effort*' [her italics] of imagination and sympathy and 'does not follow automatically from self-interest.' But because I argue that altruism is caused by self-interest it doesn't follow that self-interest automatically causes altruism. *Of course* it doesn't. All too often it leads to overtly selfish behaviour. Her statement misrepresents my argument against altruism in a way that makes it look absurd.

———◦———

So far I have concentrated on the avoidance of guilt as the decisive motivation underlying altruism. I wonder if there are any other underlying motives?

I mentioned earlier that when I was at the Western School I used to meet Miss Lovell where she parked her car and carry her case to the classroom.[19] No doubt I was sympathetic towards her by the standards of a boy of eight, but my inner motive (pathetic though it may have been) was to suck up to her in the hope that I would be her favourite. At a deeper level, I wanted to gain the affection of a substitute mother figure.

There are adult versions of this emotion, especially if we are emotionally insecure and immature. We can be extra nice and kind to people because we have an excessive inner need to be liked. However successfully or otherwise I may have sought to rationalize my extreme 'theory Y' management style[92] as being in the mutual interests of my staff and my employers, and however sympathetic a person I may genuinely be, I have to face the harsh truth that I had an excessive inner need to be liked by all my staff – at least to the extent that this is ever possible. I avoided being the 'tougher' boss some people might reasonably argue I should have been in order to satisfy this inner, immature need and to compensate for my emotional insecurity.

Partly to pursue further the nature of our inner needs when we appear to act altruistically and partly to consider cases that friends have suggested disprove my argument against altruism (not just cases that, consciously or unconsciously, I may have selected to support it), I will take two final examples.

The first is bravery. I am always moved by the obituaries of officers in the army who earned medals by doing astonishingly brave things in the Second World War, putting their own lives at risk out of concern for the safety of the soldiers under their command. The argument put against me is that nothing could be more genuinely and unequivocally altruistic: there couldn't possibly be any underlying, self-regarding motive for risking their lives for the sake of others. They were just exceptionally brave men with exceptional concern for their fellow soldiers. It is as simple as that.

But is it? By now, you will appreciate that I agree with Mary Warnock that the source of their actions was commendable concern for the soldiers under their command. They wouldn't have done what they did just for the hell of it. I must say, however, that I do find it difficult to identify the nature of their inner need, presumably because I simply can't imagine being so brave myself. But can you really imagine that these brave officers were *not* fulfilling some kind of inner need? Can you really answer this question by saying 'Yes, I don't think they were fulfilling *any* kind of inner need'? However you look at it, I suggest that they wouldn't have done what they did if they hadn't had some kind of inner need to do so. Which brings us back to Mary Warnock's trivialization of my argument – you do what you want to do. The nature of these officers' underlying want, whatever else it may have been, was complex and far from trivial. I don't, incidentally, think there is much, if any, difference between an 'underlying *want*' and (to use the expression I have used so far) an 'inner *need*'.

Not being a qualified psychoanalyst, I can't express a professional view but, not being without experience in this field, I may perhaps venture to speculate. Might there not, in some cases, have been an unconscious need, stemming from deep emotional insecurity, to be seen as a hero or martyr – and certainly not as a coward – in the eyes of their fellow soldiers (and in their own eyes)? You will have seen from my psychoanalysis that the highest conscious motives can be polarized reactions to the basest unconscious ones. Might not some have had a masochistic streak in their make-up and enjoyed the thrill of dicing with death? At any rate, I have little doubt that Freud would have talked in terms of a deeply-buried 'death instinct' or 'death wish', the emotional recognition of which was the last of all the fundamental insights to emerge from my own unconscious mind when I was 71 years old.[192]

Be that as it may or may not be, for my part – however hard I try to think otherwise – it seems unarguable that these officers were fulfilling an underlying want or need or instinct that was not trivial but complex and profound. And remembering the close connection between insecurity ('mummy doesn't love me') and guilt ('mummy says I'm naughty'), I suspect that an element of guilt comes into the picture somewhere along the line. Being the sort of people they were, could they have lived with the guilt they would feel if they had left their soldiers to their fate?

The second case friends have put to me as disproving my argument against altruism is that wondrous glory of humanity, human love – particularly what is perhaps the greatest love of all, a mother's love for her children. Such love, they say, is by definition altruistic.

Oddly enough, I find this an easier case to answer. To start with, I suggest that, unless they are a mistake or result from rape, we produce our own children in the first place not for their sakes but for ours – to fulfil the deepest of all our needs. Indeed, some people go so far as to say it is overwhelmingly selfish to bring children into the world to suffer in this vale of tears.

I will first take such a simple example that it scarcely needs explaining, firstly because I am looking to see whether we have any underlying motive other than the avoidance of guilt when we behave altruistically, and secondly because my wife's initial reaction when I asked her about it was telling.

Suppose your children are playing in the front garden and you shut and lock the front gate so they can't run out into the road. The source of your action is sympathy on stilts, as they say. But the decisive, immediate cause of your action is stark, staring fear – fear that they might be run over and killed. You want to avoid the inexpressible grief you would suffer if they were. Nevertheless, I would think your fear is more than tinged with the unbearable guilt you'd have to live with for the rest of your life if your children were killed as a result of your negligence. Of course, when you act so instinctively, your mind works instantaneously without analysing the underlying reasons for your action.

When I put this example to my wife and asked her to give an immediate answer to why she would shut and lock the gate, she said, 'because I love them (the children).' So even in so glaringly obvious a case of fulfilling a self-regarding need, without thinking – instinctively – she said her motive was altruistic. It took only a moment's discussion for her to see that the truth of the matter was otherwise. But my point is to illustrate what I have said before. We like to think we are acting purely altruistically even in a case where it is so clear that this was not our primary motive.

Suppose now there are two mothers, each with the same total love for their two children. In each case, one is two years old and the other six months old. Both mothers are the same age, equally well off and have the same professional qualifications. They both want to pursue their professional careers. One employs a nanny and goes out to work. The other stays at home to look after her children herself, at least until they are older. Although in practice there would be many variables in comparing the two mothers, let us assume for the purpose of argument that their circumstances and personalities are exactly the same and both have exactly the same total love for their children. On the basis of that hypothetical premise, it must be the case that the first mother thinks her children will be no worse off if she goes out to work, while the second mother thinks they would be. (I make no moral judgement about these alternatives.) So the first mother doesn't feel guilty about fulfilling her wish to go out to work, while the second one would feel unbearably guilty if she did so and didn't look after her children herself. It is not that she is more loving but that she is more guilty at the thought of leaving her children to be looked after by someone else.

More generally, assuming we are reasonably normal people, we want to do our best for our children. We try to bring them up as best we can within our emotional limitations. As I have said before, there is no such thing as perfect parents. And we try to have them educated as well as possible within our material limitations. But precisely because the source of our behaving in this way is such great love, we would feel correspondingly great guilt if we didn't behave in this way. The greater the love, the greater the guilt. We would feel we had failed to fulfil the most important obligation of our lives, an obligation to the children we brought into this world to fulfil our own most fundamental of needs. We couldn't bear this, so we try to avoid it. Looked at another way, we want them to grow up good and happy people because otherwise our own happiness will suffer. These, too, are self-regarding motives.

Here again I asked my wife why we did our best for our children in the ways I have described. Again, she said it was because we loved them. This time it took lengthy cross-examination by an ex-lawyer to convince her that, although our love was the source of our action, our ultimate motive was self-regarding.

Overall, I do not think I have succeeded in finding underlying motives for our altruistic behaviour that were not primarily the avoidance of guilt or where that was not at least ancillary to other motives.

***

In the last paragraph of her book, Mary Warnock argues that, if children go to 'a good school' (the nature of which she beautifully describes and includes 'moral and spiritual education'), they 'will *want*' to do things well, 'will *want*' to be good people and 'will *want*' to be ethically good. Only if they have this '*underlying* private *want*' can they be 'relied on to try for the ethically best in the public sphere'. Coincidentally, she went to the same school as Isabel, St Swithun's, where she (Mary Warnock) says, 'It was assumed that the true purpose of school was to make us good'.

Her emphasis on 'want' is ironic in the present context. Earlier, when criticizing my argument against altruism, she regarded 'wanting' as an uninteresting motive for altruistic action. Yet here, in her final conclusion of all, an 'underlying want' suddenly becomes a prerequisite for ethical behaviour. The irony is that in the final paragraph of her book she unwittingly endorses my argument against the possibility of altruism.

In the closing pages of her chapter dealing specifically with altruism, Mary Warnock concludes with a quite complex passage based, to start with, on a helpful metaphor. I can't quote over two pages, but I have read them literally dozens of times and did many drafts of the following summary of those pages, so anxious was I to ensure that it was fair and objective.

She says that we human beings realize that we are all in the same precarious boat. We also realize that if our boat – our precarious society – sinks, we will *perish*. So it's all hands on deck: to *survive* we must all co-operate, if necessary restraining our own wishes in the process. It is our realization of this need to co-operate that, in the final analysis, makes altruism possible. Altruism is central to private morality which in turn is central to public ethics, directed to the common good. So in creating our ethical systems, we are fulfilling a *'fundamental need* of human nature'. (This time she uses the word 'need' rather than 'want'!) These are the final words in her chapter designed to disprove my argument against the possibility of altruism. In fact, they constitute a powerful endorsement of my argument.

It seems clear that what, in a nutshell, she is saying is that, when we co-operate with each other – when we 'give and take' – we are fulfilling a fundamental need to survive. My only qualification would be that we do not 'realize' this, save *in extremis* (as witness the way in which we all helped each other out in the second World War, when the need to survive was paramount in our minds[36-7]). Generally speaking, it is a need so ingrained – by the process of our evolution from primates – in the deepest, unconscious recesses of our human minds that our altruistic behaviour is instinctive. Subject to that qualification, Mary Warnock's conclusion accords with my own: that when we restrain our wishes for the sake of others – when we behave 'altruistically' – we are fulfilling the most fundamental need of all – to survive rather than perish.

What could be more self-regarding than that?

CHAPTER 13

The Determined Mind

T HERE ARE SEVERAL versions of determinism. Put simply in my terms, it is that two things make us human beings what we are. These are our genes and our environment in its widest sense – everything that happens to us from the moment of our birth (perhaps even in the womb). Being what we therefore are and cannot help being, in any given situation we cannot help behaving in the way we do. We are bound to think what we think, to feel what we feel and to make the decisions and choices we make. So however much we may *consciously* feel – and like to feel – that we have free will, this is an illusion.

Whether it is our genes or our environment that contribute most to making us what we are is an open question. In his book, *They f*** you up: how to survive family life*, Oliver James opts for our environment as being the dominant factor in the development of our personalities. Concentrating on early infancy, he demonstrates the crucial role of unempathetic care in causing personality disorder, which has been shown actually to change the infant's brainwave patterns from healthy to abnormal. Other recently published studies have found a large body of evidence that homosexuality often has a significant environmental component, particularly where a mother is dominant and over-protective and inhibits a boy's agressional masculinity.

Other experts place more emphasis on our genes as determining factors in the development of our personalities. Such is the pace of research in this field that Matt Ridley, the best-selling author of *Genome*, has recently (in 2003) published another book entitled *Nature via Nurture*. He suggests that genes are neither puppet masters or blueprints nor just the carriers of heredity. Rather they are active during life and switch each other on and off in response to the environment. In other words, our environment actually causes a material change to our genes.

Incidentally, both views lend strong support to my own view about the materiality of the mind – particularly Oliver James' reference to healthy and abnormal brain waves. (See, for instance, my reference to 'instant negative brain waves'.[200])

Mary Warnock begins her criticism of determinism by again putting the cart before the horse. Having accurately described my views as being that it is never true to say that we could have acted otherwise than we did, she says she must briefly dispose of at least some versions of this theory, otherwise we will be led into a 'dead-end'. She has made up her mind that my theory leads to a 'dead-end' and so *has* to dispose of it quite briefly. She should have considered my theory in depth and with an open mind *before* working out where it leads. Here, too, she makes the illogical assumption that, as it leads to what she regards as dead end, it cannot be true.

She goes on to say, in summary, that determinism means we couldn't praise or ascribe any moral merit to humans, any more than we do to animals. Neither could we blame or punish them. We put them outside the scope of these ethical attitudes.

These are such strong words that I must respond in some detail.

I suggest that it is not only consistent with my determinism but *more* logical for me to treat people as human beings who are responsible for their actions, even though I don't think they are. This is, of course, paradoxical, the Oxford Dictionary's definition of a paradox being 'a seemingly absurd or self-contradictory statement or proposition which when explained may prove to be well-founded or true'. Let me explain.

As a determinist, I argue that people's genes and environment determine their behaviour. On the other hand, Mary Warnock argues that they do not determine people's behaviour but presumably accepts that they must at least have some lesser effect. If that were so, it would be correspondingly less important to influence people's environment, for instance by praising and rewarding or blaming and punishing them. In practice, she does of course think it right to treat people in this way so that their environment has the maximum beneficial effect on their behaviour, short of determining it. But, to the extent of that shortfall, it is logically more important for me to treat people in a similar way because I think that a 'good' environment has a correspondingly greater beneficial effect – a determining effect – on their behaviour.

Mary Warnock's answer is that determinism depends on the 'rather disagreeable' view that there is no justification for punishing or rewarding people and that the people we punish or reward are 'suckers' because they think they deserve their punishments or rewards when they don't.

She then gives an account of a visit she paid to a school for severely disabled children in New York whose teaching method was 'behaviour modification'. Although the children couldn't understand what was meant by doing well or badly, the teacher had been told that they responded by rewards (such as being given some sweets) if they did well in their work and to punishments (such as being spoken to harshly) if they did badly. This particular teacher, however, was too human and too loving to do anything except say they were doing well even when they were not. Mary Warnock concludes from this that, if determinism is true, the use of ethical concepts is 'futile because impossible'.

Perhaps I'm missing something. I'm afraid I don't see why, because one teacher in America dealing with disabled children behaved in this human and loving way, determinism means that the use of ethical concepts is impossible and therefore futile. On the contrary, if this teacher was 'too human and too loving to *do anything except*' behave as she did and it was '*impossible*' for her not to use ethical concepts, Mary Warnock's own words show that this episode was a classic example of determinism at work, in describing which she herself uses ethical concepts! I can't imagine that any man loves his grandchildren more than I do. But when my five year old grandson recently punched his three year old sister for no apparent reason (except that it was determined by sibling rivalry), I didn't say, 'Never mind, dear, you couldn't help it. Here are some Smarties.' I found it quite possible and logical to say, 'That's naughty, dear – you mustn't do it again.' (I always prefer to say 'that's naughty' rather than '*you* are naughty'.) Why, because I am a determinist, was I behaving in a rather 'disagreeable' way or treating my grandson as a 'sucker'? I was treating him with the respect he deserved.

Mary Warnock then considers in some detail the 'supposed' sciences, such as the social sciences, and includes psychology among them in a passage that refers to 'Freudian determinism' (a version of 'psychological determinism'), whereby, as we have seen from Chapter 9, our actions are (unconsciously) conditioned by our past experiences rather than by our conscious 'rationalizations'. I have insufficient academic knowledge (though plenty of practical experience) of Freud's theories to know whether he alleged that *all* the choices we make in life are determined by such motives, but would be surprised if he did. I am always amused by the self-mocking remark he is supposed to have made: 'Sometimes a cigar is just a cigar.' In other words, when people (like me) smoke cigars, they are not always driven to do so by their powerful unconscious symbolism (phallus, brown shit, sucked in the mouth) with the many permutations I have described earlier.[174] I do not think my decisions to go to Oxford or to apply for a job with the Surrey County Council or, in retirement, to play tennis on Thursdays rather than Saturdays were dictated by 'Freudian determinism', though other decisions certainly were, for example my decision to join the Royal Artillery. [179]

Paradoxically, therefore, although I have experienced the reality of Freud's unconscious and agree with him that there is no such thing as free will, I share Mary Warnock's rejection of Freudian determinism if it is supposed to apply to *all* the decisions and choices we make.

She goes on to point out that the natural sciences, including neurophysiology, assume that every event is caused by a preceding series of events. In other words, everything is causally determined. It is interesting to see how she deals with this.

She accepts that our brains are physical objects but argues that the crucial question is whether causal laws could '*even in principle* (that useful defensive phrase)' be identified which could predict how they will cause our actions. For her, the essence of the problem is predictability.

She later explains that biological theory proves that everyone is unique. For example, the cells in our brains move about and interconnect in unpredictable ways. It follows, she argues, that predictability is '*in principle*' impossible. Later, she asserts that our reaction to the infinite variety of our environments is unpredictable '*in principle*'. It is rather strange that, having implicitly criticized this phrase when it could be used against her, she then herself uses it twice as 'clinchers' to support her key conclusion – that human behaviour is unpredictable 'in principle'.

Although it is interesting and important to understand the scientific reasons why each of us is unique, it seems to me that it is obvious to the point of being almost a truism. Do you know anyone who doesn't think that we are all different? I recall the precise and moving words spoken by a Catholic priest at the funeral of my late Aunty Jane some time ago: 'No-one quite like Jane has ever existed before and no-one quite like her will ever exist in the future.'

Although, therefore, I agree with her unsurprising conclusion that we are all unique, I do not see why it follows that our behaviour, though clearly unpredictable in practice, is also unpredictable *in principle*. Just as there is no uniformity between the arrangement of the cells in our brains, so there is no uniformity between the weather in Winchester and the weather in millions of other places in the world. In practice, the best weather forecasters do not currently have the knowledge and techniques to forecast whether it will rain in Winchester at 11.15 a.m. a week next Thursday. But this does not mean that whether it will rain here at that time is not governed by causal laws and so is unpredictable *in principle*.

The counter argument is that this is an inappropriate analogy because, in one important respect, the human brain is fundamentally different. In his book entitled *Free Will*, D.J. O'Connor, former Professor of Philosophy at the University of Exeter, points out that electrons jump from one orbit to another within the atoms in our brains without any assignable cause. I quote: 'The general opinion of experts in this field (although with a few distinguished exceptions, including Einstein) is that there are no causal laws governing these events [jumps of electrons] and that their occurrence is accordingly unpredictable. And this unpredictability [unlike the unpredictability of the weather] is not just a matter of fact due to the limitations of human knowledge, skill or intelligence; such events are unpredictable *in principle* [his italics].' This is the same reasoning as Mary Warnock's – including the italicization of *in principle*.

It goes without saying that I am in no position to dispute the findings of leading experts in quantum mechanics and physics. I nevertheless presume to wonder how anyone can assert without qualification that scientists of any kind, including neurophysiologists, will *never* be able to identify causal laws governing these jumps of electrons and so will *never* be able to predict how the electrons will jump. Even if we assume now that no such causal laws exist, I presume to ask how we know that these jumps do not themselves affect what Professor O'Connor calls 'the large-scale workings of our brains' in such a way as to determine, or contribute to the determination of, our behaviour? According to Professor O'Connor, distinguished experts give different answers to my question. Yet it must surely be the case that, if the answer to my question is that these jumps of electrons *do* have this effect, it supports my case for determinism. If, on the other hand, the answer is that they do *not* have this effect, it does not seem to me to advance the argument one way or the other. Either way, we could not control random jumps.

Mary Warnock's next argument is that there are more important explanations of human behaviour than purely scientific ones. She has in mind the many natural reactions to other people which we all share. An example she quotes is that we have a natural resentment if someone purposely treads on our toes, but not if he or she did so by mistake. Such spontaneous reactions 'entail' that we treat people as capable of acting responsibly and making deliberate choices.

This is a persuasive argument which made me wonder, not for the first time, whether I should change my mind about determinism. But I couldn't stop puzzling about it. There seemed to be something wrong somewhere. Eventually I saw what it was. She makes an unargued quantum leap from the premise that we instinctively *treat* people as responsible [having free will] to the conclusion that we have to believe that they *are* responsible [have free will]. This, as I see it, is yet another non-sequitur.

In the course of this part of her argument, Mary Warnock points out that there are some people, like young children, old people suffering from senile dementia and psychopaths, who are exceptions to her conclusion that people have free will and so can be held responsible for their actions. Taking the last category, the essence of her argument is that, since psychopaths are abnormal, we can exempt them from the responsibility we attribute to normal people. In fact, she says, it is 'self-evident' that we couldn't be persuaded by the *'theory'* [her italics] of determinism that we must treat everyone like animals and psychopaths and so become inhuman. Note, by the way, how she emphasizes the word 'theory'. Her implication is that determinism is 'only a theory' so doesn't count for much. But why is my view a theory and hers not?

The trouble with her argument is that it has no bearing on my argument in favour of determinism. In this context my argument is that their genes and environment determine that some people are psychopaths and others are not and that in this determinist sense neither are responsible for what they are and so for what they do. Mary Warnock uses 'responsible' in the way we use it in every day language, not in the determinist sense of the word. She says, for instance, that we can exempt people from responsibility if they make a *'pardonable* mistake', a concept with moral overtones which has nothing to do with determinism *per se*. This is why her argument is irrelevant to the issue in hand.

In any case, in her own terms her logic is flawed. In saying that there is an 'abnormal' exemption from the rule that we are responsible, she is implying that there *is* such a rule. An exception does not prove the rule but assumes the rule exists.

Finally, so far as Mary Warnock's arguments go, may I refer back to the last paragraph of her book which I discussed at the end of the previous chapter, in which she says that the environment of a good school means its pupils *'will* want' to do everything well, *'will* want' to be good people and *'will* want' to be ethically good. Only if they have this 'underlying private want' can they be *'relied on'* to try for the ethically best in the public sphere. Assuming she is not being over-optimistic in suggesting that all the pupils will turn out to be such paragons of virtue, it seems to me that this is in fact a good example of environment determining behaviour – behaviour, moreover, which she found it quite possible to say was ethical!

Let us see what Thomas Nagel has to say about determinism in *What does it all mean?* Having put both sides of the argument, he says that he can't accept determinism: 'If I thought that everything I did was determined by my circumstances and my psychological condition, I would feel trapped. And if I thought the same about everybody else, I would feel they were like a lot of puppets. It wouldn't make sense to hold them responsible for their actions any more than you hold a dog or a cat or even an elevator responsible'.

This adds nothing to Mary Warnock's arguments, which I have already discussed. (I venture to suggest that he can't know how he would feel if he were something he isn't: that is to say, a determinist like myself.) But the interesting thing is that he goes on to say that, on the other hand, he's not sure he understands how responsibility for our choices makes sense if they are *not* [his italics] determined. He concludes: 'It's not clear what it means to say *I* [his italics] determine the choice, if nothing about me determines it. So perhaps the feeling that you could have chosen a peach instead of a piece of cake [the amusing example he uses] is a philosophical illusion, and couldn't be right whatever the case'. He qualifies this by adding that, to avoid this conclusion, you would have to explain what you *mean* [his italics] if you say that you could have chosen differently and what the world would have to be like if this were true. I will discuss later the practical consequences of Mary Warnock's views – as well as my own.

I should perhaps say a brief word about *'soft* determinism'. In *The Science of the Mind*, Owen Flanagan, who was Class of 1919 Professor of

Philosophy at Wellesley College and wrote this book while a Visiting Scholar at Harvard, advocates one version of soft determinism, which he describes as a disparaging name for his compatibilism, so called because it attempts to reconcile the theories of determinism and free will. He summarizes his complex case for compatibilism by saying that, whatever the various types of causes for our behaviour may be, if the 'proximate cause' of our actions is processing by conscious features of our brains (such as adapting quickly to new situations, knowing, remembering and planning), these features 'can count as' constituting free will.

To answer Professor Flanagan in detail would take up more space than I would wish. Suffice it to say that his theory does not seem to contradict my argument that we are bound to know what we know, to remember what we remember and to plan what we plan. Furthermore, since I can only take his words as I find them, to say that processing by the features of the brain he describes can 'count as' free will seems to be saying no more than, for instance, that a close, lifelong friend can 'count as' a member of our family, when in fact he or she is no such thing.

———◦◦———

I had intended to finish this chapter here were it not that I have just been moved to tears by an item on the Sky television news channel (for the record at 12.30 p.m. on Sunday, 10 March, 2002). A reporter was interviewing a young lady in India who spent her life looking after people who had leprosy and other contagious diseases and lived in abject poverty. She had already caught leprosy once and had been cured but knew she might catch it again or catch another awful disease. What moved me so much was her sheer goodness. When she goes to her grave, she will probably be unrecognized by the world at large. (I often think of wonderful people who will have 'unvisited tombs' – that moving expression used by George Eliot in the last paragraph of *Middlemarch*.)

The reporter asked if she would continue spending her life in this way. When I heard her reply, I instantly made a note of her exact words: 'There is absolutely no doubt in my mind that I *have* to be doing this.'

The rest is silence.

———◦◦———

The rest *would* have been silence had it not been that two friends sent me copies of an article in *The Times* of 26 February 2003 about an interview with the ebullient and the combative Daniel Dennett – one of the most famous philosophers in the world. He is the Distinguished Arts and Sciences Professor at Tufts University in Boston in the United States. I have since read the book on which he bases the article in *The Times*. Although it is a long and, to my mind, rather complex book, the article in *The Times* well summarizes his arguments in favour of his own brand of compatibilism. I will therefore confine my comments to the salient points he makes in that article.

While he accepts the neuroscientists' materialistic view of the human brain, he believes that our being composed of genes and cells does not disprove the idea that we have free will. He gives the example that as we evolve, we can use more and more information to override the tendencies that our genes have built in us. 'For example, we can wear glasses if we are genetically geared to be short-sighted and we can eat healthy food if our genes predispose us to heart disease. Hence evolution has bestowed on us the intelligence to direct our destinies.' This may seem impressive at first sight but a moment's thought tells us that his two examples mean nothing more than that the present generation has two options that previous ones didn't (to wear glasses or to eat healthy food), a statement which, apart from being blindingly obvious, has no bearing on the question of determinism as I defined it at the beginning of this Chapter. The fact that Julius Ceasar couldn't wear glasses because they had not been invented in Roman times has nothing to do with the nature of my own decision to wear glasses while I was at Oxford. It is a blatant *non sequitur* to imply that the invention of glasses means that my decision to wear glasses was made freely rather than determined. Furthermore, I believe he is quite wrong to confuse the issue by implying that the expression 'we have the intelligence to direct our destinies' is equivalent to 'we have free will'.

Later he gives what he calls a trivial example. 'If I throw a brick at your head, you'll duck. The brick was going to hit you, but of course it wasn't going to hit you because you were caused to see the brick which caused you to decide to duck, and so you ducked and it went over your head. Thank goodness for determinism. If you couldn't count on that, you wouldn't have had any idea that the brick might actually hit you. But maybe what your really need right now is £200,000 and, as you see the brick coming, *it occurs to you*, "Maybe I can sue this guy who hurled the brick at me. I'll stand here and take it on the face." *So it is not inevitable that you'll duck.*'

I do not understand why that example proves that, despite

determinism, we retain an element of free will. As a matter of fact, his four words 'it occurs to you' well illustrate a fundamental aspect of my case for determinism which I develop in some detail in Part IV: you do not choose your thoughts – quite beyond your control, they just *occur to you* and cannot be other than they are. On that basis Professor Dennett's example supports my version of determinism because whether you duck or remain standing depends on whether or not the thought happens to occur to you to take the brick on the face so that you can sue for damages.

He goes on to say that 'people think that if their choices are caused, then they are inevitable. That's just wrong. People think that's not real freedom, but of course it is.' The only thing that is clear about this statement is that it is as obscure as it is dogmatic. Yet it is the fundamental plank on which he rests his case for free will.

What in effect he does in that statement is to begin by repeating the premise that, taking the above example, it was not inevitable that you ducked because the thought of suing for damages might have occurred to you, and then to go on to conclude that this is real freedom on your part.

As to the premise, let us suppose that in the same situation the thought of suing occurred to Mr Jones but not to Mr Smith. If we accept for the time being my view in Part IV that our thoughts can never be other than they are, it was inevitable that Mr Jones remained standing and that Mr Smith ducked. In other words it is as true to say that their behaviour was inevitable as to say that it was caused.

As to his conclusion, I believe that Professor Dennett is again guilty of emotive terminological inexactitude by equating 'real freedom' with 'free will'. Among the meanings 'real freedom' most naturally evokes is when we say, for example, that there is no real freedom unless we live in a fully fledged democracy. To make matters worse, his book is even entitled Freedom Evolves, apparently because he emphasizes that we have an ever increasing number of choices, when – if we are supposed to be talking about free will – the relevant question is whether, in making those choices, we are exercising free will. 'Freedom evolves' is a statement which is as unexceptional as it is emotive: a suitable title for a book about the history of the Soviet Union in the last quarter of the 20th Century, but – to say the least – a confusing title for a book the purpose of which is to demonstrate the existence of free will.

It is interesting that in his book Professor Dennett is at pains to use the word 'inevitable' in its proper sense.: that is to say, as meaning 'unavoidable' (defined by the Oxford Dictionary as 'not able to be avoided'). If we express positively the double negative in his statement that it was not inevitable that you would duck, he is saying no more than that you were able to avoid (were capable of avoiding) ducking. This reveals what seems to me to be a fundamental fallacy in his reasoning. The fact that we have the ability or capacity to avoid a certain course of action does not necessarily mean that, if we decide to avoid it, we are exercising our free will in the process. This is, surely, just another version of the non sequitur in his previous example where he says 'we can wear glasses' (are capable of wearing glasses). I comment further on this particular example of the misuse of words in Appendix III.

Finally I will take his third example. I quote: 'If you get a speeding ticket and you decide to fight it in court on the basis of brain damage, you don't want to win the suit because you'd get your licence revoked and you'd be put in an institution. You wouldn't want that – you'd say, "Gimme the fine and let me back on the road." People *want* to be held responsible.' In asserting that you would say, 'Gimme the fine' because you '*want* to be held responsible', Professor Dennett is agreeing with what I have said earlier in my critique of Mary Warnock's book. If it is your (underlying) want or (inner) need to be held responsible that causes you to ask to be fined, he could hardly have given a better example of my version of determinism at work. It is becoming wearisome to have to point out yet again that it does not follow that people *are* responsible because they want to be.

The interviewer and writer of the article about Professor Dennett, Anjana Ahuja, says that they both felt they had freely chosen to meet at a particular London hotel. This, as I have said in other contexts, proves nothing but itself – nothing except that they felt they made their choice of hotel freely. The possibility does not seem to have occurred to them that they – being they – couldn't have felt otherwise: that they were not free to feel that they had chosen freely – they were bound to. Arijana Ahuja says that it would be 'disconcerting' to feel that their choice of venue was determined. So what? In defining my version of determinism, I was careful to emphasize that we like to feel that we have free will.

I have no objection to waxing lyrical or indulging in poetic licence when appropriate. But phrases used by Professor Dennett such as 'Free will is like the air we breath and it is present everywhere we want to go' do not advance his cause but are emotive substitutes for rational argument. I am tempted to say it is *hot* air.

I am increasingly of the view that lengthy and complex philosophical argument can sometimes obfuscate rather than illuminate the truth. Conversely, simple examples can sometimes be an effective means of illuminating the truth. But they can also expose the fallacies underlying more intricate discourses. In my opinion, the examples given by Professor Dennett in his interview with Anjana Ahuja fall into the latter category.

CHAPTER 14

Pigs of the Fields

I OFTEN ENJOY walking along the lane that leads from my home in Olivers Battery on the southern edge of Winchester to the charming village of Hursley. A couple of hundred yards along the lane on the right hand side is a large pig farm on which hundreds of pigs live in open fields. Scattered round the fields are scores of little huts in which they sleep in the night and shelter from the weather's worst extremes during the day. I observe these splendid creatures with the greatest of pleasure. They spend nearly all their time munching whatever morsels of food they can find by nuzzling their snouts into the grass or mud. Sometimes they wander up to a trough near the gate on which I lean to watch them and they eagerly guzzle water from the trough.

The adult pigs don't know that one day they will die. They aren't conscious that they are alone, isolated from other pigs, tiny specks on a planet moving round a sun many million of miles away at a speed of many thousands of miles an hour. They have no concept of eternity – the 'always was' and 'always will be'. They don't look at the stars and try to imagine the unimaginable – space without end. They don't appreciate that the countryside in which they live is beautiful or that the pylons that cross parts of it are not. They don't realize that it is their mating that produces baby pigs. They don't fall in love with other pigs or just plain love them. They don't hate them either. They feel neither hope nor despair, neither hubris nor humility. They don't see the funny side of other pigs or of themselves. They neither laugh nor cry.

Occasionally, for no reason that I can detect, these otherwise docile creatures rush at each other emitting loud and, by their standards, fierce squeals and tussle with each other, fighting as best they can in the absence of horns to lock or sharp claws or long teeth with which to tear each other apart, which seemingly they would if they could. But they don't feel insecure or guilty about their aggression or anything else.

Like human creatures, they follow their inclinations whithersoever they may lead. They don't choose to. They just do. Unlike human creatures, they haven't tried to improve on nature or harness it to their own needs. Their natural instincts remain basic and simple. They fulfil them unconstrained by artificial taboos. Come the Spring, the delightful baby pigs run around and play with each other. Whenever they feel like it, which is quite often, they dash up to their mothers and fight to find a teat from which to guzzle milk to their heart's content.

Pigs are nevertheless more sensitive creatures than many. If artificially confined in a restricted indoor environment, they are liable to suffer from stress and so, with their immune systems weakened, to contract illnesses such as pneumonia. But the pigs living in the open fields down the lane wander into their own little huts only when they feel like it. They are at one with nature and with themselves. They don't suffer from the depression, anxiety or other mental illnesses that we humans, the more civilized and at odds with nature we become, have increasingly to endure. Neither are they prone to suffer from most of the other physical illnesses, such as cancer of the udder, which correspondingly beset humankind. By their uncomplicated standards, the baby pigs grow up into contented, healthy and mature adults.

Lucky pigs! Or are they?

Part IV

CHAPTER 15

Reflections

AS I APPROACH the end of my life, it is only natural to want to look backwards and reflect on the meaning, if any, it may have had. It is also inevitable that I should occasionally look forwards and contemplate my life's more or less imminent ending. The opening words of a poem by Heinrich Heine (set to music on one of Brahm's great lieder) come to mind as I write; 'Der Tod, das ist die kühle Nacht'. Death is the cool night.

I want first to explore the implications in human terms of my conclusion in favour of determinism. By human terms I mean specifically humanist, as opposed to divine or supernatural, terms.

We know that Mary Warnock thinks that it is impossible for determinists like me to be other than inhumane and that we must logically treat everyone like animals and psychopaths.

My own view is otherwise. I suggest that it is entirely consistent with determinism to behave in ways which are profoundly humane and christian (to use a small 'c' as we are at this stage focusing on humanism).

Let us take an example and consider the case of people who are 'always getting themselves into trouble' and 'always making a mess of their lives'. If you believe that they are exercising their free will and so have only themselves to blame, it would be consistent with that belief to say that 'they got what they asked for' and so eventually to run out of sympathy for them. If, on the other hand, you believe that such people are bound to do what they do and so in this sense are not responsible for their actions, it would be inconsistent to say 'they got what they asked for' but consistent – though sometimes easier said than done – to have infinite compassion for them. I am not suggesting that all determinists or only determinists would behave in this way in practice: only that to do so would be consistent with their philosophy. It would also be consistent to forgive those who have caused us to suffer: to turn the other cheek.

There is another significant way in which, if you are a determinist, it would be consistent to be humane and christian. It would be consistent – again though easier said than always done – 'to hate the sin but love the sinner'. This is because you believe the sinner is not in the determinist sense responsible for being a sinner or for the sins he or she commits. Again, I am not suggesting for a moment that such an attitude is the exclusive prerogative of determinists. Clearly, for instance, there are many millions of non-determinist Christians who hate the sin but love the sinner, which is far more commendable because they believe the sinner is free to choose to be a sinner and to sin, though sadly I am bound to say there are also some so-called Christians who take an unloving, self-congratulatory and condemnatory attitude to those who do wrong.

Be that as it may, and at dire risk of sounding 'holier than thou', I venture to say that there have been occasions when, in my own small way, I have found it possible to act in a more kindly way than I would have done had I not believed in determinism. For my part – and from empirical observation of some other people who share my views – it is simply untrue to say that determinism is only a theory with no practical consequences in terms of human behaviour.

Another moral 'upside' of determinism is that it is illogical to be boastful about our positive achievements in life.

It could be said that determinism has 'left wing' consequences, an expression which can be used as a term of abuse just as can 'right wing'. An example of the supposed left wing consequences is the allegation that determinists would have to have as much (if not more) sympathy for criminals as for the victims of their crimes because they think that criminals can't help being criminals. So, the argument goes, they would have to be 'wet' left-wingers, soft on crime and criminals. But more than one logical consequence can flow – as we have already seen – from the same premise. We could equally well say that determinists would have to be 'dry' right-wingers, tough on crime and criminals, because they think that such a policy creates an environment which determines that other would-be criminals are deterred from committing crimes. In passing, I have never forgotten the occasion at a Conservative Party Conference some years ago when the right wing Michael Howard actually received a prolonged ovation for uttering the ultimate truism that 'criminals cause crime'. Not that politicians of different persuasions always refrain from such banalities.

In this context, I am reminded of a moving incident that occurred many years ago when I was working for the then Cumberland County Council and was acting as Clerk to the Court of Quarter Sessions. The jury had found a young, educated couple guilty of some kind of minor fraud. They were sitting in the dock hugging each other and sobbing, with tears pouring from their eyes, waiting for the judge to come back into the Court and sentence them. When he came back, he was trying desperately to restrain his own tears and haltingly said (I can remember almost his exact words) 'I find it very hard to do my duty to society, which demands that I send you both to prison for two years'. I am not suggesting that this profoundly humane judge must have been a determinist. I don't suppose he'd ever thought about it, any more than I had at whatever age I then was. I am only suggesting that his attitude was consistent with determinism.

By way of contrast, I would bet my bottom dollar that the judge who said that Roy Whiting was 'in no way mentally ill' was not a determinist. In my view, he should have thanked his lucky stars that it was Roy Whiting and not himself who was in the dock[204].

———•———

So far I have limited my reflections to the relationship between determinism and humanism. I now want to widen the scope of my reflections by considering the implications of my psychoanalysis and of my conclusions about the material, immature, selfish and determined mind vis-à-vis the spiritual and the supernatural. I propose to dive in at the deep end and straightaway to grapple with the fundamental question of the existence or otherwise of a creationist, all-powerful and all-loving God.

Let me say at once that, although it is hardly surprising that Freud was an atheist, I have not myself found anything in my psychoanalysis that necessarily disproves the existence of God. I have gone out of my way to emphasize more than once that my insights into my unconscious, horrifying to religious people though some of them may be, did not remove an underlying feeling of spirituality in the deepest recesses of my brain. Furthermore, the fact that my religious experiences, such as taking holy communion from Father Mullarkey and praying in awe before a crucifix, transpired to be sublimations of sexual or other primitive impulses in the primitive part of my unconscious (my id) does not mean that they were not sublime, genuinely religious experiences. On the contrary, it could be said that, being sublimated, they were by definition sublime, just as Wagner's music, though sublimated breaking of wind, is sublimely and truly beautiful. ('Beauty is truth, truth beauty.')

I will never forget the face of a very old man amidst a bustling crowd of people worshipping at the foot of a crucifix in a church in Sofia when we visited Bulgaria many years ago when it was still behind the Iron Curtain. I was moved to tears by the absolute faith and sublime awe that shone out from his fading eyes, deeply sunk in a heavily, greyly bearded face etched and furrowed with the human suffering of a long lifetime: so sure seemed his patent and patient belief that he would soon be at peace with his maker for all eternity. Yet awe is an emotion tinged with fear, the sort of fear that had been contained within my unconscious until I experienced those *aweful* insights when sitting before that overly large crucifix in Westminster Cathedral.[184]

If we have evolved from our primate origins by a process of continuous divine creation, it can also be argued more generally that God in his wisdom consummated his creation of the human psyche by superimposing, as it were, our unconscious superego, thereby creating a sophisticated conscious mind capable of rising above its primitive roots and developing a rational religious belief. Unlike Darwin himself, I have never felt that his theory of evolution, so far as I understand it, disproved the existence of a creationist God. Far from it. That His creation is a continuous and continuing process seems to me to be far more likely than the concept that He caused the 'big bang', or whatever it was that set in train the creation of the universe, and then sat back and simply watched His divine plan unfold.

That said, I am bound to say that I find it more plausible that the human psyche created primitive gods and, in the fullness of time, the God of Christianity, Judaism and Islam than the other way round. In the course of evolution we became conscious that we were conscious and so became *self-conscious* and aware of the ultimate isolation of our individuality, a process re-enacted in microcosm as babies grow into the childhood from which they never quite escape ('nor in their inmost hearts ever quite wish to'[44]). There being no such thing as perfect parents here on earth, we developed an overwhelming psychological need to create the notion of God as a perfect Father who, moreover, was immortal and so, unlike our imperfect mortal parents, would never abandon us in our hours of suffering in this life and would continue to give us his unconditional love in the next. This seems to me to be confirmed by the fact that, although Hinduism and Shintoism involve a diverse range of deities, the only great religion or philosophy that does not depend on the existence of a deity is Buddhism, the essence of which is precisely to achieve a state of Nirvana in which there is neither joy nor suffering nor *sense of self (self-consciousness)*.

If we extend this line of thought to, say, the Oedipus and Electra complexes, it again seems more likely that, evolution having incorporated them into our psyche, it was we human beings who created the Christian notion of the virgin birth (as, if I recall aright, did the ancient Egyptians in relation to one of their own gods) in order to satisfy man's unconscious yearning for the exclusive love of an otherwise virgin Mother and women's corresponding need for the individual attention – dare I say attentions? – of an otherwise celibate Father. The concept of the virgin birth resolved an unbearable paradox. Men were able to love and worship a supreme surrogate Mother, and women a divine surrogate Father, who had not betrayed them at the very moment of their conception by having sexual relations with each other. Men did not need to kill God in order to enjoy the exclusive love of Mary, nor did women need to kill Mary in order to enjoy the exclusive love of God.

Even so, it is not logically impossible that God created us with psychological mechanisms attuned to believing that He existed in heaven and caused his Son to be born on earth by a process (the virgin birth) at which those mechanisms would not unduly baulk. It is not logically impossible to envisage a scenario in which it was part of God's divine plan that our psyche should evolve with an inherent capacity to love Him and the mother of His son untainted by irreconcilable conflicts.

———

Turning now to my philosophical views about the human condition, I will first briefly consider my conclusion about 'the immature mind' because it is not unconnected with what I have just been saying.

I have always vividly remembered a television interview given by Jung just before he died in 1961. When asked by the interviewer whether he believed there was a God, he replied: 'I don't believe there is a God. I know there is.' I could see in the close-up of his ageing, wise face the power and depth of his intuitive certainty and was deeply impressed by the apparent humility and maturity of a person who, despite the defects in his character, was one of the important thinkers of the twentieth century. Yet suddenly I felt confused. Part of me felt that his statement was arrogant and childishly simplistic. Looking back on it now as a 'both/and' person, I see no exceptional dichotomy in his personality. Is it not inevitable that we all have the weaknesses inherent in our strengths? Do not the former necessarily mirror the latter and vice-versa? Can we have convictions without being arrogant or always be unsure without lacking conviction? And if Jung displayed childish characteristics, what is so wrong with that? As I visualize Jung's face filling that television screen over forty years ago, the saying springs to mind 'out of the mouths of babes...'.

Be that as it may, I am unconvinced that my conclusion about the immature mind advances the argument about the existence of God one way or the other.

The same is true of my conclusion about 'the selfish mind': that fulfilling a self-regarding inner need or want or instinct is always our decisive motivation even when we behave altruistically. It could reasonably be said that the mechanism of the brain that leads people to behave in ways which are altruistic in their effects is a God-given mechanism, just as I earlier argued that the unconscious mind in all its infinite complexity could be the God-given instrument whereby human beings are enabled – by a process of sublimation – to reach the peak of sublime belief. In this instance, however, I do not find it so difficult to envisage that God created the mechanism of guilt to guide us towards Christian behaviour and attitude. He could hardly have devised a more natural and comprehensible device. If we feel guilty at the thought of doing the wrong thing, so we darned-well should!

Nor do I find my conclusion about 'the material mind' necessarily incompatible with the existence of God. Descartes thought that the mind must be separate from the physical brain because otherwise when we die (are 'brain dead') there would be nothing left – no spirit or soul – that lives on and can go to heaven (or, presumably, hell). Later thinkers who followed in Descartes' footsteps, notably Malebranche, sought to overcome the problem of how the mind could operate on the brain by hypothesizing that, since God's creation was a continuous process, His all-pervasive presence was the instrument whereby the two interacted with each other, a theory which is surely the weakest link in the chain of Cartesian thought. I hope it is not too cheap a jibe to suggest that on any such showing even God would have his hands too full! On my own argument that even our spiritual feelings are physical phenomena generated by our brains, it is not impossible that this spiritual element in our brains constitutes our soul. The materiality of the mind and the existence of God are not necessarily mutually exclusive.

In full circle, this brings us back to 'the determined mind', this time to consider its spiritual and supernatural, as opposed to its humanist, implications. In the context of the existence or otherwise of God, the implications are of such overriding significance that it is timely to admit how unqualified I am to have reached the conclusion that the functioning of the mind is determined (in a deterministic sense) or, for that matter, any other conclusions about the nature of the human mind.

To be so qualified, I should have to be a professional – indeed a Professor – in all aspects of philosophy, medicine, theology, neuroscience, neurophysiology, behaviourism, physics, metaphysics, chemistry, quantum mechanics, social science, sociology, biology, social biology, evolutionary biology, epistemology, cognitive science, comparative religion and logic – a list which is no doubt by no means exhaustive. Although this is a *reductio ad absurdum* on the basis of which no-one could have a valid opinion about almost anything, it is a cogent reminder of the fallibility of our mortal minds.

I appreciate, too, that – apart from attending some lectures on philosophy since I retired – I have read only half a dozen books out of an enormous range of relevant literature. For instance, the 'Guide to Further Reading and Bibliography' at the end of D.J. O'Connor's *Free Will* lists 227 books and articles for further reference. I counted 35 such references on one of the eleven pages of the 'Bibliography' at the end of Owen Flanagan's *The Science of the Mind* – a total of about 385 books or articles. In passing, this book comprises 366 pages, many of which are well nigh incomprehensible to the lay reader – and, I should add, the lay author! Opening it at random I find on page 105: 'If we let uS = unconditional stimulus, and let uR = unconditional response, we can write the general law governing unconditional reflexes as follows: for all uS and uR, uS → uR, where Probability (uR, given uS) = ~ 1'. On page 171 I find: 'Kohlberg's theory has problems of varying degrees in satisfying the criteria Piagetians normally lay down for membership in the class of bona fide stage theories, namely universality, structured wholes, invariant sequence, no regression and integration.' As a last example, on page 328 I read: 'The "ineffable" pink of one's current visual sensation may be richly and precisely expressed as a

95Hz/80Hz/80Hz "chord" in the relevant triune cortical system.' So there you have it!

It is also material to point out at this stage that, as well as being a both/and rather than an either/or person, I tend to over-analyse everything in life, to the point of being unable to make up my mind about anything. I am invariably left in two minds. I am particularly averse to people concluding discussions of complex issues, apparently to their satisfaction, by saying 'it's the principle of the thing'. My late father use to say that people who did so were generally talking nonsense. Over the years, I have come to understand more and more what he meant. After all, if there is only one principle involved, there is really no question to ask. If there is more than one principle, there is certainly a question to ask. But to answer it simply 'on principle' not only begs the question but also smacks of prejudice and bigotry, often of the worst kind. The same is true of an appeal to 'common sense' when it suits us. Mary Warnock, for instance, says that she wants to defend 'the common-sense view' that there is a subject-matter for ethics. Even Descartes appeals to 'the light of natural reason', which is not all that different, when pushed for an answer.

The purpose of this wayward homily as an introduction to the further consideration of determinism is to show how surprisingly contrary to my nature it is that I should feel reasonably sure of my view about so controversial a subject particularly as, contrary to my every instinct, it is an overriding stumbling block to belief in God, even by deploying the most tortuous of arguments.

Determinism makes it impossible for me to overcome what philosophers and theologians have long called 'the problem of evil'. Granted the undeniable evil in this world of ours, it is difficult enough for non-determinist religious people to reconcile the notion of the all-powerful God of Christianity and other religions with that of their all-loving God. They agonize about the dilemma that, their God being all-powerful, He could have prevented the wretched suffering that we human beings whom He created have so often to endure. As he does not, how can it be true that he has infinite love for each and every one of us? Taken on its own I do not find this incredible. As mere finite mortals, it is a wonderful and mysterious paradox that we can give more than one person *all* our love. I do not, for instance, give my wife, four children and six grandchildren only one eleventh of my love but love each of them totally and absolutely. So, therefore, an infinite God could give an infinite number of human beings His total and absolute love. But where was His love for millions of human beings when they were being shovelled into gas chambers during the Holocaust? Being all-powerful, He could have stopped this happening but chose not to.

As I understand it, religious people answer this in two main ways. In a highly condensed form, they are that God works in mysterious ways His wonders to perform and that such grotesque evil is the fault of human beings, not His, because He created them with the freedom to choose between sinning and not sinning. I am not psychologically disinclined to recognize that some 'truths' can be mysterious and above logic. Thus my oft-quoted 'beauty is truth, truth beauty' is not demonstrable by a process of logic but, despite that, is to my mind a meaningful, if mysterious, proposition. The essential point, however, is that, although some truths may be *above* logic, they cannot be *contrary* to logic. If determinism be true – if human beings are not free to choose between good and evil, between sinning and not sinning – it is logically impossible to say that the evil in the world is their fault. It follows that, whereas religious belief makes it difficult to reconcile the 'all-powerfulness' and 'all-lovingness' of God, determinism makes it downright impossible.

Determinism also strikes at the heart of the concept of civilization and civilizations themselves. From the earliest moments when primates became recognizably human, they formed groups or societies to ensure their own survival. In order that there should be some semblance of order they created rules and punishments for breaking those rules. Both rules and punishments became more sophisticated and numerous as civilizations became more complex, sometimes by coalescing, as we can see from the current debate about laws for the European Community. Yet all such laws depend on the assumption that the citizens of the states who create them are responsible for their actions. If they are not so responsible, all laws are based on a fiction – a necessary and desirable fiction, but a fiction nonetheless. That may be a difficult consequence of determinism, but the temptation to put the cart before the horse – to conclude that, because it has consequences which are difficult to grapple with, it cannot be true – is a temptation, as ever, to be resisted if we are to argue rationally rather than emotionally.

In this context, I was fascinated by a summary in Oxford Law News (issue 7) of the inaugural lecture by John Gardner, who was elected Professor of Jurisprudence in 2000. The lecture was entitled 'The Mark of Responsibility'. Amongst his arguments, Professor Gardner says that, in a trial in which the defence is anxious to reduce murder to manslaughter, it is more moral for the accused to claim responsibility and argue that his action was reasonable in the light of the provocation he faced than to claim 'diminished responsibility': it would be better to 'assert his basic responsibility'. (This is remarkably similar to Professor Dennett's 'Gimme the fine' example.[227]) It seems quite extraordinary to me that in a key lecture about responsibility under the law, the Professor of Jurisprudence at a University recognized as the world leader in legal philosophy apparently fails to address the fundamental underlying issue of free will versus determinism.

———·•·———

I had anticipated that I would reach the conclusion that in no sense could the existence or the non-existence of God be proved or disproved by logical deduction, thereby leaving it open to us to believe in the mystery either of His existence or of His non-existence (or remain in doubt one way or the other.) I refer to the mystery of His non-existence advisedly because, when I contemplate the intricate beauty of nature and the immensity of the wonders of the universe, emotionally I find His non-existence as difficult to comprehend as His existence.

What I had not anticipated, particularly as a both/and person for ever in two minds, was that my belief in determinism would lead me to the conclusion that a God who is at once all-powerful and all-loving cannot logically exist.

I recognize that this conclusion depends on whether I have 'proved' that its premise – determinism – is true. I have a limited understanding that there are different kinds of so-called proof, such as 'philosophical' and 'scientific' proof. It is arguable that the greatest achievement of Karl Popper (probably the greatest philosopher of science of the twentieth century) was to show that even scientific theories cannot be verified, only falsified: thus, though science is the closest we can get to knowledge, it is never perfect knowledge.

In discussing determinism I have not been able to adopt a scientific approach because it cannot be tested by scientific experimentation. The most I have been able to do is to test my theory against its possible falsifications, which I have previously called the counter arguments. If I have falsified all the falsifications, have I not proved determinism to the limited extent that it is possible to prove anything?

———◦———

It occurs to me to wonder whether my conclusion about the determined mind is consistent with my conclusions about the material, immature, and selfish mind. If not, they cannot all be right. It seems to me that not only are they consistent but in fact positively support each other. Thus we could combine my conclusions about the selfish and determined mind by saying that we are always bound to fulfil an inner need or want or instinct of one kind or another. My conclusion about the material mind sits comfortably with determinism because it is reasonable to suppose that a material mechanism works by means of cause and effect, a concept which is inherent in determinism. My view about the immature mind, while not inconsistent with determinism, does not advance the arguments about it one way or the other.

In the course of writing these reflections, a further thought about determinism in the context of evil has occurred to me. It is that the evil that men do, again taking the Holocaust as a prime example, is less incomprehensible if the Nazis were not exercising their free will than if they were. To put it more positively, I find it more credible that they were bound to do what they did than that they freely chose to.

At one of my philosophy classes a few months ago, the lecturer was talking about the various so-called proofs of God and mentioned that one philosopher, William Paley, gave the example of finding a clock or watch in a jungle. I pricked up my ears, instantly recalling the incident when Monsignor Elwes tried to reconvert me to Catholicism at Oxford[53] and thinking to myself that I knew this was going to be a silly argument. Presumably Monsignor Elwes had picked up this idea at some theological college but had forgotten how to explain it properly. It is called 'the argument from design'. Expressed more fully, it is on the lines that if you found such a clock or watch and examined it, you would have to conclude that some Mind had been behind its complex and beautiful construction with its delicate, inter-reacting myriad parts in harmony with each other and designed to achieve a purpose – the purpose of telling the time accurately. Put like this, I found the argument from design powerfully compelling. I remembered being moved by obituaries of famous scientists and surgeons who, the more they had learnt about the awesome complexity and wonderful harmony of the many parts of the human body, all working towards the sustenance of life, the more convinced they had become that there must have been a divine Creator. There could be no design without a Designer. Coincidentally, the argument is well put in the November 2002 edition of Awake, one of the magazines published by the Watchtower Bible and Tract Society, whose publications two nice ladies (Jehovah's Witnesses) regularly deliver to my house. An article about a new scientific discovery about our eyes concludes: 'Clearly, the more we learn about life, the more we see evidence of often subtle, yet truly profound design. Such insights move many to echo the Bible's words of praise to the Creator: "I shall laud you because in a fear-inspiring way I am wonderfully made. Your works are wonderful, as my soul is very well aware." – Psalm 139.14.' In the cool light of subsequent reflection, however, I have been unable to stop asking myself why a loving Creator should have designed our brains with the capacity to cause and undergo incomprehensible suffering and our bodies with the capacity to incur dreadful illnesses and diseases (like the Black Death and AIDS) with all the untold agony that ensues: or why, if he is benign, he should have designed a planet with volcanoes, earthquakes, hurricanes, floods, droughts and other natural phenomena that regularly kill tens of thousands of innocent human beings. An all-powerful Creator could have designed us and our planet free of such evil and awfulness but chose not to.

I often think to myself that some of the greatest minds, Einstein and Jung among them, believed in God. I recently put this to a friend who is an unashamed atheist. (Why should I disassociate an atheist from shame?) He replied that some of the greatest minds had been atheists – Darwin, Freud and Bertrand Russell spring to mind – which deflated my enthusiasm.

Try as I may with my limited experience, knowledge and capacity for thought, I am always driven back to determinism. Indeed it seems clear to me that, being me, it was determined that I would end up being a determinist: I was bound to be, bound to think in the way I do. We do not independently or artificially manufacture the thoughts that come to mind. We cannot choose to stop them coming to mind or make them other than they are. We think what we think and feel what we feel. We cannot help falling in love or with whom we fall in love, or being heterosexual, gay, lesbian, bisexual or paedophiliac. But we don't have to take such extreme examples. That this thought – that we don't have to take such extreme examples – came to mind was beyond my control. I did not freely choose that it should. It just did. In ordinary language, I could now choose to cross that sentence out in order to show that I am free from the so-called shackles of determinism. Yet, if I didn't think in the way I cannot help thinking, I wouldn't have added that last, equally unsolicited sentence either. As I sit here at my desk, I can feel that there is 'something about me' (Thomas Nagel) making me decide to leave it in.

So, too, anyone reading what I have just written will be thinking something about it – typically 'of course I can make choices' or 'determinism is a cop-out'. But he or she will not be choosing to be thinking what he or she will be thinking. It will not be possible for his or her thoughts to be other than what they will be. One person with whom I recently discussed determinism concluded – unaware of the irony – by saying 'I see what you mean, but I still can't help thinking that I am in control of my life'!

The same is true of feelings. If some readers feel, say, disturbed or annoyed by what I have written, they will not be choosing to feel disturbed or annoyed. It will not be possible for them to feel differently. Our thoughts and feelings at any one microsecond in time can only be what they are and, as I see it, they alone determine our actions and so-called choices.

Why, then, is it that so few people apparently agree with my view about determinism? My experience is that Mary Warnock was right when she said that we instinctively treat people as being responsible for their actions but was wrong to assume that it follows that people are responsible. As most people instinctively dismiss determinism, they do not bother to think about it. Why should they? Abstracted from its fundamentally important consequences, which *a fortiori* they do not think about either, determinism is not in itself the most interesting of our human characteristics such as those I suggested were not enjoyed (or endured) by the 'pigs of the fields'[(229)]. It can also be 'sold' rather unimaginatively and inadequately. In *The Science of the Mind*, for instance, Owen Flanagan is for once dangerously close to expressing something vaguely resembling an emotion when he describes Aldous Huxley's statement that 'we are conscious automata' as a 'brazen pronouncement'. Huxley's statement may be an accurate description of determinism, but if determinists conjure up the vision that we humans are nothing more than cleverer automata than the Daleks in *Dr Who* they do less than justice to their cause and invite a dismissive reaction.

Instinctive resistance to believing in determinism is rather like the resistance to believing in Freud's theory of the unconscious. Such resistance can be overwhelmingly powerful, sometimes and sadly to the detriment of mentally ill people who pull out all the stubborn stops of their resistance (conscious but mainly unconscious) in order to avoid seeking the psychiatric help they so clearly need. The same is true of people suffering serious psychosomatic illnesses such as alcoholics, anorexics and agoraphobics. Indeed, it is often the case that the greater the mental or psychosomatic illness, the greater the resistance to recognizing it as such.

An otherwise intelligent person I know recently said he did not 'believe in' Freud because he was 'such a nasty man'. But then so were Wagner and Picasso, which does not mean their music and paintings were not sublime masterpieces. Some years ago, I even read an article in the *Sunday Times* by a serious writer whose name I have forgotten, who, in his desperation to denigrate Freud, asserted that it was not he who discovered the unconscious Oedipus complex but Sophocles in the fifth century BC because he wrote his play about Oedipus unknowingly killing his father and marrying his mother, on discovering which he gouged out his own eyes. On that basis, we might just as well say that Homer discovered the unconscious evil eye by writing about the Cyclops round about 800 BC.

The trouble is that Freud's theory is particularly hard to 'prove'. Advocates that Freud was in essence, if not in every respect, 'right' – amongst whom I count myself – have to argue in a circle: 'You reject Freud because of your unconscious resistance to his views'. Yet to refer to unconscious resistance is assuming what we are seeking to prove. At the end of the day, I can only say to people: 'Go away, find someone like Dr Lester and be treated by him, and then come back and have another discussion in ten years' time.' On the other hand, it was quite obvious to me that Dr Lester listened to variations on my own unconscious insights as a matter of regular daily routine. So far as he was concerned, listening to such outpourings was just another day at the office.

The validity of the claim by Freudian analysts that their clinical observations verify Freud's theories has been doubted by Karl Popper in his book *Conjectures and Refutations: The Growth of Scientific Knowledge*, written in 1968. His argument is that Freudian analysts have preconceived views and so are 'looking for' verification. I can only say that in my case

Dr Lester didn't have to look very hard. I dished out large helpings of verification and served them up to him on a plate. Moreover, I did not 'look for' the insights I described in Part II – indeed, I strongly resisted recognition of many of them. Nor did I have a vested interest in verifying Freud's theories. Speaking for myself – and not for my analyst – it seems clear to me that, insofar as my insights during and long after my analysis verify Freud's theories, such verification cannot reasonably be dismissed as spurious.

Not to believe in God makes it difficult to find meaning in our lives: impossible, in fact, to find an Ultimate Meaning. That was easy enough for me as a young Roman Catholic. If my memory fails me not, the first two questions and answers of the Catechism, which we learnt by heart parrot-fashion, were:

'Q.Who made you?

A.God made me.

Q.Why did God make you?

A.God made me to know, love and serve Him in this world and to be happy with Him in the next.'

Meaning enough in those few words. I am envious of people – including friends for whom I have the highest regard – who have not lost or who have discovered their Christian faith and receive profound comfort from it in life's darkest moments. At such times, I should like to be able to pray for others or for myself. I should like to believe that when I shuffle off this mortal coil I will be for ever reunited with those I love – my wife, children and grandchildren – with a composure free from the anxiety which can sometimes be the price we pay for love in this world.

Quite by chance, I recently came across a book by Gerald Priestland entitled *Something understood: an autobiography*. During his time as a broadcaster, he accumulated a devoted following, particularly during his years as the BBC's religious affairs correspondent. He regards his book as 'a story of victory over depression'. All through his remarkable BBC career, he felt himself 'pursued by the Furies'. Eventually, he had a complete breakdown and underwent analysis for a period of less than six months. I quote:

'He [the psychiatrist] conducted me through a long and sometimes tearful pilgrimage of understanding and forgiving from which all the characters, including [my parents and] myself, at last emerged as having done their best by the light they had, misunderstanding and misunderstood, but all in the end to be loved for what they are...So long as I believed that I was a boy who hated his parents, of course I was rotten and worthless and guilty of willing their death. But in fact I had showed plenty of evidence that I was a *good* [his italics] son and had brought them pride and pleasure.'

He eventually found happiness from his conversion to Christianity, specifically by becoming a Quaker – a member of the Society of Friends, the greatest blessing being that it really was a society of friends. He expressed profound gratitude to George Gorman, who used to conduct sample weekends for 'enquirers', when 'he dispensed exactly the kind of religious philosophy I was waiting to hear.' On one occasion, George Gorman told him: 'I spend a lot of time de-guilting people who have been torn and smashed by their sense of sin. Quakers are around witnessing to the goodness of life, starting at the opposite end to original sin. No matter how rotten it looks, we believe that life is good, valuable and loving...In loving and accepting other people, you are beginning to love yourself. For the truth about life is love; and the truth about love is that it is God.'

Whereas Gerald Priestland's book is the story of his journey, via one form of analysis, from atheism and severe depression to Christian belief as a Quaker, mine is the opposite story of a journey, via another form of analysis, from Christian belief as a Roman Catholic to atheism and comparatively mild depression. (I have never contemplated suicide as he did when his breakdown led him to the depths of despair.) Nevertheless, our paths in life – our experiences and insights – have much more in common than might at first sight appear to be the case.

Apart from the obvious similarity of our unconscious guilt about our aggressive feelings towards our parents (particularly our mothers), I have in mind his statement that through his analysis he had come to realize that his parents, though *misunderstanding and misunderstood* (as profoundly true and moving an expression of our human condition as I have ever come across), had done their best. Dr Lester once said to me – I remember his exact words – that my mother had loved me 'as best she could: that she couldn't do better wasn't her fault but her parents' who couldn't help it either' (heavy shades of determinism?).

Although Gerald Priestland's analysis did not need to scour the bottom of the Freudian barrel, he had insights that rang a clear bell of recognition in my mind. He says, for instance, that at most of his meetings as a Quaker, the room was bare and unadorned and the worship mostly in silence 'but at least I was not confronted with that tortured figure on the crucifix telling me that I had helped to nail him there.' Perhaps he was half-consciously aware of the revelation I experienced before the crucifix in Westminster Cathedral: that I had castrated Christ by nailing him to the cross and deserved to be punished for that sin, for my other sins and for the sins of the world. Furthermore, in the course of his analysis it emerged that all his hard work and perfectionism were ways of satisfying authority so that it need never investigate his real motives, especially his 'appalling hatred of his mother.' This sheds a new light on the unconscious reasons for my own hard work and perfectionism, as exemplified by my unhealthy and harmful compulsion to achieve exceptional academic excellence at Oxford. He also came to understand that he had been taken from his mother's breast too early and says: 'the truth is that part of us never grows up', which is equivalent to my conclusion about 'the immature mind'. 'The Furies' that had pursued him sound very like what I have described as 'the dark shadows' that sometimes overwhelmed me. The significant difference is that, whereas he eventually found happiness through his conversion to religion, I have done so despite my rejection of religion.

As I anticipated, it is when we come to wrestle with the problem of human suffering that our paths diverge, never to converge. He says he found helpful, and will never forget the outburst of the poet, P. J. Kavanagh, when he (Gerald Priestland) suggested that we deserved something better than most of us get: 'I don't see what we have deserved. I cannot see why people think things should be better than they are. It seems to me that we get more than we deserve.' I suggest that in its context 'more' can only mean more that is good rather than more that is bad: that we *deserve* (that most guilt inducing of words) to suffer more than we do.

It is not a good morning for me to comment calmly and analytically on P.J. Kavanagh's outburst. Late last night (28 January 2003), I flicked casually from one television channel to another. On the first channel was an account of social workers dealing with appalling cases of parents' cruelty to their children. The second channel showed police investigations into paedophiles, including horrifying pictures of child abuse. The third was about Jewish children in Prague being sent to

England just before the Second World War. There was an old speckled film showing their chubby little hands waving goodbye from the windows of a departing train, their parents, crowding and jostling on the platform, in return waving their handkerchiefs and shedding tears of unimaginable grief at the departure of their beloved children, knowing that they were unlikely ever to see them again but not yet that they themselves would soon be departing by train, not for England but for the gas chambers. In desperation, I flicked across to the news, only to witness the gathering storm clouds of war over Iraq. Glancing at the paper this morning, there was an account of Zimbabweans currently being tortured to death and an article about the Chinese who were hung by their tongues with meat-hooks during the Japanese invasion of China before the Second World War. I aver unequivocally – 'with words that weep and tears that speak' – that those innocent children, those parents standing on Prague station, and those of so-called 'God's children' being tortured horrendously to death avowedly were *not* getting better than they deserved: they did *not* deserve greater suffering, if such be conceivable even by the monstrous beasts who, in the name of some perverted cause, perpetuate such disgusting, filthy crimes against humankind. At least the cruellest of non-human animals 'know not what they do'.

Such examples are only the tip of the twentieth century's iceberg of evil whose deep darkness was so often lashed by the swirling tides and raging torrents of the cruel sea. Speaking at random and in round figures, I have in mind the bloody Second Boer War; the First World War (with over one million soldiers being killed or wounded just in the Battle of the Somme); the massacre of a million Chinese during the Japanese invasion in the thirties; the ruthless disregard for life, sometimes of father, son or brother, in the Spanish Civil War; the Second World War, with the unrivalled horrors of the Holocaust involving the cold-blooded, pitiless murder of six million Jews, over three hundred thousand German casualties at the Battle of Stalingrad alone, many millions of Russians randomly slaughtered on the Eastern Front, the thousands left entombed in their own melted fat after the carpet-bombing and fire storms of Hamburg and the horrific deaths and injuries of untold thousands of Japanese civilians following the dropping of atom-bombs on Hiroshima and Nagasaki; the Korean War and the defeat of the Americans in Vietnam, each with their own untold horrors; the genocide of a million human beings in Rwanda and, more recently, of tens of thousands of Muslims and others in the former Yugoslavia in the name of ethnic cleansing; the madness of confrontation between different tribes, exacerbated by their different religions, in Northern Ireland, the Middle East and elsewhere; and other wars so countless as to be nameless. None of these wars – none of the wars in the brief history of humankind – was launched in the name of humanism.

To praise P.J. Kavanagh's outburst in aid of reconciliation between suffering and the existence of a loving God is all very well for those of us living comfortably in the middle class of middle England. We may well count our blessings. But to bury our heads in the sand and to suggest that suffering such as I have described was 'better' than was deserved by those who had to endure it, strikes a dagger at the very heart of the notion of an all-loving, all-powerful god. Moreover, it is not only a question of the headlines writ large about the broad sweep of history but also of the unwritten personal tragedies and sorrows that we so often witness in our daily lives. To take but one recent example from my own experience: I have witnessed the work of the Children's Hospice, Naomi House. Let no-one take the blinkered view and tell me that the parents and children in residence there do not deserve better – let alone deserve worse – than they are getting.

The other way in which Gerald Priestland tackles the problem of evil is the one which I have suggested is the classic way of so doing: he regards human beings as free to choose. He points out that two people can have much the same experience of life (as in many ways have he and I, despite our very different professional careers) and yet one can emerge as believing, the other disbelieving. 'God', he says, 'has to make belief in Himself *optional* or there is no human freedom and no divine love.'

I italicized 'optional' in order to illustrate the trap of terminological inexactitude into which those who argue against determinism can so easily fall. Properly speaking, optional means 'available to be chosen' (see the Oxford Dictionary): it does not mean 'choosable by the exercise of free will'.

So, too, the definition of 'choice' in the Oxford dictionary is emotionally neutral: 'an act of selecting or making a decision when faced with two or more possibilities'. When people say 'of course we can choose between various options', I do not doubt that in one sense they can. Nonetheless, they are almost invariably unaware that they are not only begging the question of free will versus determinism but also implicitly answering it by assuming that they make their choices freely, unconstrained by their mental processes which I have argued cannot be other than they are.

These examples illustrate a crucial and largely unrecognized vicious circle where people instinctively use words in an emotive and inaccurate way which implies that they have free will and then use those words to support their view that they do indeed have free will. That may be only human. But it is the antithesis of detached, rational argumentation. (I give other examples of ambiguity in the use of words in Appendix III.)

It was because Gerald Priestland thought that he was free to choose to believe in God, 'who has to make belief in Himself optional', that he discovered his belief in 'divine love' and found his salvation in both the psychological and religious senses, the mutually enriching correlation between the two being the most enviable and wonderful consequence of religious belief. It is because I think that it was inevitable that he would reach his destination of divine love that I find myself unable to follow in his footsteps.

I have long come to realize that a major problem for atheists is to explain life, and especially human consciousness. I put this to one of the lecturers, Mike Smithhurst, at my philosophy course during a coffee break. I was fascinated to learn that consciousness (as well as life) is one of the salient current issues in the philosophical world. This was later confirmed when I happened to read the 'Preface to the Second Edition' of Owen Flanagan's *The Science of the Mind*, where he says that he had added a new final chapter entitled 'Consciousness', which reflects his most recent thinking about 'the hardest problem in the science of the mind'. This chapter, like the rest of his book, is an intellectual tour de force.

As to life itself, I had often wondered whether scientists could put all the relevant chemicals in a test tube and so replicate the beginning of life on our planet. I was not surprised to discover that scientists had indeed conducted such experiments which had gone some, but not the whole, way to producing DNA. The chemistry of the experiments he describes is way beyond my understanding, but he concludes that no-one is yet sure exactly how life evolved because we are not certain what the primeval organic materials were or in what amounts they subsisted, whether the consummating action took place in the seas or in the marshes, and what form of life was the very first to arise. Later he says that 'we know that

DNA is the basis for life and that the brain is the basis for mind' and 'a Darwinian machine'. Owen Flanagan explains that the best estimates at the time of writing in 1990 were that the brain consists of roughly 100 billion neurons. Recalling the number of permutations in which fifteen coloured cards can be arranged[156], the number of permutations of 100 billion neurons is mind-blowing – more than enough to make us all unique! Moreover, a typical neuron has synaptic connections emanating on average from of the order of 3,000 other neurons. This is on average: some have as many as 10,000. According to the Oxford Dictionary a synapse is 'a junction between two nerve cells, consisting of a minute gap across which impulses pass by diffusion of a neurotransmitter'.

A conservative estimate is that the total number of distinct neural states is $10^{100,000,000,000,000}$. Even if we assume that 99 percent of these states do not add up to anything 'cognitively worthwhile', that still leaves $10^{99,999,999,999,998}$ states – conscious or unconscious – capable of doing worthwhile 'cognitive labour'.

In passing, I found it interesting that neurotransmitters do not just function to turn neurons on or off but are also involved in how things feel qualitatively (which differentiates the brain from a computer). Hence neurotransmitter levels are becoming increasingly implicated in diseases such as anxiety disorders and clinical depression. Some extremely effective new antidepressants work by inhibiting the reabsorption of serotonin by the neurons releasing it. While I do not pretend to understand that, it again confirms my point in 'The Material Mind' (Chapter 10) that feelings, like memories and thoughts, are physical phenomena. None of which – to repeat myself, hopefully not *ad nauseum* – disproves the existence of a creationist God. On the contrary, *taken by itself*, it is a spell-binding reinforcement of the argument from design.

Owen Flanagan's final paragraph concludes that, if we look to work in the areas of the philosophy of mind, neuroscience, neuropsychology and certain segments of cognitive science, the problem of consciousness is beginning to yield. 'Understanding consciousness with consciousness is a wonderful, giddy idea and yet at the same time a genuine possibility. So let the fun begin.'

Little more than ten years after Owen Flanagan wrote this, some neuroscientists have already begun to have their fun. According to an article by Jonathan Leake, the Science Editor, in the *Sunday Times* of 9 March 2003, Francis Crick (a Nobel Prize winner) claims already to have found the group of cells – a small set of neurons – in the human brain responsible for generating consciousness and self-awareness explaining why, as I have put it[236], we became conscious that we are conscious. His latest research, based on years of experimentation and studies of the brain, apparently proves his case. Christof Koch, professor of neuroscience at the California Institute of Technology, who co-authored Francis Crick's latest research, says: 'It is clear that consciousness arises from biochemical reactions within the brain.' Although other scientists are not entirely convinced, Colin Blakemore, professor of neuroscience at Oxford University, is amongst those who support this view. Where I have the temerity to differ from these eminent scientists is that I do no see why these findings about 'the material mind' disprove the existence of a creationist God. Such a God could surely have created the relevant small set of neurons. For me, determinism stands alone as the determinant of the non-existence of God.

———

Is there any sense in which those like myself who, however reluctantly, have come not to believe in God, can make sense of our lives or find meaningful meaning in them, particularly in the light – or rather against the darkness – of the problem of evil? It all depends, of course, on what we mean by meaning. However interminably philosophers may argue about the meaning of meaning, for the likes of determinists like myself, there can, as I said above, be no Ultimate Meaning: we can only grapple to find finite meanings in our daily lives.

Many years ago, I read a book by W. Beran Wolfe entitled *How to be happy though human*. To the best of my recollection, its broad thrust was that, as we only have finite minds, not only can we never hope to solve infinite problems, such as the existence or otherwise of God, but it is a waste of our minds' time – indeed, it is a positive abuse of our minds even to try to do so. If I say – as I do – that I can see the merits of that argument, the thought springs involuntarily to my mind that it is inconsistent with my own conclusion that the non-existence of God is as proven as anything can ever be. How can I have it both ways? Is it not an irresolvable paradox? And can we ever 'prove' a negative? On reflection, I think I remain on firm ground because my chain of reasoning is based on the material, determinist and finite working of the human brain. It is from the *finite* and *positive* premise of determinism that I draw the *infinite* and *negative* conclusion that there cannot be an all-powerful God who is also a God of love. I am not sufficient of a logician to know whether I am hoist by my own logical petard on the grounds that a conclusion about the infinite cannot logically follow from a finite premise. For my part, I cannot see why it cannot logically follow. Although most people with whom I have discussed my views have not accepted the premise – certainly at first sight – they have all accepted that, granted the premise, the conclusion is irrefutable.

Does it follow, then, that all is doom and gloom? That we are merely intelligent automata doomed to the gloom of determined suffering? That human suffering is pointless, devoid of all meaning?

While it does follow from determinism that this is the unpalatable truth and nothing but the unpalatable truth, it does not follow that it is quite the *whole* truth. I have argued before that we are much more than intelligent automata. Furthermore, to overcome suffering and despair requires perseverance, more so, perhaps, than any other human experience. There can therefore be blessings in having suffered and despaired, however limited. It can, for instance, be a character-forming and 'growing experience' that leads to greater maturity and hence to greater mental well-being in the longer run (though this is of little comfort at the time). Moreover, if we have never suffered we can never be as fully conscious as we would otherwise be that we are as happy as we are when we *are* happy. I myself am profoundly thankful for my mental well-being precisely (but not only) because it was not ever thus.

It is also true that, if we have not ourselves suffered, we cannot by definition know what it is like to suffer and so, though we may be sympathetic people, we cannot empathize with other people's suffering to quite the same extent. (I have included this amongst the blessings of suffering, though if carried to neurotic extremes it can be self-destructive without achieving anything positive for those dear to us who we know are suffering.) One of the significant conscious psychological bonuses of the story of Christ's crucifixion is that believers feel comforted that His extreme suffering showed how profoundly He empathized with their own. More (literally) mundanely, the 'I know how you feel' approach of some kinds of psychotherapists can help to give limited relief to some patients, though its efficacy can, in my view, be overstated and simplistic.

The philosophy advocated in *How to be happy though human* is that, having cast aside our ill-judged attempts at infinite speculation about infinite concerns, we should simply get on with our finite lives and do our best to find meanings in contented human relationships (sexual and otherwise), in comradeship, in useful work we are good at and in enjoying fulfilling hobbies. Such meanings are sufficient unto the day. Beyond that, we should stoically accept the world for what it is, warts and all.

I remember this approach being astonishingly successful in an interview on television many years ago given by John Stonehouse, the high-profile Member of Parliament, who was in a state of such appalling breakdown that he manufactured his own bizarre disappearance. It was years after the event and it was clear that he had received prolonged psychiatric treatment of one kind or another. The essence of what he said was that he used to think – or try to – that the world was a wonderful place and was profoundly unhappy. Now he knew it was a rotten world and had found happiness through stoical, philosophical resignation. Amen to that!

There are grounds for optimism about the future of the world, though we need to be, amongst other things, professional 'futurologists' and 'cross-culturalists' if we are to have an informed view. The theme of one of my philosophy courses was prejudice about cultures other than our own: the difficulty, for instance, of overcoming our ingrained mind-set that 'Western' Christian civilization is superior to other civilizations.

Books that are required reading in this context are: *The clash of civilizations and the remaking of the world order* by Samuel P. Huntington and *The cultural imperative: global trends in the 21st century* by Richard D. Lewis (whom I have had the pleasure of meeting because his wife, Jane, sometimes plays tennis with Isabel). Both books exude remarkable knowledge of the great number of diverse cultures in the world. Comfortingly, Samuel Huntington concludes that a global war involving the core states of the world's major civilizations is highly improbable. More positively, Richard Lewis concludes that 'the West, in spite of the huge forthcoming advances in Eastern and Islamic societies [China being the most notable example] will continue to acquit itself well in the twenty-first century'.

Successive generations tend to be pessimistic about the generations that succeed them. I myself, however, am optimistic that, set against the twentieth century, the twenty-first century augurs relatively well. There will no doubt be further terrorist attacks following – amongst others – those against the Twin Towers on 11 September 2001. I believe that the more acts of terrorism there are, the more the major powers and other countries of the world will increasingly unite to combat terrorism, which will at least be a better state of affairs than the world in which I have lived much of my life and in which the major powers were constantly at hot or cold war with each other. We may be horrified at the thought of future terrorist attacks, though the statistical probability of their affecting us personally must be close to zero. This is infinitely better than it was to live through the cold war when we constantly lived in fear of total and personal obliteration.

The number of people killed on the worst night of the blitz in Coventry was nearly three times more than the two hundred people killed in the terrorist attack in Madrid on 11 March 2004, and that was in just one night of the blitz on just one British city, the Battle of Britain itself being just one of thousands of battles in just one of the major wars of the twentieth century. I vividly remember a picture on the front page of the *News Chronicle* (long since extinct) showing the battlecruiser, HMS *Hood*, when it was announced that she had been sunk with the loss of more than 1,400 crew, who suffered the ghastly death of slowly drowning – nearly half as many human beings as those killed in the terrorist attack on the Twin Towers. The *Hood* was just one of the many hundreds of ships sunk during the Second World War. The loss of British Commonwealth warships in the Mediterranean alone between 10 June 1940 and 8 September 1943 included 14 cruisers and 47 destroyers. In just one year the Germans lost 244 submarines. My source for these figures is *War at Sea* by Capt S.W. Roskill. They are small extracts just from Part I of Volume III.

Prominence is rarely given by the media to good news. It seems to me that the most important single factor that will enhance our welfare and minimize our destruction of each other and of our planet is to encourage the spread of contraception in an effort to ensure that human numbers decline. (Let us hope against hope that the next Pope will be progressive in this respect.) If that be right, every newspaper should have emblazoned across its front page a United Nations report which, according to Sarah Baxter in the *Sunday Times* of 2 February 2003 (page 27!), will have buried within it figures that will show that average fertility rates world-wide will decline to Western levels by 2050. Women are likely to bear an average of only 1.85 children in all countries. Alarmist predictions by doom-mongers of a world population of more than 10 or 11 billion will not be reached, according to the author of the authoritative report, Larry Heligman of the UN population division. The number is more likely to grow just beyond the 8 billion mark, where it will begin to level off and decline. By 2075, the world's population should have shrunk by half a billion. In Iran, where women bore an average of 6.5 'soldiers for Islam' at the height of Khomeini's revolution in the early 1980s, family planning has already brought the figure down to just 2.75. Similar downward trends can also be seen in such populous countries as Indonesia, India, Tunisia and Brazil.

Another recent short article locked away in the *Sunday Times* was alarmingly headed: 'North Pole ice cap will have melted in 80 years'. Yet in the last paragraph, Jonathan Leake, the Environment Editor, points out that the melting of the North Pole will not – as I had assumed – contribute to a rise in sea levels, as all the ice is floating. (Is this not why Archimedes jumped out of his bath and shouted 'eureka' over 2000 years ago?) Although it is otherwise with the southern icecap, which sits above sea level on a buried continent, and although polar bears and seals may not survive, the loss of the northern icecap would open up the Northwest Passage and enable ships to save thousands of miles on journeys between Europe and the Far East, and increased rainfall will probably allow more plankton to grow and so boost fish stocks.

I sometimes think someone should produce a newspaper confined to giving good news. Imagine a headline saying: 'Thirty million British men did not rape anyone yesterday'. Certainly the examples I have given bear on two of the most important issues relative to the future of our planet. Yet everyone to whom I have mentioned them was – like myself – pleasantly surprised, not to say astonished. And there are further grounds for optimism. At a business dinner some ten years' ago, I was sitting next to the Chairman of one of the largest oil companies in the world (Shell or BP?), who said that in the next (twenty-second) century people would look back at the era of oil and its concomitant pollution as an unfortunate blip in the history of humankind. I believe it probable that the United States of America, if ever forced to face up to the prospect of the environmental equivalent of Pearl Harbour, will take the lead in reducing pollution.

Progress has been well defined as the creation of a new set of problems. In the twenty-first century an iron curtain will not hang between East and West, apartheid in South Africa will remain a thing of the past and there will be some semblance of continuing peace in Northern Ireland, though in each case the new problems created by progress remain in varying degrees to be resolved. I had not expected to see any of those events occur in my lifetime. Isabel and I were in Berlin three weeks before its infamous wall came tumbling down and went through 'Checkpoint Charlie' to witness the devastating contrast of East Berlin. If anyone had then suggested that the wall would not be there three weeks later, we would have thought them stark-staring mad. I suspect we would think someone no less mad were he or she to suggest that the Israeli-Palestinian problem will be solved in the foreseeable future. The American invasion of Iraq has certainly created a new set of problems. Only time will tell whether they will lead to progress.

We can at least hope that the increasing globalization of communications will do more to promote toleration than to provoke discord. There will certainly be further substantial advances in medical science and illnesses such as cancer will be curable, perhaps even preventable. There will be greater understanding of the working of the human brain and so in the understanding and treatment of mental illnesses.

In *The cultural imperative*, Richard Lewis does not fight shy of strong criticism of the United States: he does not pull his punches. Nevertheless, following the passage I quoted above, he adds that 'Western society – active, throbbing, in every sense self-perpetuating – has a momentum all of its own. If such social vibrancy is Western in essence, it is epitomized in the United States. As Hamish McRae wrote recently as he watched America arise phoenix-like from the ashes of Ground Zero, "*the future starts here* [his italics]".'

Let us dare to be hopeful about that future.

In other respects, too, the picture of the human condition is by no means as black or as bleak as the one I have painted. I was recently stopped in Winchester High Street by two young American Mormons. They asked me whether I believed in God, to which I gave a truthful negative answer. When one them asked me why, I explained how I found His existence irreconcilable with the evil in the world. His reply was: 'But what about the good in the world? There is more good than evil.' Although that is unquantifiable, it may well be true. Is it not at least encouraging that so many men and women in all societies and walks of life behave in ways which are christian and Christian? Is it not comforting that their

My grandchildren – back row, left to right, Charlotte, James, Michael;
front row, left to right, Claudia, Tom, Harry.

goodness ranges across the board from – at one extreme – the life-long devotion displayed by millions of people towards poor, starving and diseased people living in impoverished countries throughout the world to – at the other extreme – the small acts of kindness and compassion so often shown by many of us lesser mortals in our day-to-day lives? As a determinist, I ask whether it is not wondrous that so many human beings so often feel an inner need to behave in a sympathetic and humane way and are determined – in both senses of the word – to fulfil that need? My answers to these questions being in the affirmative allows me to answer the question I posed in the last three words of Chapter 14 ('Lucky pigs! Or are they?') in the negative. When I think on such things, I am glad I am a human being rather than one of 'the pigs of the fields'.

The paramount need to give love (and so, as Gerald Priestland well says, to receive it) is a common factor – the highest common factor – in non-fundamentalist, un-bigoted Christianity and other religions as well as in agnostic or atheistic humanism. The paramount need for parents to give and show their love for their children is even consistent with the views of the cynical, atheist Freud. Love of others for what they are, for better or for worse, is the bedrock on which the well-being of humanity should be founded. Only in this wise can we build the firm ramparts which are necessary to support and contain the unconditional love without which misunderstanding and being misunderstood run riot and we flounder aimlessly on the rocks of man's inhumanity to man.

I know little about moral philosophy. But among a plethora of intellectually complex theories I have not myself stumbled across a better synthesis, however simplistic, than that contained in the children's story – none the worse, perhaps even the better, for that – about Mrs Do-as-you-would-be-done-by. Understand as you would be understood. Love as you would be loved.

That is the message which, as I approach the end of my life, I leave with my four children and (at the last count) six grandchildren, for each of whom my love is 'as deep and boundless as the sea'. There is hope for the world and for humankind. The strength of the human spirit knows few insuperable bounds.

I said in my preface that these were memoirs with a difference. An unspoken reason for so saying is that in most memoirs the hero is the writer. In my case, the hero is a heroine: my wife, Isabel, whose ever-smiling strength has for more than half a century been my saving grace. I quote from the 'Rubaiyat of Omar Khayyam':

'...and thou beside me, singing in the Wilderness, is Paradise enow.'

CHAPTER 16

Full Circle

As for myself, contemplating my end, I hope – and in that sense pray – that I will yet see the snowdrops in bud and then in bloom at least several more times – the snowdrops that, in the closing words of Schumann's song that bears their name (the deliberately last of the songs in the cycle I compiled and recorded) 'presage the return of Spring.'

I was driving my car some years ago, with no idea that I was unconsciously thinking about death, when I suddenly recalled the saying once popular with philosophers: nothing comes from nothing. A different thought then sprang unannounced into my mind in the form of questions: Can something become nothing? Can anything 'pass into nothingness'? I have no notion of the scientific answer to these questions. And yet I have the mystical, spiritual feeling that my ashes will never become nothing but will mingle with the earth and be blown by the wind, somehow to become an infinite, infinitesimal part of the immensity, grandeur and wonder of continuous creation. It is due to this thought that I also included in my song cycle Gerald Finzi's great song to the words of Thomas Hardy's *Proud Songsters*, surely one of the loveliest of poems in the English language:

> The thrushes sing as the sun is going,
> and the finches whistle in ones and pairs,
> and as it gets dark loud nightingales in bushes
> pipe, as they can when April wears,
> as if all time were theirs.
>
> These are brand-new birds of twelve-months' growing,
> which a year ago, or less than twain,
> no finches were, nor nightingales,
> nor thrushes,
> but only particles of grain,
> and earth, and air, and rain.

I close my book by completing the full circle of my life's brief cycle; by reverting to my memory of Grampa Gray whose love for me I so long ago returned in full childish measure and now so wistfully recall; by recording a fleeting feeling about my ephemeral life on planet earth, ephemeral as the gentle-lapping waves of Ullswater; by saying that which I feel rather than that which I think (of which Dr Lester would have heartily approved).

I adopt as my own the defining sentence and the two closing words of Grampa Gray's poignant and beautiful summary of his own humble life which follows as appendix II to my book but is so much more than a mere appendage to the story it tells:

'I have lived a full human life... *Deo gratias.*' Thanks be to God.

Poetry in Music

A Cycle for Voice and Piano

Song	Poet	Composer
1 **Wehmut** Sadness	Joseph v. **Eichendorff**	Robert **Schumann**
2 **Du bist wie eine Blume** You are like a flower	Heinrich **Heine**	Robert **Schumann**
3 **Die rose, die lilie** The rose, the lily	Heinrich **Heine**	Robert **Schumann**
4 **Now sleeps the crimson petal**	Alfred Lord **Tennyson**	Roger **Quilter**
5 **Brown is my love**	Anon	Roger **Quilter**
6 **Les Roses d'Ispahan** The roses of Ispahan	Leconte de **Lisle**	Gabriel **Fauré**
7 **Chanson d'amour** Song of love	Armand **Silvestre**	Gabriel **Fauré**
8 **Fleur des blés** Flower of the cornfields	André **Girod**	Claude **Debussy**
9 **To an isle in the water**	William Butler **Yeats**	John **Elton**
10 **The white birds**	William Butler **Yeats**	John **Elton**
11 **Dein blaues Auge** Your blue eyes	Klaus **Groth**	Johannes **Brahms**
12 **Der Gärtner** The gardener	Eduard **Mörike**	Hugo **Wolf**
13 **Zueignung** Devotion	Hermann v. **Gilm**	Richard **Strauss**
14 **An die Musik** To music	Franz v. **Schober**	Franz **Schubert**
15 **A Green Cornfield**	Christina **Rossetti**	Michael **Head**
16 **Proud Songsters**	Thomas **Hardy**	Gerald **Finzi**
17 **Gesang Weylas** Weyla's song	Eduard **Mörike**	Hugo **Wolf**
18 **Denk'es, o Seele** Think on it, my soul	Eduard **Mörike**	Hugo **Wolf**
19 **Gebet** Prayer	Eduard **Mörike**	Hugo **Wolf**
20 **Shneeglöckchen** Snowdrops	Friedrich **Rückert**	Robert **Schumann**

The Structure of the cycle

Song 1 is a 'prologue' expressing the sadness of that inner isolation which, despite outward appearances, can so often be our human condition. Even the apparently happy song of the nightingales in Spring resounds from their 'prison tomb'.

Songs 2 to 13 are love songs.

Song 14 is a contemplative expression of thanks for the consolation that music has given the poet in life's dark moments.

Song 15 I first heard as a child and is for me a personal recollection of the innocence of youth.

Song 16 expresses resignation at the cycle of nature: dust to dust.

Song 17 can be seen as a pagan expression of hope for eternal youth.

Song 18 contemplates the possible imminence of death: intimations of mortality.

Song 19 is a Christian prayer – with philosophical overtones – for inner contentment.

Song 20 is an 'epilogue' that returns to the Spring and Schumann where we began. It gently describes the cycle of nature whereby the snowflakes of winter change to snowdrops that presage the return of Spring.

I am Sixty Years of Age

I AM SIXTY, am the father of seven children (five of them boys) all of whom are healthy and well and all doing an honourable job, and I have never earned more than £4.4.0 a week.

I am one of the innumerable army of nobodies who do the necessary work of the world.

I have lived an uneventful life, if by eventful is meant the kind of happenings that make 'copy' for newspapers. There have been no 'adventures' in the popular sense of the term. There have been no notorious achievements. I have written no great book, painted no famous picture, composed no heart-shaking music. I have not 'risen from the ranks' to become famous.

Yet, as it seems to me, I have lived a full human life. Even the limitations imposed by comparative poverty have not stultified the interests, the pleasures, the satisfaction of sheer living.

To me the earth and sky have always been enchantingly beautiful and significant; and the thrilling pleasure of common sights and sounds can be had for nothing. The fascinating interests of human life have been mine too.

The supreme human satisfaction of being in love, getting married, and being the father of children have been mine: as have the joys of comradeship.

The pleasures and deep satisfactions of communication and sharing of experiences with the saints, singers and sages of all times have been mine, and these too at small cost in these days of cheap and good reprints. Much have I travelled in the golden realms of literature.

I sometimes in quiet moments am filled with a deep thankfulness for all the good things I have found in my life, in spite of the material anxieties and hardships imposed by poverty.

When the seven children were young and all at home, the problem of feeding them, clothing them and caring for them generally was a very difficult one. Yet, I cannot remember that we were ever unhappy. Indeed mostly life was full of fun. The children were healthy and happy. They had their keen interests in games, hobbies and school-work, in all of which my wife and I shared. We read stories, we sang songs, we laughed, we played games, we were interested in all we saw and all that went on around us. It was a great life.

Now the children are all grown up and have all left home. They are scattered. The house seems very quiet. The garden and lawn tennis court are deserted. But two married daughters and one married son live in the neighbourhood and often call in.

It seemed very strange when the last of them, a boy of twenty, left home and we were quite alone. Often when we went to bed my wife would shout out several times 'Good night' to the absent children.

They are of course always in our minds and hearts. Their affairs are ours: we seem to share their lives as we did when they were at home. Indeed, sometimes our anxiety is greater: when they were at home we could go round last thing after the tumult of the day when the children were all asleep, safe and sound, after the day's activities, and feel a profound satisfaction as we said our prayers. But now they are scattered about, fighting life's battle for themselves, facing difficulties, meeting failures and successes and all life's experiences alone, and we wonder and sometimes half wish for what is impossible, that we could have them all in our care again, and put life right for them in the old way.

And the affair is all the more complicated now that I have two grandchildren – boys aged 6 and 8 – who come nearly every week and fill the house with the old joyous tumult. Once again I am telling the old stories and playing the old games. Once again I have to answer innumerable questions.

So I shall never be lonely, never without deep, loving, human interests.

Has life been worth living? It has, thank God.

Is life worth living? It is, thank God.

What of the future? Better still, I believe, thank God.

Deo Gratias.

8th March, 1938   **Ernest Frank Gray**
                                                                Assisi
                                                                Kings Road
                                                                Alton, Hants.

The Misuse of Words

THE MISUSE OF WORDS even applies to the word 'free' itself. In *The Times* of 27 February 2003, Steven Rose, Professor of Biology of the Open University, in commenting on the interview with Daniel Dennett[224], says that we are 'free to make our own future' (a statement which echoes Daniel Dennett's pronouncement that we can direct our destinies), having earlier given an example that purports to prove his case: 'I am *free* [as a result of evolution] to lift my arm above my head because of neurophysiological sequences that begin with my brain – but I would not be [free to do so] if particular nerves were severed or brain regions lesioned'. The trouble with this example is that, like David Dennett[223], he confuses our capacity to do something with free will. He should have first said that 'I am *able* to lift my arm… but would not be *able* to do so if…' and only then gone on to consider whether his action in lifting his arm was free or determined. Having myself – before reading Professor Rose's comments – experimented with lifting or not lifting my arm and felt that something inside me made my choice (or, to avoid the same pitfall, my selection of one of the available alternatives) inevitable, I took the opportunity to conduct an experiment at a seminar of my philosophy group at which I was invited to talk about determinism. I began by saying that I would count '5, 4, 3, 2, 1, zero' and asking those present either to raise or not to raise an arm when I said zero. I gave them each a piece of paper and asked them to write 'yes' if they raised their arm and 'no' if they didn't, and then write down the reasons for their decisions. Their answers were as follows:

1. 'Yes: a quick thought said "do it" and there was no reason not to.'
2. 'No: I thought most people would and so I didn't.'
3. 'Yes: I felt I had to, it was the right thing to do.'
4. 'Yes: don't know why.'
5. 'No: I didn't want to do the expected thing.'
6. 'Yes: no particular reason. I just did.'
7. 'Yes: no reason not to.'
8. 'Yes: I wanted to be co-operative and do something positive.'

9. 'No: no conscious awareness of choice.'
10. 'Yes: like a NASA lift off.'
11. 'Yes: no particular reason.'
12. 'No: don't know.'

When I then suggested that, whether or not they had been able to identify the thought processes that had led to their decisions, those thought processes had just 'occurred to them' beyond their control, I wasn't hung, drawn and quartered! In fact, they all seemed at least to recognize what I was suggesting. When people couldn't ascribe their decisions to an identifiable cause (e.g. case 6: 'I just did'), their answers were suitably deterministic! But what about the cases where people gave reasons for their decision? Take case 10 ('like a NASA lift off') as an example. Did the person concerned *volunteer* to think about the analogy with the count-down to the launching of a rocket into space and so put up his or her arm? Or did the analogy occur to him or her *involuntarily*? It is surely hard to gainsay that an affirmative answer to the latter question is the truth of the matter – both in this case and in the other cases where people gave reasons for their choices.

It now occurs to me (!) that I might well have clarified my case for determinism if I had throughout used the words 'voluntary' and 'voluntarily' instead of 'free' and 'freely'. Put the other way round, perhaps I should have coined a noun 'involuntarism' the better to describe determinism.

Three last thoughts about the use of language in ways which pre-suppose that we have free will:

'Free will' is often confused with 'willpower'. Some people have objected to my case for determinism by saying something like: 'Of course I've got free will because I've got such strong willpower.' My own view is exactly the opposite. From empirical observation, they of all people are patently 'driven' by their willpower. The greater their willpower, the more blatant their involuntarism.

It can also be unduly emotive continually to use the word 'responsible' as equivalent to 'having free will'. In one sense this is fair enough, but it has the negative connotation that determinists like myself are necessarily 'irresponsible' people.

I myself have said more than once that 'I nearly changed my mind about determinism'. When we say 'I changed my mind', what and where is the 'I' or 'self' that is separate from our 'mind' and – by implication – freely, voluntarily and without constraint instructed it to think differently? (Philosophers argue interminably and – dare I say – abstrusely about the concept of the self.). Instead of saying 'I changed by mind', we should – strictly speaking – say 'my brain generated a different thought'. Even if we make a distinction between our brains and ourselves, it is our brains that tell us what to do and not we who tell our brains what to do.